THE
ultimate
GRILL
BOOK

JG
PRESS

Research & Text
Joan Griffiths
Mary Jane Swanson

Coordinating Editor
Deborah Thomas Kramer

Design
Joe di Chiarro

Illustrations
Guy Porfirio
Sally Shimizu

Calligraphy
Sherry Bringham

Jacket Design
Murray Greenfield

Photography by Tom Wyatt
Additional photography: Victor
Budnik: 76, 113, 121; Glenn
Christiansen: 65, 85, 173, 192;
Darrow Watt: 116, 153, 168;
Nikolay Zurek: 53.

Photo stylists: Susan Massey-Weil: 29,
45, 48, 56, 73, 80, 88, 101, 108,
116, 137, 140, 145, 148, 189, 200;
Lynne B. Morrall: 53; JoAnn
Masaoka Van Atta: 1, 6, 12, 21, 24,
32, 37, 40, 60, 68, 76, 93, 96, 104,
113, 121, 124, 129, 132, 156, 161,
164. 176, 181, 184, 197.

Jacket: Photography by FOODPIX

Published in the U.S.A.
by JG Press, Inc.

Distributed by
World Publications, Inc.

The JG Press imprint is a
trademark of JG Press, Inc.
455 Somerset Avenue
North Dighton, MA 02764

ISBN 1-57215-276-1

Printed in the U.S.A.
by Quebecor World

Foreword

In the mostly mild climates of the West, barbecuing happens year-round. But in colder regions, it is especially in spring–when days grow longer and warmer–that back-yard chefs start migrating outdoors to their barbecue equipment. Soon, grills start to sizzle, and you smell the first tantalizing aroma of the barbecue season.

Whether it's because of fresh air, glowing coals, succulent foods, or the primitive appeal of fire, an outdoor grill creates something much more enjoyable than just an outdoor meal. A barbecue relaxes people, whets the appetite, kindles laughter, and turns the simplest food into a festive event.

This book invites you to join the fun, and experience the flavors of long barbecue traditions. It offers over 300 mouth-watering recipes, both favorites and new dis-coveries, for a few or a crowd, to enjoy casually, outdoors, or more formally in the dining room.

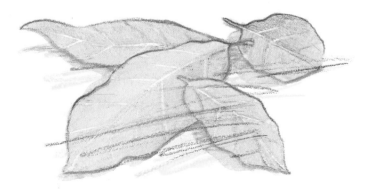

Contents

Venetian Mixed Grill (page 195) offers a savory sampling of six meats: chicken thighs, sausages, skirt steak, lamb and veal chops, and calf's liver. Alongside, serve juicy tomato halves, grilled polenta, and artichokes.

Grilling Basics

EQUIPMENT, TECHNIQUES & COOKING CHARTS

Barbecuing is one culinary art that even a novice back-yard chef can master with ease. For satisfying results, you need only use your equipment properly and learn a few basic skills.

In this chapter, you'll find general information on charcoal-fueled barbecues and fire starters, followed by complete directions for building a fire and barbecuing by direct and indirect heat. The charts on pages 15 to 18 tell you the temperatures and times for grilling a variety of meats, poultry, and seafood; you'll also find basic directions for smoking and spit-roasting.

To test our recipes (and the times in our grilling charts), we used a charcoal-fired barbecue with 2-inch pressed long-burning briquets—still the most popular barbecue-fuel combination on the market today. If you're interested in cooking with a gas-powered barbecue, turn to page 13. To learn more about other fuel choices, including wood cooking chunks and mesquite charcoal, consult page 14.

CHARCOAL-FUELED BARBECUES

Charcoal-fueled barbecues come in three basic styles: open braziers, covered kettles, and boxes with hinged lids.

Open braziers are designed for open grilling over direct heat (see page 10). They're best suited to cooking pieces of food that lie flat and are no thicker than 2 inches—steaks, chops, hamburgers, fish steaks and fillets, and chicken pieces. For grilling roasts, whole birds, and thick pieces of meat, braziers aren't always reliable, since covered cooking is typically makeshift (a foil tent often serves as the "lid"). Roasts and whole poultry can, however, be spit-roasted on an open brazier with the appropriate attachments (see page 19).

Open braziers come in a variety of sizes, from table-top portables and hibachis to very large (often custom-fashioned) built-in brick barbecues. Some braziers feature a movable cooking grill that can be raised or lowered to adjust the distance from the firebed and thus control the heat. But in most types, including the model we used for testing, the grill is fixed 5 to 6 inches above the coals.

Covered kettles provide the same even heat an oven does, making them an ideal choice for cooking whole fish, whole poultry, roasts and other thick cuts of meat by indirect heat (see page 10).

This sort of barbecue may also be used uncovered for direct-heat cooking, though many manufacturers recommend that you always cover the grill to speed up cooking and conserve fuel. Of course, quick-cooking foods such as hamburgers, steaks, and chops are easier to watch and tend if the lid is off—but covering the barbecue does help prevent flare-ups and charred foods.

Kettle barbecues are available in various sizes; the 18- to 24-inch-diameter models are the most popular. Dampers on the lid of the kettle and beneath the firebed allow you to adjust the flow of air and control the heat. If the food is cooking too fast, reduce the heat by closing the dampers a bit; to increase the heat, open the dampers and let in more air.

Barbecue boxes with hinged lids work on the same principle as covered kettles: the lid turns the barbecue into an oven, and adjustable dampers allow you to control the fire temperature.

Barbecue boxes tend to be the most elaborate and expensive charcoal-fueled units on the market. Some are portable, others are mounted on wagons, and still others are permanently mounted on pedestals. In most boxes, the distance between food and coals can be adjusted by raising or lowering the grill or fire grate; many models have a built-in air temperature thermometer that allows you to check the inside temperature when the lid is down. Some units come with spit-roasting attachments.

Like kettle barbecues, boxes can be used with the lid up for direct-heat cooking.

STARTING THE CHARCOAL

When we refer to charcoal, we mean the 2-inch pressed briquets widely sold in grocery stores. The various brands differ somewhat in density and composition; some kinds burn longer than others. We based our testing on long-burning briquets; if you buy a fast-burning type, you'll obviously need to use more charcoal to maintain an even heat throughout the cooking time.

To ignite long-burning briquets, choose one of the following starters.

Fire chimney. Stack briquets inside the chimney on top of wadded sheets of newspaper, then light. In about 30 minutes, you'll have burning coals ready to use; remove the chimney and spread the hot coals for cooking. (To make your own fire chimney, remove the top and bottom of a 2-pound coffee can; then punch holes just above the bottom edge, using nails or a can opener that makes triangular holes.)

Electric starter. This is one of the easiest, cleanest, and—in the long run—least expensive charcoal starters you can buy. Set the starter on a few briquets in the firebed and pile more briquets on top; then plug in the starter. After 10 minutes,

Hibachi

Tabletop grill

Portable covered
barbecue

Covered
kettle

Gas-fired barbecue

remove the starter from the pile (if you leave it in the coals for long periods of time, the heating element will burn out quickly). In about 20 more minutes, the coals will be ready to spread.

Solid starter. These small, compressed, woodlike blocks or sticks light easily with a match and continue to burn with no attention until the coals are ready for cooking (in about 30 minutes).

Liquid starter. If you use a liquid starter, be sure it's a product intended for charcoal, and follow the manufacturer's instructions closely. *Never* pour liquid starter on hot coals—this could cause a dangerous flare-up.

Self-starting briquets, impregnated with a liquid starter, are easily ignited with a match. Though more expensive than regular briquets, they also heat up more quickly. Do not add these impregnated briquets to an existing hot fire. Use regular briquets when additional charcoal is needed to maintain heat.

Propane starter. To use this starter, simply stack the briquets around the burner; then light the burner and proceed as directed by the manufacturer.

HOW TO BARBECUE BY DIRECT & INDIRECT HEAT

Almost all the recipes in this book call for either direct- or indirect-heat cooking—and these are the two simplest barbecuing methods. The two techniques differ in how the coals are arranged and in whether the barbecue is covered. For direct-heat grilling, any barbecue is satisfactory; to cook by indirect heat, you'll need a model with a lid.

The charts on pages 15 to 18 state the preferred grilling method—direct or indirect—for each cut of meat, fish, or poultry. In each recipe in this book, the recommended method is indicated by a symbol:

  Direct heat (open grilling)   Indirect heat (covered grilling)

To barbecue by direct heat, open the bottom dampers if your barbecue has them; for a covered barbecue, remove or open lid. To build the fire, spread briquets on the fire grate in a solid layer that measures at least 2 inches larger all around than the grill area required for the food. Then mound the charcoal and ignite it. When the coals have reached the fire temperature specified (see next page), spread them out into a single layer again.

Set the grill in place at the recommended height above the coals. Grease the grill, then arrange the food on the grill. Watch carefully and turn as needed to ensure even cooking. If you're using a baste that contains sugar, ingredients high in sugar (such as catsup or fruit), or a large proportion of fat, apply it during the last part of cooking and turn the food frequently to prevent scorching. Also keep a water-filled spray bottle handy to extinguish any flare-ups.

To maintain an even heat, scatter about 10 briquets over the firebed every 30 minutes.

To barbecue by indirect heat, open or remove the lid from a covered barbecue; open the bottom dampers. Pile about 50 long-burning briquets on the fire grate and ignite them. Let the briquets burn until hot (usually about 30 minutes). Using long-handled tongs, bank about half the briquets on each side of fire grate; then place a metal drip pan in the center.

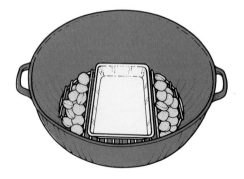

Set the cooking grill in place 4 to 6 inches above the pan; lightly grease the grill. Set the food on the grill directly above the drip pan. If you're grilling meat, place it fat side up; if the meat has been marinated, drain it briefly before placing it on the grill. Cover barbecue and adjust dampers to maintain an even heat.

Add 5 or 6 briquets to each side of the fire grate at 30- to 40-minute intervals as needed to keep the fire temperature constant, starting when you arrange the coals for cooking.

FIRE TEMPERATURE

In our charts and in all the recipes in this book, we specify desired fire temperatures at the start of cooking as *hot*, *medium*, or *low*. Here's how to determine the temperature of your fire.

Hot. You can hold your hand close to the grill for only 2 to 3 seconds. Coals are barely covered with gray ash and may have low flames around them.

Medium. You can hold your hand at grill level for 4 to 5 seconds. Coals are well covered with ash and may glow red through the ashy coating.

Low. You can hold your hand at grill level for at least 6 to 7 seconds. Coals are covered with a thick layer of ash.

BARBECUE TOOLS & ACCESSORIES

The world of barbecuing offers a full range of gadgetry, both useful and frivolous. For everyday use and care of your barbecue, just a few tools are necessary: long tongs for adjusting hot coals and turning foods; long-handled spatulas and forks for turning foods while they cook (be sure not to puncture juicy meats with a fork); drip pans (either disposable foil or inexpensive aluminum) for catching meat and poultry juices while barbecuing by indirect heat; mitts for emergency adjustment of the grill and removal of drip pans from the firebed; and a stiff metal brush for scrubbing the grill.

For special spit-roasting attachments, see page 19. You'll find descriptions of smoke-cooking equipment on page 20.

SPECIAL TIPS FOR BARBECUING

When preparing the recipes in this book, keep these tips in mind.

■ Our recipes were tested with the cooking grill 4 to 6 inches above the coals. If your grill is closer, the cooking time will be shorter.

■ Use a water-filled spray bottle to extinguish flare-ups.

■ Salt food *after* cooking (salt draws out juices).

■ To prevent steaks and chops from curling, slash edge fat at 2- to 3-inch intervals, cutting *just to meat*.

■ To test roasts or thick steaks for doneness, insert a meat thermometer in the thickest part (not touching bone). To ensure accuracy, repeat the test in several places (if possible).

A WORD ABOUT OUR NUTRITIONAL DATA

For our recipes, we provide a nutritional analysis stating calorie count; grams of protein, carbohydrates, and total fat; and milligrams of cholesterol and sodium. In general, the nutritional information applies to a single serving, based on the largest number of servings given for each recipe.

The nutritional analysis does not include optional ingredients or those for which no amount is stated. If an ingredient is listed with an option, the information was calculated using the first choice. Likewise, if a range is given for the amount of an ingredient, values were figured using the first, lower amount.

In this book, you'll find numerous recipes for marinades and sauces containing high-sodium ingredients such as soy sauce and chicken broth. If you wish to reduce the sodium level in these recipes, consider using light (reduced-sodium) soy sauce and unsalted or low-salt chicken broth.

Lightly blistered, then split and stuffed, Grilled Chiles Rellenos with Shrimp (page 99) are heated on the barbecue. Diners top servings with salsa and sour cream, then enjoy chiles as a side dish or light entrée.

GAS

BARBECUES

The many models of gas barbecues now on the market offer an alternative to charcoal grills. Their simple no-fuss, no-mess approach to barbecuing is undeniably appealing: they save you the work of building the fire and cleaning up the ashes. And because most units require only brief preheating, you can start cooking in a matter of minutes—a definite advantage when time is short or the weather is unpleasant. On the other hand, gas barbecues are expensive compared to charcoal grills, ranging in price from around $150 to over $500. Moreover, if you enjoy the deep, rich "charcoal" flavor of foods cooked over coals, a gas grill may not give you the results you want.

How gas grills work. Gas units are fueled by either bottled or natural gas. Those fueled by bottled gas usually roll on wheels, but they're heavier and more difficult to move than their charcoal counterparts. Natural gas units are mounted on a fixed pedestal and must be connected to a permanent gas line.

Direct & indirect heat. In general, gas barbecues have two or three stainless steel burners, each with a separate control that allows you to regulate the flame from high to low, depending on the amount of heat required. To cook by direct heat, light both burners if you need to use the entire grill area; use just one burner if you're only cooking a few hamburgers.

To cook by indirect heat, turn one burner on and leave the other off; place the food to be cooked over the off burner. Remember, though, that many gas models are small, limiting the size of the roast or bird you can cook. Full-size, covered charcoal grills accommodate larger pieces of meat and poultry than do most gas barbecues.

Most manufacturers of gas units recommend you do *all* cooking with the lid closed.

Distributing the heat. To distribute the heat from the burners, most gas units use lava rock, either crushed or in various shapes: disks, briquets, pyramids. When meat juices drip on the hot rock, smoke rises to penetrate and flavor the food. The rock's shape doesn't have much effect on the cooking efficiency; just be sure you have enough rock, and position it carefully to form a single, solid layer.

Instead of lava rock, a few units have a gridwork of porcelainized metal "flavorizer bars." These do a good job of distributing heat and minimizing flare-ups.

Cooking grids. The majority of gas grills have cooking grids that come apart in two or three sections, making them easy to remove for cleaning. Some grids can be positioned at different heights above the heat source; others have a single fixed position.

Cooking time. In gas grilling, as in any kind of barbecuing, a number of factors influence cooking time: wind and weather, the food's shape and density and its temperature when placed on the grill, and so on. And because gas barbecues do differ from charcoal-fueled models, cooking times may not be identical to those we give in our charts and recipes. In most cases, though, times are about the same on gas and charcoal grills, provided you use the same temperature (hot, medium, or low) specified for barbecuing over coals and set the grids 4 to 6 inches above the heat. If the grids are closer to the heat, the cooking time may be shorter. Once you've consulted the manufacturer's directions and cooking information and used your particular unit a few times, you'll be able to make any necessary adjustments in temperature and time.

FUELS FOR COOKING

While charcoal briquets are still the barbecue chef's favorite fuel, two relative newcomers to the market—mesquite charcoal and cooking chunks of fragrant hardwoods—are gaining in popularity.

THE MESQUITE MYSTIQUE

Mesquite charcoal, made by charring the wood of the southwestern mesquite tree under special commercial conditions, is popular among many home and restaurant chefs. Aficionados claim this fuel produces a hotter fire and gives foods a more intensely smoky flavor. In our taste tests, we found that mesquite-grilled beef, pork, and veal gained little additional flavor, but fish and poultry did take on a smokier taste. We also found that mesquite burned hotter. However, while pressed briquets are uniformly shaped to provide even heat, mesquite coals range from 4-inch chunks to tiny shards. The fire is hotter where large lumps jut upward; for more even heat, break up big pieces.

The amount of mesquite you'll need depends on whether you're grilling by direct or indirect heat (see page 10). For indirect-heat barbecuing, use a volume of mesquite equal to 50 briquets—about 7 quarts or 5 pounds.

Look for mesquite charcoal in 6¾-, 8-, 15-, and 40-pound bags at well-stocked supermarkets and cookware shops. Make sure you buy mesquite *charcoal,* not mesquite wood or briquets laced with mesquite splinters.

To ignite mesquite, open your barbecue's bottom dampers and mound the coals on the fire grate. Ignite (see "Starting the Charcoal," page 8). Expect the coals to flame and spark a bit as they catch. In about 30 minutes, they should be well spotted with gray ash and ready for cooking.

Arrange the hot coals for barbecuing by direct or indirect heat as directed on page 10. To maintain an even heat, every 30 to 45 minutes, add about 4 cups of mesquite to the fire (2 cups to each side if cooking by indirect heat).

COOKING OVER HARDWOODS

Dried fragrant hardwoods such as alder, apple, hickory, mesquite, and oak are now available to patio chefs. These woods have two basic uses. You can soak the wood in water, then place it atop burning charcoal to smolder and give off smoke that flavors the food (see page 20). Or you can cook directly over burning wood chunks or the coals they form, as described below. The best foods to grill over a hardwood fire are those that require *hot* coals—beef patties, fish steaks, and many other foods listed in the charts on pages 15 to 18. If a food is best grilled over low to medium coals, don't cook it over a hardwood fire.

Hardwoods used as cooking fuel (often labeled "cooking chunks") are packaged in assorted sizes, including 2-inch chunks, 7-inch sticks, 10-inch logs, and pressed logs made from sawdust and wood scraps. Small chunks and logs ignite quickly; pressed logs are a bit harder to start. To cook 4 pounds of ground beef patties or steaks rare to medium-rare, allow about 2 pounds of wood (8 to 10 chunks or 4 to 6 small logs). This much wood will burn for about 35 minutes, including 15 minutes for start-up.

You'll find cooking chunks packaged in 6- to 8-pound bags or boxes at well-stocked supermarkets, hardware stores, and garden supply centers, and in mail-order catalogs.

To ignite cooking chunks or logs, loosely crumple several sheets of newspaper and place them in the center of the fire grate. Stack chunks or logs mixed with kindling on top of the paper; then ignite with a match. When most of the wood is blazing and streaked with white ash (after 10 to 15 minutes), arrange the pieces in a single layer, sides just touching. Set the cooking grill about 4 inches above the wood. The flames should just touch the grill (they'll die down soon).

Place foods on the grill directly over the burning wood; turn them often during cooking. If you're grilling foods that cook for more than about 20 minutes, add more wood around the fire to maintain an even heat.

GRILLING BEEF

Cut of Meat	Weight or Thickness	Grilling Method	Fire Temperature	Test for Doneness & Approximate Cooking Time
Standing rib roast	3½–5 lbs.	Indirect	Hot, banked	Meat thermometer registers 135°–140°F (R), 150°F (M), 160°F (W). 24–26 min./lb. (R).
	6–8 lbs.	Indirect	Hot, banked	Meat thermometer registers 135°–140°F (R), 150°F (M), 160°F (W). 18–22 min./lb. (R).
Boned & tied roasts (rib, sirloin tip, crossrib)	3–5 lbs.	Indirect	Hot, banked	Meat thermometer registers 135°–140°F (R), 150°F (M), 160°F (W). 24–26 min./lb. (R).
Steaks (T-bone, New York, Porterhouse, top round, sirloin; chuck steak if marinated or tenderized)	1 inch	Direct	Hot	Cut meat to test. 5–6 min./side (R).
	1½ inches	Direct	Medium	Meat thermometer registers 135°–140°F (R), 150°F (M), 160°F (W). 8–9 min./side (R).
	2–2½ inches	Direct	Medium	Meat thermometer registers 135°–140°F (R), 150°F (M), 160°F (W). 12–15 min./side (MR).
Flank steak	1–1½ lbs.	Direct	Hot	Cut meat to test. 5–7 min./side (MR).
Skirt steak (cut into serving-size pieces)	⅛–¼ inch	Direct	Hot	Cut meat to test. 1½–2 min./side (R).
	½ inch	Direct	Hot	Cut meat to test. 2½–3 min./side (R).
Boneless cubes	¾ inch	Direct	Hot	Cut meat to test. 5–6 min. *total* (MR).
	1 inch	Direct	Hot	Cut meat to test. 8–10 min. *total* (MR).
	1½ inches	Direct	Hot	Cut meat to test. 15 min. *total* (MR).
Ground beef patties	1 inch	Direct	Hot	Cut meat to test. 4–5 min./side (R), 5–6 min./side (M), 6–7 min./side (W).

(R) Rare; (M) Medium; (MR) Medium-rare; (W) Well done

GRILLING LAMB

Cut of Meat	Weight or Thickness	Grilling Method	Fire Temperature	Test for Doneness & Approximate Cooking Time
Leg, bone-in	5–7 lbs.	Indirect	Hot, banked	Meat thermometer registers 135°–140°F (R), 150°F (M), 160°F (W). 18–20 min./lb. (R).
Leg, boned & tied	4–5 lbs.	Indirect	Hot, banked	Meat thermometer registers 135°–140°F (R), 150°F (M), 160°F (W). 25–27 min./lb. (R).
Leg, boned & butterflied	4–5 lbs.	Indirect	Hot, banked	Meat thermometer registers 135°–140°F (R), 150°F (M), 160°F (W). 12–14 min./lb. (R).
Shoulder, bone-in	5–7 lbs.	Indirect	Hot, banked	Meat thermometer registers 135°–140°F (R), 150°F (M), 160°F (W). 18–20 min./lb. (R).
Shoulder, boned & tied	4–6 lbs.	Indirect	Hot, banked	Meat thermometer registers 135°–140°F (R), 150°F (M), 160°F (W). 25–27 min./lb. (R).
Rack	2–3 lbs.	Indirect	Hot, banked	Meat thermometer registers 140°–145°F (MR). 18–20 min./lb.
Chops (loin, rib, shoulder); leg steaks	¾ inch	Direct	Hot	Cut near bone to test. 4–5 min./side (MR).
	1 inch	Direct	Hot	Cut near bone to test. About 5 min./side (MR).
	1½ inches	Direct	Hot	Cut near bone to test. 6–7 min./side (MR).

(Continued on next page)

GRILLING BASICS **15**

Cut of Meat	Weight or Thickness	Grilling Method	Fire Temperature	Test for Doneness & Approximate Cooking Time
Boneless cubes	¾ inch	Direct	Hot	Cut meat to test. 5 min. *total* (R), 6–8 min. *total* (M), 8–10 min. *total* (W).
	1 inch	Direct	Hot	Cut meat to test. 6 min. *total* (R), 8 min. *total* (M), 12 min. *total* (W).
	1½ inches	Direct	Hot	Cut meat to test. 12 min. *total* (R), 15 min. *total* (M), 18–20 min. *total* (W).
Ground lamb patties	¾ inch	Direct	Hot	Cut meat to test. 4–5 min./side (MR).
	1 inch	Direct	Hot	Cut meat to test. 5–6 min./side (MR).

(R) Rare; (M) Medium; (MR) Medium-rare; (W) Well done

GRILLING PORK

Cut of Meat	Weight or Thickness	Grilling Method	Fire Temperature	Test for Doneness & Approximate Cooking Time
Half leg (shank or butt), bone-in	6–8 lbs.	Indirect	Hot, banked	Meat thermometer registers 150°–155°F. 25–30 min./lb.
Loin roast, half, bone-in	4½–6 lbs.	Indirect	Hot, banked	Meat thermometer registers 150°–155°F. 22–24 min./lb.
Loin roast, half, boned & tied	3–5 lbs.	Indirect	Hot, banked	Meat thermometer registers 150°–155°F. 20–22 min./lb.
Loin roast, rib or sirloin end, bone-in	3–4 lbs.	Indirect	Hot, banked	Meat thermometer registers 150°–155°F. 28–30 min./lb.
Shoulder roast (picnic or butt), bone-in	4–6 lbs.	Indirect	Hot, banked	Meat thermometer registers 150°–155°F. 26–29 min./lb.
Shoulder roast (picnic or butt), boned & tied	3–5 lbs.	Indirect	Hot, banked	Meat thermometer registers 150°–155°F. 30–32 min./lb.
Tenderloin (fold and tie thin end underneath for even thickness)	½–1 lb.	Indirect	Hot, banked	Meat thermometer registers 150°–155°F. 18–22 min. *total*.
Chops (loin, rib, shoulder); leg steaks	¾ inch	Direct	Medium	Meat near bone is no longer pink; cut to test. 4–5 min./side.
	1 inch	Direct	Medium	Meat near bone is no longer pink; cut to test. 5–7 min./side.
	1½ inches	Direct	Medium	Meat near bone is no longer pink; cut to test. 8–10 min./side.
Spareribs	2½–3 lbs., whole slab	Indirect	Hot, banked	Meat near bone is no longer pink; cut to test. 1–1¼ hours *total*.
Spareribs, country-style	3–4 lbs., cut into serving-size pieces	Indirect	Hot, banked	Meat near bone is no longer pink; cut to test. 1–1¼ hours *total*.
Boneless cubes	¾ inch	Direct	Hot	Meat is no longer pink; cut to test. About 8 min. *total*.
	1 inch	Direct	Hot	Meat is no longer pink; cut to test. 12–14 min. *total*.

GRILLING VEAL

Cut of Meat	Weight or Thickness	Grilling Method	Fire Temperature	Test for Doneness & Approximate Cooking Time
Leg, bone-in	8–9 lbs.	Indirect	Hot, banked	Meat thermometer registers 165°–170°F.* 20–22 min./lb.
Leg, boned & tied	3–4 lbs.	Indirect	Hot, banked	Meat thermometer registers 165°–170°F.* 32–34 min./lb.
Shoulder roast, bone-in	7–8 lbs.	Indirect	Hot, banked	Meat thermometer registers 165°–170°F.* 18–20 min./lb.
Shoulder roast, boned & tied	3–4 lbs.	Indirect	Hot, banked	Meat thermometer registers 165°–170°F.* 32–34 min./lb.
Chops (loin)	¾ inch	Direct	Hot	Cut near bone to test. 5–6 min./side (M).
	1 inch	Direct	Hot	Cut near bone to test. 6–7 min./side (M).
	1½ inches	Direct	Hot	Cut near bone to test. 8–9 min./side (M).

*Veal cooked to 165°–170°F is cooked medium-well—
   tender and juicy throughout, but no longer pink.

(M) Medium

GRILLING FISH & SHELLFISH

Type of Fish or Shellfish	Weight or Thickness	Grilling Method	Fire Temperature	Test for Doneness & Approximate Cooking Time
Whole fish (with or without head and tail)*	½–1 lb. (1–1½ inches thick)	Indirect	Hot, banked	Flakes when prodded in thickest part. 6 min./side.
	3–5 lbs. (2–2½ inches thick)	Indirect	Hot, banked	Flakes when prodded in thickest part. 30–35 min. *total.*
	5–7 lbs. (3 inches thick)	Indirect	Hot, banked	Flakes when prodded in thickest part. 45 min. *total.*
Steaks & fillets**	½ inch	Direct	Hot	Flakes when prodded in thickest part. 2–3 min./side.
	¾ inch	Direct	Hot	Flakes when prodded in thickest part. 3–4 min./side.
	1 inch	Direct	Hot	Flakes when prodded in thickest part. 4–5 min./side.
	1½ inches (2–3 lbs.)	Indirect	Hot, banked	Flakes when prodded in thickest part. 15–18 min. *total.*
Boneless cubes	1 inch	Direct	Hot	Flakes when prodded in thickest part. 8–10 min. *total.*
Shrimp	Medium-size (30–32 per lb.)	Direct	Hot	Shrimp turn pink. 1½–2½ min./side.
Scallops	About 1-inch cubes	Direct	Hot	Opaque throughout; cut to test. 5–7 min. *total.*
Clams	Medium-size	Direct	Hot	Shells pop open. 3–4 min. *total.*
Oysters	Medium-size	Direct	Hot	Shells pop open. 4–6 min. *total.*

*Rub whole fish with salad oil before grilling.
**Place heavy-duty foil under large fillets instead of putting
   them directly on the grill.

GRILLING POULTRY

Type of Poultry	Weight or Thickness	Grilling Method	Fire Temperature	Test for Doneness & Approximate Cooking Time
CHICKEN, whole	3–4 lbs.	Indirect	Hot, banked	Meat thermometer inserted in thigh registers 185°F.* 1–1¼ hours.
	6–7 lbs.	Indirect	Hot, banked	Meat thermometer inserted in thigh registers 185°F.* 1½–1¾ hours.
Halved or quartered	3–4 lbs. *total*	Direct	Medium	Meat near bone is no longer pink; cut to test. 40–50 min.
Cut up	3–4 lbs. *total*	Direct	Medium	Meat near bone is no longer pink; cut to test. Dark meat 35–40 min.; white meat 15–20 min.
Breast halves, bone-in	½–¾ lb. *each*	Direct	Medium	Meat near bone is no longer pink; cut to test. 15–20 min.
Whole legs, thighs attached	8–10 oz. *each*	Direct	Medium	Meat near bone is no longer pink; cut to test. 35–45 min.
Drumsticks or thighs	4–6 oz. *each*	Direct	Medium	Meat near bone is no longer pink; cut to test. About 35 min.
Wings	3–4 oz. *each*	Direct	Medium	Meat near bone is no longer pink; cut to test. About 30 min.
ROCK CORNISH GAME HEN, whole	1–1½ lbs.	Indirect	Hot, banked	Meat near thighbone is no longer pink; cut to test. 45–60 min.
Halved	1–1½ lbs. *total*	Direct	Medium	Meat near bone is no longer pink; cut to test. 30–40 min.
TURKEY, whole	9–15 lbs.	Indirect	Hot, banked	Meat thermometer inserted in thigh registers 185°F.* 15 min./lb.
	16–22 lbs.	Indirect	Hot, banked	Meat thermometer inserted in thigh registers 185°F.* 12 min./lb.
Halved	10–12 lbs. *total*	Indirect	Hot, banked	Meat thermometer inserted in thigh registers 185°F.* 1½–2 hours.
Breast halves, bone-in	2½–3 lbs. *each*	Indirect	Hot, banked	Meat near bone is no longer pink; cut to test. 1–1½ hours.
Drumsticks or thighs	1–2 lbs. *each*	Direct, covered	Medium	Meat near bone is no longer pink; cut to test. 55–65 min.
Boneless cubes	1 inch	Direct	Medium	Meat is no longer pink in center; cut to test. 12–15 min.
Breast steaks	½ inch	Direct	Medium	Meat is no longer pink; cut to test. 7–9 min.
DUCK, whole (prick skin with a fork before grilling)	4–5 lbs.	Indirect	Hot, banked	Meat near bone at hip socket is no longer pink; cut to test. 2–2½ hours.
Cut up	4–5 lbs. *total*	Indirect	Hot, banked	Meat in thickest part is still slightly pink; cut to test. Legs and wings 40 min.; breast 10–15 min.
SQUAB, butterflied	1 lb.	Direct	Hot	Breast meat is pink near bone; cut to test. 15–20 min.
QUAIL, butterflied	3–4 oz.	Direct	Hot	Breast meat is still slightly pink near bone; cut to test. 7–8 min.

*Insert meat thermometer in thickest part of thigh, not touching bone.

SPIT-ROASTING

In spit-roasting, the diameter of the meat and its distance from the heat determine cooking time.

Bone-in roasts, boneless roasts, and poultry are all suitable for spit roasting. In every case, it's important to balance the meat on the spit. Use a ruler to find the center of each end of a roast; the spit should enter and exit at these points.

Choose *bone-in roasts* of fairly uniform shape, cutting off any bony extensions. Run spit through the meaty section, as close to the center of the roast as possible. For leg of lamb, run the spit through the meat from the center of the thickest end, keeping the length of the leg parallel to the spit. Roll and tie *boneless roasts* into evenly shaped cylinders and run the spit through dead center. Tie wings and legs of *poultry* closely to the body; run spit through the neck and body openings. Position meat in center of spit; secure with spit forks.

The firebed. Imagine a wall extending straight down from the spit to the firebed. Then, starting from about 2 inches behind this imaginary wall,

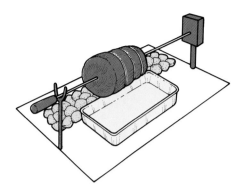

arrange the coals in a solid 6-inch-wide band reaching 3 to 4 inches beyond each end of the spitted meat. Place a metal drip pan directly beneath the spit, with one side touching the coals. To maintain a constant fire temperature, add 5 or 6 briquets every 30 minutes, spacing them evenly.

Adjusting the distance between meat & fire.
In general, position the spitted meat so its surface is about 5 inches from the coals. To adjust the distance, you can raise or lower either the spit or the firebed, depending on your barbecue.

Meat Cut or Bird, Weight & Preparation	Dimensions or Diameter	Test for Doneness & Approximate Cooking Time
Pork loin (4–11 lbs.): Roast may include shoulder end of loin; if so, have blade bone removed and tie end to hold compactly.	An irregular oval, 3½–4 inches by 6–6½ inches	Meat thermometer registers 150°–155°F. About 2½ hours.
Leg of lamb (5½–6½ lbs.): Cut shank bone off at joint.	An irregular oval, 3½–4 inches by 7½–8 inches	Meat thermometer registers 135°–140°F (R), 150°F (M), 160°F (W). 2–2½ hours (M).
Beef standing rib roast (from 3-rib size up to about 12 lbs.): Use small end of standing rib; cut rib bones off close to meaty portion.	Meaty section 6½–7 inches across; bony section 9–10 inches across.	Meat thermometer registers 135°–140°F (R), 150°F (M), 160°F (W). 4–4½ hours (R).
Boneless pork loin end or pork shoulder roast (about 2½ lbs.)	3–3½ inches	Meat thermometer registers 150°–155°F. About 1½ hours.
Boneless leg of lamb roast (3½–4¾ lbs.)	4¼–4¾ inches	Meat thermometer registers 135°–140°F (R), 150°F (M), 160°F (W). 2–2¼ hours (M).
Boneless leg of pork roast (6½–7½ lbs.)	4½–5 inches	Meat thermometer registers 150°–155°F. About 3½ hours.
Beef rib eye or sirloin tip roast (4–12 lbs.): Wrap with a thin layer of fat.	5–5½ inches	Meat thermometer registers 135°–140°F (R), 150°F (M), 160°F (W). 2–2½ hours (R).
Chicken, frying (3–4 lbs.) or roasting (6–7 lbs.)	4–4½ inches (frying) or 5½–6 inches (roasting)	Meat thermometer inserted in thigh registers 185°F. 80–90 minutes (frying), 2¼–2½ hours (roasting).
Rock Cornish game hens (1¼–1½ lbs.)	3–3¼ inches	Meat near thighbone is no longer pink; cut to test. 70–80 min.
Turkey (12–14 lbs.)	7½–8 inches	Meat thermometer inserted in thigh registers 185°F. 4¼–4¾ hours.

(R) Rare; (M) Medium; (W) Well done

FLAVORING FOODS WITH SMOKE

Flavoring foods with the smoke of fragrant woods is an ancient cooking art still very much in style with modern patio chefs. On these pages, we offer two alternative techniques for smoking beef, pork, lamb, fish, and poultry. *Quick smoke-flavoring* can easily be accomplished on a covered barbecue; *smoke-cooking* requires a special piece of equipment called a smoker.

WOODS FOR SMOKING

Whether you choose smoke-flavoring or smoke-cooking, your first consideration will be what type of wood to use. Consult the chart on page 23 for ideas; for each kind of meat, we include a list of appropriate woods. These dried woods can be purchased in 2- to 3-inch chunks, small logs, twigs, chips, or sawdust; the size determines how long the wood must be soaked before using.

If you want to experiment with garden cuttings, choose the same unsprayed woods listed in the chart, or try peach, pear, apricot, pecan, or black walnut. Break clippings into small twigs and cut limbs into chunks or short lengths. Green wood may be used as is; if the wood is dry, soak it in water. *Do not* use random garden clippings, which may contain poisonous plants such as oleander. Also avoid the wood of cedar, fir, pine, spruce, and eucalyptus; their smoke gives food a bitter, resinous taste.

QUICK SMOKE-FLAVORING

If you own a covered barbecue, you can add a delicate smoke flavor to foods as they cook by indirect heat. Start by soaking your choice of wood chips or chunks in water—20 minutes for chips, 45 to 60 minutes for chunks. Then prepare the barbecue fire for indirect heat (see page 10); sprinkle each pile of coals with 1 cup wet wood chips or top with one wood chunk. Set the cooking grill, food, and lid in place and adjust dampers as needed to maintain an even heat. Cook as the recipe directs. Add more wet wood chips about every 30 minutes, when you can no longer see smoke coming from the vents. (There's no need to add extra chunks—they burn longer than chips.)

SMOKE-COOKING

Very slow, even cooking in a smoker produces succulent, smoky-flavored meats, fish, and poultry that taste as good or better than high-priced commercial products. Many types of smokers are sold in hardware, department, and outdoor supply stores; various smokers are also available from mail-order catalogs specializing in outdoor equipment.

One of the most popular units is the water smoker, which uses steam to keep the inside temperature low and even. Thanks to the steam and the long, slow cooking, foods remain moist and have plenty of time to absorb the swirling smoke.

As the illustration on page 22 shows, a water smoker looks like an elongated covered barbecue. In the base is a heat source (charcoal, gas, or electric); directly above it is a water pan. Two or three cooking racks are inside, and a domed lid with a temperature gauge fits on top.

Our smoke-cooking directions and the times given on our smoking chart apply to a charcoal-fueled water smoker. If you have a different type of unit, check the manufacturer's directions for cooking information.

Preparing the food. To prepare foods for smoking, you can brush them with olive oil or salad oil, or soak them in a spicy-sweet brine. Brining has several advantages—foods stay moister, the salty-sweet brine complements the smoky flavor, and the shelf life of the food is tripled. (Without brining, smoked foods can be kept only as long as those cooked by any other method.)

■ *Brining.* To make the brine, you'll need a container made from a noncorrodible material such as plastic, glass, or stainless steel; make sure it's large enough to hold 10 pounds of meat, fish, or poultry.

In the container, combine 3 quarts **cool water,** 2 cups firmly packed **brown sugar,** 1½ cups **salt,** 3 cloves **garlic** (halved), 2 teaspoons **whole black peppercorns,** and 4 **bay leaves.** Stir briskly until sugar and salt are dissolved. Then add **foods to be smoked,** submerging them in brine. Let fish, spareribs, and small birds (quail, squab, game hens) stand at room temperature for 1 hour; brine turkey breast, whole chicken, duck, and pheasant for 2 hours at room temperature. Cover 2½- to 4½-pound rolled and tied beef, pork, or lamb roasts and let soak for at least 8 hours (or until next day) in the refrigerator.

After the food has soaked for the recommended time, lift it from the brine and rinse thor-

Colored a rich mahogany, this smoked turkey (page 23) cooks slowly over smoldering hickory chips in a water smoker. Serve the bird hot for a holiday meal, or offer it cold at a picnic with assorted pickled fruits.

...Smoke-cooking

oughly under a thin stream of cool water, rubbing gently to release salt. Pat the food dry, then set it on a rack and let dry until the surface feels tacky (30 to 60 minutes). At this point, you may cover and refrigerate brined foods until next day.

Setting up the smoker. We did our testing in a charcoal-fueled water smoker, using 2-inch pressed charcoal briquets. If your water smoker is powered by gas or electricity, follow the manufacturer's directions.

■ *Starting the fire.* Begin by checking the chart on the facing page for the approximate cooking times of the foods you're smoking. For up to 5 hours of cooking, allow 8 pounds of briquets—a level charcoal pan in most units. For more than 5 hours, you'll need about 12 pounds of charcoal—a heaping panful in most units. Open all vents and ignite the charcoal, using one of the methods suggested on pages 8 and 10. When the coals are hot (about 30 minutes), it's time to add wet or green wood for smoke.

■ *Adding wood.* Consult the chart for the amount and type of wood to use, keeping in mind that one wood chunk (or small log) weighs about 4 ounces and is equivalent to 2 cups of wood chips, twigs, or sawdust.

We recommend you start with the minimum amount of wood listed—the smoke should enhance, not overwhelm, the taste of the food. If you want a smokier flavor, increase the amount of wood the next time you smoke-cook. Soak dry chunks or logs in water for 45 to 60 minutes; soak smaller pieces for just 15 to 20 minutes. Lift wood from water, let drain, and distribute *all* of it over the hot coals.

■ *Adding water to make steam.* Line the water pan with foil for easy cleaning, then set the pan in place over the hot coals. Fill pan with 3 quarts hot tap water.

■ *Adding food.* Pat foods (both brined and unbrined) dry, then brush with olive oil or salad oil to prevent the surfaces from drying out. Set the cooking racks in place; arrange food on racks in a single layer, allowing 1 inch between pieces. If you want to smoke several foods with different cooking times, place the smaller pieces on the top racks so they can easily be removed when they're done. Also remember that foods above will drip on those below; stack with care, so incompatible flavors won't mingle.

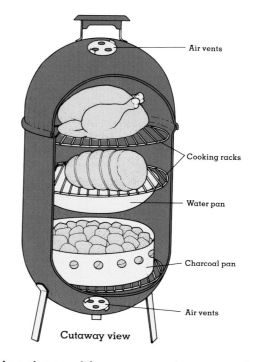

Air vents
Cooking racks
Water pan
Charcoal pan
Air vents

Cutaway view

During the smoking process. A water smoker functions practically unattended. You'll probably need to add more water after 3½ to 4 hours, but otherwise keep the door closed unless you're testing for doneness or adding coals or water to adjust temperature. Opening the smoker too often allows heat and smoke to escape.

Check the temperature gauge occasionally; it should consistently read 170° to 200°F. When the heat drops too low, try opening the vents. If the temperature stays too cool for more than 30 minutes, add a few extra coals. When the heat rises above 200°F, close the vents slightly; if that doesn't work, add cool water to the water pan. (In some smokers, water can't be poured directly into the pan from the outside. In this case, pour it through the racks, not over the food.)

Checking foods for doneness. Test foods for doneness as the chart directs, making a small cut into the center of the food if necessary. Keep in mind that the smoke may tint foods a bright pink just beneath the browned surface.

SERVING & STORING SMOKED FOODS

You can serve smoke-cooked foods hot or cold. To serve foods cold, let them cool after smoking, then wrap tightly and refrigerate. Unbrined smoked foods can be stored 1 to 3 days depending on size— 1 to 2 days for small pieces, 2 to 3 days for medium or large ones. Brined foods keep three times as long.

SMOKE-COOKING GUIDE

Type of Meat	Weight or Thickness	Best Woods for Smoking	Number of 2- to 3-inch Wood Chunks	Test for Doneness & Approximate Cooking Time
BEEF				
Boneless roasts (rib, sirloin tip, crossrib)	3½–4½ lbs.	Grapevine, hickory, oak, mountain mahogany, mesquite	2–4	Meat thermometer registers 135°–140°F (R);* or until done to your liking. 4–5 hours (R).
PORK				
Boneless loin	2½–3 lbs.	Alder, apple, cherry, grapevine, hickory, mesquite	2–6	Meat thermometer registers 155°–160°F.* 4–5 hours.
Bone-in loin or leg section	About 4 lbs.	Same as above	2–6	Meat thermometer registers 155°–160°F.* 5–7 hours.
Spareribs	Full slab	Same as above	1–3	Meat pulls easily from bone. 4–5 hours.
Sausages, such as Italian	1 inch	Same as above	1–3	Meat is firm and no longer pink in center; cut to test. 3–4 hours.
LAMB				
Leg, boned & tied	3½–4½ lbs.	Apple, cherry, oak	2–4	Meat thermometer registers 135°–140°F (R);* or until done to your liking. 4–5 hours (R).
FISH				
Whole, small**	About 1 lb.	Grapevine, hickory, oak, mesquite	1–3	Flakes when prodded in thickest part. About 1½ hours.
Fillets**	1–1½ inches thick	Same as above	1–3	Flakes when prodded in thickest part. 1½–2½ hours.
POULTRY				
Turkey, whole	12–14 lbs.	Alder, apple, cherry, grapevine, hickory, mesquite, oak	2–4	Meat thermometer inserted in breast registers 165°F.* 6–8 hours.
Turkey breast, bone-in	4–5 lbs.	Same as above	2–4	Meat thermometer registers 165°F.* 4–6 hours.
Chicken, whole	3½–4½ lbs.	Same as above	1–3	Meat near thighbone is no longer pink; cut to test. 4–6 hours.
Duck	4½–5 lbs.	Same as above	2–4	Breast meat is moist but firm near bone; cut to test. 4–5 hours.
Pheasant	About 3 lbs.	Same as above	2–4	Breast meat is moist and faintly pink near bone; cut to test. 4–6 hours.
Rock Cornish game hen	About 1½ lbs.	Same as above	1–3	Meat near thighbone is no longer pink; cut to test. 3–5 hours.
Squab	About 1 lb.	Same as above	1–3	Breast meat is moist but firm near bone; cut to test. 3–5 hours.
Quail	3–6 oz.	Same as above	1 or 2	Breast meat is moist but firm near bone; cut to test. 1½–2 hours.

*Insert meat thermometer in thickest part of meat or poultry, not touching bone.
**Choose fish such as salmon, trout, sturgeon, white sea bass, sablefish, tuna, bonito, mackerel, or yellowtail.

*Savory toppings stack up on 12-inch Mexican Platter Burger
(page 26): Cheddar cheese, green chiles, tomatoes, guacamole,
and sliced olives. Feature this show-stopping sandwich at
a back-yard party for ten.*

Beef

BURGERS ■ STEAKS ■ RIBS ■ ROASTS

From burgers to steaks, ribs to roasts, you're sure to please when you barbecue beef.

When friends stop by for a swim or a post-game party, treat them to a platter-size hamburger or *fajitas*—sliced skirt steak to be tucked into warm tortillas. Or, if you feel like splurging, choose a festive whole beef tenderloin or a boneless New York strip. And don't neglect the less expensive cuts such as chuck and brisket. Marinated before grilling and served rare or medium-rare, they're tender and juicy, rivaling the more prestigious steaks and roasts in flavor.

For parties as well as more casual times, you can easily devise your own recipes for barbecued beef. Pair one of our marinades or sauces (page 27) with your favorite cut of beef; then follow the basic grilling times and techniques on page 15.

(Pictured on page 24)

MEXICAN PLATTER BURGER

Preparation time: About 25 minutes

Grilling time: About 15 minutes

Using two rimless baking sheets as "spatulas," you can flip this platter-size hamburger neatly and easily.

> 1 round loaf (1½ lbs.) French bread
> ½ cup (¼ lb.) butter or margarine, at room temperature
> 1 tablespoon chili powder
>   Toppings (directions follow)
> ¼ cup prepared taco sauce
> 3 tablespoons instant minced onion
> 2 cloves garlic, minced or pressed
> 2 teaspoons *each* chili powder and oregano leaves
> 1 teaspoon *each* ground cumin and salt
> 2½ pounds lean ground beef
> 8 ounces thinly sliced Cheddar cheese

Using a long, serrated knife, cut bread in half horizontally.

In a small bowl, beat butter and the 1 tablespoon chili powder until blended; spread evenly over cut sides of bread. Set bread aside. Also prepare toppings and set aside.

In a large bowl, combine taco sauce, onion, garlic, the 2 teaspoons chili powder, oregano, cumin, salt, and beef; mix well. Turn meat mixture onto a large baking sheet lined with wax paper; pat into a round patty 1 inch wider than bread (meat patty will be approximately 12 inches in diameter).

Holding both ends of baking sheet, invert meat patty onto a lightly greased grill 4 to 6 inches above a solid bed of medium coals. Lift off wax paper.

Cook for about 7 minutes, then turn. To turn, use 2 rimless baking sheets. Using one baking sheet as a pusher, slide patty onto second sheet. Then hold patty between baking sheets; invert sheets to flip patty. Slide patty back onto grill, cooked side up; overlap cheese slices on top. Continue to cook until done to your liking; cut to test (about 7 more minutes for medium-rare).

Slide cooked burger back onto one baking sheet; keep warm. Place bread halves on grill, cut side down, and heat until lightly toasted. Cut top half of bread into wedges; keep warm. Slide burger onto bottom half of bread. Arrange toppings over burger. Cut into serving-size wedges; accompany with bread wedges. Makes 8 to 10 servings.

Toppings. Halve and pit 2 medium-size ripe **avocados;** scoop flesh into a bowl and mash with a fork. Stir in 3 tablespoons **lemon juice** and season to taste with **garlic salt** and **liquid hot pepper seasoning.** Also have ready 2 cans (4 oz. *each*) **whole green chiles,** drained, split, seeded, and flattened; 2 medium-size **tomatoes,** sliced; and 3 large **pitted ripe olives,** sliced.

Per serving: 680 calories, 33 g protein, 46 g carbohydrates, 40 g total fat, 121 mg cholesterol, 1123 mg sodium

Greek Platter Burger

Cut and butter bread as directed for **Mexican Platter Burger,** but substitute 2 cloves **garlic** (minced or pressed) for the 1 tablespoon chili powder.

For the toppings, beat 2 small packages (3 oz. *each*) **cream cheese** (at room temperature) until smooth; stir in 4 ounces **feta cheese,** crumbled. Also have ready 1 large mild **red onion,** sliced; 2 medium-size **tomatoes,** sliced; 1 jar (6 oz.) **marinated artichoke hearts,** drained; and a **mint sprig.**

For the meat patty, combine 3 tablespoons *each* **lemon juice** and **instant minced onion;** 3 cloves **garlic** (minced or pressed); 2 teaspoons **oregano leaves;** ¾ teaspoon **ground coriander;** 1 teaspoon **salt;** ¼ cup *each* finely chopped **fresh mint** and **parsley;** and 1 pound *each* **lean ground beef** and **lean ground lamb.** Mix thoroughly. Shape and grill as directed for **Mexican Platter Burger,** but omit Cheddar cheese.

Per serving: 560 calories, 27 g protein, 44 g carbohydrates, 30 g total fat, 118 mg cholesterol, 1025 mg sodium

MARINADES, SAUCES & BUTTERS FOR BEEF

The robust flavor of beef calls for a marinade, butter, or sauce of equally assertive character. We suggest herbed wine, pungent mustard, or teriyaki-style marinades, a pair of classic barbecue sauces, and butters seasoned with shallots or blue cheese.

You'll find basic grilling times and techniques for beef on page 15.

MARINADES

A marinade containing wine, vinegar, or citrus juice is the best choice for less tender cuts such as chuck, flank, skirt, or round steaks: the acidic liquid helps tenderize the meat.

Marinate the meat in a close-fitting dish, pan, or bowl, or use a heavy-duty plastic bag. A marinating time of at least 4 hours—or preferably until the next day—will give you the tenderest and most flavorful meat; if you must cut the time short, you might want to apply an unsalted meat tenderizer just before cooking.

Wine & Garlic Marinade. In a bowl, stir together 1 cup **dry red wine,** 2 tablespoons **red wine vinegar,** 2 cloves **garlic** (minced or pressed), 1 teaspoon **oregano leaves,** and 2 tablespoons **salad oil.** Makes about 1¼ cups.

Dijon Marinade. In a bowl, stir together ½ cup **salad oil;** ¼ cup *each* **white wine vinegar,** finely chopped **shallots,** and **Dijon mustard;** and 2 cloves **garlic** (minced or pressed). Makes about 1 cup.

Teriyaki Marinade. In a bowl, stir together ⅔ cup **soy sauce,** ⅓ cup **honey,** 2 teaspoons grated **fresh ginger,** 3 tablespoons **dry sherry,** ½ cup **salad oil,** 1 clove **garlic** (minced or pressed), and ½ cup thinly sliced **green onions** (including tops). Makes about 1¾ cups.

BASTING SAUCES

Basting with one of these two sauces adds zippy flavor to tender cuts of beef that don't need marinating—ground beef or steaks such as sirloin, T-bone, New York, Porterhouse, or tenderized chuck. To prevent scorching, apply the sauces during the last few minutes of cooking; pass any remaining sauce at the table.

Beef Barbecue Sauce. Melt ½ cup (¼ lb.) **butter** or margarine in a small pan over medium heat; add 1 clove **garlic** (minced or pressed) and ¼ cup minced **onion.** Cook, stirring often, until onion is soft (about 10 minutes). Stir in 3 tablespoons **catsup;** 2 tablespoons *each* minced **parsley, lemon juice,** and **red wine vinegar;** 1 teaspoon *each* **dry mustard** and **liquid hot pepper seasoning;** ⅛ teaspoon **ground red pepper** (cayenne); and ¼ cup **beer.** Bring to a boil; then reduce heat and simmer, uncovered, until flavors are blended (about 5 minutes). Makes about 1 cup.

Heavy-Duty Barbecue Sauce. Heat 2 tablespoons **salad oil** in a 2- to 3-quart pan over low heat. Add 1 clove **garlic** (minced or pressed) and cook, stirring often, until garlic is golden (about 5 minutes). Stir in 1 can (6 oz.) **tomato paste,** ½ cup **light molasses,** ¼ cup *each* **prepared mustard** and **soy sauce,** 3 tablespoons **Worcestershire,** 2 tablespoons **red wine vinegar,** and 2 teaspoons **ground sage;** then season with 1 to 3 teaspoons **liquid hot pepper seasoning** and ½ to 1 teaspoon **pepper.** Simmer, uncovered, until flavors are blended (about 10 minutes). Makes about 2 cups.

SEASONED BUTTERS

A seasoned butter offers a simple way to flavor beef. Brush the melted butters over meats as they cook, or just spoon softened butters atop meats hot from the grill. To let the flavors blend, prepare the butters at least 1 hour (or up to 1 week) ahead.

Shallot Butter. Melt 2 tablespoons **butter** or margarine in a wide frying pan over medium heat. Add ½ cup finely chopped **shallots** and cook, stirring, until soft (about 10 minutes). Add 2 tablespoons **dry sherry** and cook until liquid has evaporated. Let cool thoroughly, then combine with ½ cup (¼ lb.) **butter** or margarine (at room temperature) and ¼ teaspoon **salt.** Beat until fluffy; cover and refrigerate for up to 1 week. Makes about 1 cup.

Blue Cheese Butter. In a bowl, combine 1 cup (½ lb.) **butter** or margarine (at room temperature) and ½ cup (about 2 oz.) crumbled **blue cheese.** Beat until well blended. Cover and refrigerate for up to 1 week. Makes about 1¼ cups.

(Pictured on facing page)

LEBANESE HAMBURGERS

Preparation time: About 45 minutes

Grilling time: About 12 minutes

Start by slow-cooking the onions to bring out their sweetness. Then quickly grill the spicy beef patties and serve the two together.

  1 **tablespoon** *each* **ground cinnamon and paprika**
  1 **teaspoon salt**
  ¾ **teaspoon ground red pepper (cayenne)**
  ½ **cup (¼ lb.) butter or margarine**
  4 **large onions, sliced**
  4 **small tomatoes, cut into ½-inch-thick slices**
     Yogurt Sauce (recipe follows)
  3 **pounds lean ground beef**
  ½ **cup water**
  6 **pocket breads,** *each* **about 7 inches in diameter, cut into halves**

Combine cinnamon, paprika, salt, and red pepper; set aside. Melt 6 tablespoons of the butter in a wide frying pan over low heat. Add onions and cook, stirring often, until pale golden and very soft (about 40 minutes); stir in half the spice mixture after 20 minutes. Transfer cooked onions to a heat-proof dish and place in a 300° oven.

Melt remaining 2 tablespoons butter in frying pan over medium heat; add tomatoes. Cook for 1 to 2 minutes on each side. Distribute tomatoes and any juices over onions; return to oven.

Prepare Yogurt Sauce; cover and refrigerate.

In a bowl, blend remaining spice mixture with beef and water; then shape into 12 patties, each about 4 inches in diameter. Also stack pocket breads and wrap in heavy-duty foil. Place patties and foil packet on a lightly greased grill 4 to 6 inches above a solid bed of hot coals. Cook, turning once, until meat is done to your liking; cut to test (about 12 minutes for medium). Serve patties in pocket bread, with onion mixture and Yogurt Sauce. Makes 12 servings.

Per serving: 402 calories, 24 g protein, 24 g carbohydrates, 23 g total fat, 91 mg cholesterol, 509 mg sodium

Yogurt Sauce. In a serving bowl, stir together 2 cups **plain yogurt,** 1 clove **garlic** (minced or pressed), and 2 tablespoons minced **fresh mint.** Makes about 2 cups.

Per tablespoon: 9 calories, .7 g protein, 1 g carbohydrates, 2 g total fat, .9 mg cholesterol, 10 mg sodium

TACO BURGERS

Preparation time: About 15 minutes

Grilling time: 4–6 minutes

Cradle a beef patty and some refried beans in a warm corn tortilla; add tomatoes and avocado, then drizzle with taco sauce.

  1 **can (about 1 lb.) refried beans**
  2 **medium-size tomatoes, sliced**
  1 **large ripe avocado, pitted, peeled, sliced, and tossed with 2 teaspoons lemon juice**
  1 **pound lean ground beef**
  1 **small onion, chopped**
  ¼ **cup fine dry bread crumbs**
  1 **egg, beaten**
  1 **teaspoon Worcestershire**
  ⅓ **cup canned diced green chiles**
  ¾ **teaspoon ground cumin**
  6 **corn tortillas**
     Prepared taco sauce

Place beans in a pan and heat through; keep warm. Place tomatoes and avocado in separate dishes.

In a bowl, combine beef, onion, bread crumbs, egg, Worcestershire, chiles, and cumin. Mix well, then shape into 6 rectangular patties, each about ⅜ inch thick.

Place patties on a lightly greased grill 4 to 6 inches above a solid bed of hot coals. Cook, turning once, until browned and done to your liking; cut to test (4 to 6 minutes for medium-rare). To serve, heat tortillas on grill just until softened (15 to 20 seconds), turning often with tongs. Spread some beans on a tortilla; then place a meat patty, tomatoes, and avocado slices on one side and drizzle with taco sauce. Fold other side of tortilla over meat and vegetables; eat out of hand. Makes 6 servings.

Per serving: 406 calories, 23 g protein, 36 g carbohydrates, 19 g total fat, 93 mg cholesterol, 475 mg sodium

Warm sautéed onions, juicy tomato slices, and spicy beef patties are all tucked into pocket bread for tempting Lebanese Hamburgers (facing page). A dollop of cool, minty yogurt sauce tempers the spirited seasonings.

CAL-MEX BURGERS

Preparation time: 10–15 minutes

Grilling time: 10–12 minutes

Jack cheese, green chiles, and pinto beans hide inside these barbecued hamburgers. Serve them in warm flour tortillas with complementary toppings.

   1½ pounds lean ground beef
    1 medium-size white onion, chopped
    6 slices (1 oz. *each*) jack cheese
    ¼ cup canned diced green chiles
    ¼ cup canned pinto beans, drained
       Salt and pepper
       Butter or margarine
    6 flour tortillas, *each* about 8 inches in diameter
       Prepared taco sauce
       Fresh cilantro (coriander) sprigs
       Thinly sliced tomatoes

Mix beef and onion, then divide into 6 equal portions and shape each into a patty about 6 inches in diameter. Cut cheese slices diagonally in half to make triangles. Arrange 1 triangle on half of each meat patty so tips of cheese touch edges of meat.

Evenly spoon chiles over cheese, then evenly top with beans and sprinkle with salt and pepper. Arrange remaining cheese triangles on top. Fold plain half of meat patty over filling and pinch edges together to seal, forming a half-moon of stuffed meat.

Place patties on a lightly greased grill 4 to 6 inches above a solid bed of hot coals. Cook, turning as needed, until patties are browned on both sides and meat in center is done to your liking; cut to test (10 to 12 minutes for medium-rare).

Meanwhile, lightly butter tortillas. Stack, wrap in foil, and place at side of grill to warm. Turn package over several times to heat evenly.

To serve, place a stuffed meat patty on a tortilla and top with taco sauce, cilantro, and tomatoes; then fold tortilla over meat. Eat out of hand. Makes 6 servings.

Per serving: 487 calories, 31 g protein, 27 g carbohydrates, 28 g total fat, 105 mg cholesterol, 539 mg sodium

SOY-DIPPED HAMBURGERS

Preparation time: About 10 minutes

Marinating time: 1–2 hours

Grilling time: About 10 minutes

These hamburgers are a good choice for a picnic: you can shape the meat patties at home, then marinate them en route to the picnic site.

   ½ cup *each* soy sauce and water
    1 clove garlic, minced or pressed
    2 teaspoons grated fresh ginger
    2 tablespoons Worcestershire
    6 tablespoons firmly packed brown sugar
    3 pounds lean ground beef
    8 hamburger buns or French rolls, split and buttered
       Thinly sliced tomatoes
       Green bell pepper rings

In a bowl, mix soy, water, garlic, ginger, Worcestershire, and sugar. Shape beef into 8 patties, each about 1 inch thick; place in a large heavy-duty plastic bag. Pour soy marinade over patties in bag; seal bag securely and rotate to distribute marinade. Place in a shallow baking pan. Refrigerate (or place in a picnic cooler) for 1 to 2 hours.

Lift patties from marinade and drain briefly (reserve marinade). Place patties on a lightly greased grill 4 to 6 inches above a solid bed of hot coals. Cook, turning once and basting several times with marinade, until done to your liking; cut to test (about 10 minutes for medium-rare). When you turn patties, place buns, cut side down, around outside of grill to toast. Serve patties on buns, with tomatoes and bell pepper rings. Makes 8 servings.

Per serving: 534 calories, 34 g protein, 37 g carbohydrates, 29 g total fat, 118 mg cholesterol, 1408 mg sodium

CRUNCHY ONION BURGERS

Preparation time: About 5 minutes

Grilling time: About 10 minutes

Crisp canned French-fried onions contribute a pleasant surprise in flavor and texture to these simple beef burgers.

- 1½ **pounds lean ground beef**
- ½ **teaspoon salt**
- ¼ **teaspoon pepper**
- 1 **tablespoon catsup**
- 1 **can (3½ oz.) French-fried onions, crumbled**
- 6 **hamburger buns or English muffins, split and buttered**

Mix beef, salt, pepper, catsup, and onions. Shape into 6 patties, each about 1 inch thick.

Place patties on a lightly greased grill 4 to 6 inches above a solid bed of hot coals. Cook, turning once, until done to your liking; cut to test (about 10 minutes for medium-rare). When you turn patties, place buns, cut side down, around outside of grill to toast. Serve patties in buns. Makes 6 servings.

Per serving: 410 calories, 24 g protein, 24 g carbohydrates, 24 g total fat, 83 mg cholesterol, 542 mg sodium

STEAK SANDWICH WITH MUSHROOM SAUCE

Preparation time: 20–25 minutes

Marinating time: 2–4 hours

Grilling time: About 15 minutes

Leftover red wine marinade becomes part of the rich-tasting mushroom sauce for these open-faced sirloin-on-rye sandwiches. Garnish each serving with a sprinkling of parsley.

- ½ **cup dry red wine**
- ½ **medium-size onion, cut into chunks**
- 2 **tablespoons lemon juice**
- ¼ **cup olive oil or salad oil**
- 1 **clove garlic**
- ¼ **teaspoon** *each* **salt and pepper**
- 1½ **pounds boneless top sirloin steak, cut about 1 inch thick**
- ¼ **cup butter or margarine**
- 1 **pound mushrooms, sliced**
- 6 **slices light rye bread, buttered**
  Chopped parsley

In a blender, combine wine, onion, lemon juice, oil, garlic, salt, and pepper. Whirl until blended.

Place steak in a heavy-duty plastic bag; then pour in wine mixture. Seal bag securely and rotate to distribute marinade. Place in a shallow baking pan and refrigerate for 2 to 4 hours, turning bag over several times.

Remove steak from marinade and drain briefly (reserve marinade); set steak aside. Melt butter in a wide frying pan over medium heat. Add mush-rooms and cook, stirring, for about 5 minutes. Add reserved marinade and increase heat to high. Boil, stirring constantly, until just slightly reduced and thickened. Keep warm while steak cooks.

Place steak on a lightly greased grill 4 to 6 inches above a solid bed of hot coals. Cook, turning once, until done to your liking; cut to test (about 15 minutes for rare). When you turn steak, place bread, buttered side down, around outside of grill to toast.

To serve, let steak stand for 5 minutes, then cut across the grain into thin slanting slices. Place a few slices on each piece of toast, cover with mushroom sauce, and sprinkle with parsley. Makes 6 servings.

Per serving: 444 calories, 30 g protein, 18 g carbohydrates, 29 g total fat, 102 mg cholesterol, 402 mg sodium

Sprigs of thyme twine around skewered Skirt Steaks with Fresh
Herbs (facing page). Accompany the quick-to-cook meat with
butter-basted grilled tomatoes and corn in husks.

(Pictured on facing page)

⬡ SKIRT STEAKS WITH FRESH HERBS

Preparation time: 10–15 minutes

Marinating time: 4 hours or until next day

Grilling time: About 6 minutes

Fresh herbs add a tantalizing aroma and flavor to barbecued meats. The heat of the coals releases the herbs' volatile oils, which are absorbed by the meat juices during grilling.

- 1½ **to 2 pounds skirt steaks, trimmed of excess fat**
- ½ **cup olive oil**
- 3 **tablespoons red wine vinegar**
- 1 **tablespoon Dijon mustard**
- 1 **clove garlic, minced or pressed**
- ¼ **teaspoon pepper**
- 25 **to 30 fresh thyme, rosemary, or tarragon sprigs, *each* about 3 inches long**

Cut steaks crosswise into about 12-inch lengths, then arrange in a 9- by 13-inch dish. In a bowl, mix oil, vinegar, mustard, garlic, and pepper. Pour over meat; turn meat to coat. Cover and refrigerate for at least 4 hours or until next day, turning meat occasionally.

Soak herb sprigs in water to cover for about 30 minutes.

Lift meat from marinade and drain briefly (reserve marinade). Weave each piece of meat onto a long metal skewer, rippling meat very slightly and tucking an herb sprig between skewer and meat on both sides of meat.

Place skewers on a lightly greased grill 4 to 6 inches above a solid bed of hot coals. Cook, turning often and basting with marinade, until done to your liking; cut to test (about 6 minutes for rare). Makes about 6 servings.

Per serving: 378 calories, 22 g protein, 3 g carbohydrates, 31 g total fat, 58 mg cholesterol, 146 mg sodium

⬡ COSTA RICAN SKIRT STEAKS

Preparation time: 5 minutes

Marinating time: 4 hours or until next day

Grilling time: About 6 minutes

We first sampled this barbecued beef (*carne asada*) in the northern part of Costa Rica, where the steak strips are served with warm corn tortillas, black beans, and rice.

- 3 **to 4 pounds skirt steaks, trimmed of excess fat**
- ⅓ **cup Worcestershire**
- 2 **cloves garlic, minced or pressed**
- ⅛ **teaspoon pepper**
- ½ **cup catsup**
- ½ **teaspoon liquid hot pepper seasoning**

Cut steaks crosswise into about 12-inch lengths, then arrange in a 9- by 13-inch dish. In a bowl, mix Worcestershire, garlic, and pepper; pour over meat and turn meat to coat. Cover and refrigerate for at least 4 hours or until next day, turning meat occasionally.

Lift meat from marinade and drain briefly, reserving marinade; then mix reserved marinade with catsup and hot pepper seasoning and set aside. Place meat on a lightly greased grill 4 to 6 inches above a solid bed of hot coals. Turn meat a few times to brown lightly on both sides; brush with catsup mixture. Then cook, turning once, until meat is done to your liking; cut to test (about 6 minutes for rare). Makes 10 to 12 servings.

Per serving: 222 calories, 22 g protein, 4 g carbohydrates, 13 g total fat, 58 mg cholesterol, 266 mg sodium

VARIETY

MEATS

Variety or organ meats are rarely considered for barbecuing, yet their flavor and succulent texture make them an unusually tasty choice for any outdoor occasion. Just be sure that you don't overcook them.

GRILLED SWEETBREADS WITH FRAGRANT OILS

A day ahead, poach and separate the sweetbreads into meaty nuggets. Then simply brush the skewered morsels with seasoned oil and briefly grill.

> 1 to 1¼ pounds sweetbreads
> 1 tablespoon *each* olive oil, soy sauce, and rice wine vinegar
> 2 teaspoons chili oil
> 1 teaspoon sesame oil
> Lemon wedges

Rinse sweetbreads. Bring about 8 cups water to a boil in a 3- to 4-quart pan over high heat; add sweetbreads, then reduce heat, cover, and simmer for 15 minutes. Drain, then immerse in cold water until sweetbreads are cool enough to handle. Separate sweetbreads into naturally divided segments about ¾ inch in diameter; pull off most of the thick, rubbery membrane and easily removed tubes.

Divide sweetbread segments into 8 equal portions; thread each portion on a 10- to 12-inch metal skewer. (At this point, you may cover and refrigerate until next day.)

Stir together olive oil, soy, vinegar, chili oil, and sesame oil. Brush sweetbreads generously with oil mixture. Place skewers on a lightly greased grill 4 to 6 inches above a solid bed of medium coals. Cook,

turning skewers with tongs every 2 to 3 minutes and brushing frequently with oil mixture, until sweetbreads are well browned in spots (about 15 minutes). If flare-ups occur, move sweetbreads away from flames at once.

Push sweetbreads from skewers onto individual plates; offer lemon wedges to squeeze over individual portions. Makes 4 servings.

Per serving: 170 calories, 20 g protein, .5 g carbohydrates, 9 g total fat, 284 mg cholesterol, 367 mg sodium

GRILLED KIDNEYS

Beef, veal, lamb, and pork kidneys may be successfully grilled over charcoal. They take from 5 to 15 minutes to cook, depending on the size.

> 1 pound beef, veal, lamb, or pork kidneys
> Melted butter or margarine
> Salt and pepper

Split kidneys and remove fat and connective tissue. Brush with butter and place on a lightly greased grill 4 to 6 inches above a solid bed of medium coals. Cook, turning frequently, until browned on outside but still juicy and pink on inside; cut to test (5 to 15 minutes, depending on size). Season to taste with salt and pepper. To serve, cut into slices. Makes about 4 servings.

Per serving: 71 calories, 13 g protein, .47 g carbohydrates, 2 g total fat, 191 mg cholesterol, 66 mg sodium

LIVER, BACON & ONION SKEWERS

The familiar flavor combination of liver, bacon, and onions takes on a lively new dimension when served from a skewer. Partially cook the bacon strips first.

> 12 slices bacon
> 2 pounds baby beef liver, cut into ½-inch-thick slices
> Salt and pepper
> 1 can (about 1 lb.) small whole onions, drained

Cook bacon, a portion at a time, in a wide frying pan over medium heat until it is partially cooked but still limp (about 3 minutes). Drain on paper towels.

Remove any tubes and membranes from liver, then rinse liver and pat dry. Cut liver into 1-inch pieces and sprinkle lightly with salt and pepper. Divide bacon, liver, and onions into 6 equal portions.

To prepare each skewer, run tip of a sturdy metal skewer through one end of a bacon slice, then thread on a piece of liver and an onion; lap bacon over and pierce it. Add another piece of liver and an onion; pierce end of bacon slice, so bacon forms S-curves around liver and onions. Repeat the process, using 2 bacon slices for each skewer.

Place skewers on a lightly greased grill 4 to 6 inches above a solid bed of medium coals. Cook, turning often, until bacon is crisp and liver is browned on outside but still pink inside; cut to test (6 to 8 minutes). Makes 6 servings.

Per serving: 304 calories, 35 g protein, 12 g carbohydrates, 12 g total fat, 547 mg cholesterol, 593 mg sodium

LIVER WITH FRESH HERBS

Threaded on three parallel skewers, thick slices of liver are easy to turn. Fresh herbs tucked between skewers and meat impart a subtle flavor and fragrance.

¼ cup olive oil or salad oil
6 large onions, sliced
25 to 30 fresh sage, tarragon, or
    marjoram sprigs, *each* about
    3 inches long
½ pound sliced bacon
3 tablespoons lemon juice
2 pounds calf's liver, cut into
    1-inch-thick slices
    Salt and pepper

Heat oil in a wide frying pan over low heat. Add onions and cook, stirring often, until pale golden and very soft (about 40 minutes).

Meanwhile, soak herb sprigs in water to cover for 30 minutes. Also cook bacon in a wide frying pan over medium heat until crisp; lift out and drain on paper towels. Discard all but ¼ cup of the drippings; stir lemon juice into remaining drippings and set aside.

Remove any tubes and membranes from liver, then rinse liver and pat dry. Arrange liver slices side by side, with long sides almost touching. Weave 3 long metal skewers through liver slices at right angles to long sides, piercing each slice at least twice; space skewers at ends and middle of liver slices.

Divide herbs equally among liver slices, tucking sprigs under skewers to secure. Brush seasoned drippings over all sides of liver.

Place liver on a lightly greased grill 4 to 6 inches above a solid bed of hot coals. Cook, turning once and basting often with seasoned drippings, until liver is firm but still moist and pink in center; cut to test

(8 to 10 minutes). Wrap cooked bacon loosely in foil and warm on grill during last 2 to 3 minutes.

Transfer liver to a platter; remove skewers and cut liver into serving-size pieces. Accompany with bacon and onions. Let guests season foods to taste with salt and pepper. Makes 6 to 8 servings.

Per serving: 362 calories, 26 g protein, 16 g carbohydrates, 22 g total fat, 352 mg cholesterol, 246 mg sodium

GLAZED BEEF TONGUE

First you simmer the beef tongue until almost tender (this can be done a day ahead) and then finish cooking it in a covered barbecue for smoky flavor.

3- to 4-pound fresh beef tongue
1 large onion, chopped
1 cup buttermilk
1 tablespoon *each* Dijon mustard
    and honey
⅛ teaspoon pepper

Place tongue and onion in a 5-quart pan; cover with water. Bring to a boil over high heat; then reduce heat, cover, and simmer until meat is almost tender when pierced (about 2½ hours). Let cool in broth. (At this point, you may cover and refrigerate until next day.)

Remove skin and fat from cooled tongue (if refrigerated, let stand at room temperature for several hours before removing skin and fat). Set aside. In a small pan, combine buttermilk, mustard, honey, and pepper. Heat just until honey is dissolved. Remove from heat.

Barbecue tongue by indirect heat (see page 10), placing it on a lightly greased grill directly above drip pan. Cover barbecue and adjust dampers as necessary to maintain an even heat. Cook, basting frequently with buttermilk mixture, until meat is glazed and tender when pierced (about 1 hour). Makes 8 to 10 servings.

Per serving: 239 calories, 18 g protein, 4 g carbohydrates, 16 g total fat, 84 mg cholesterol, 117 mg sodium

(Pictured on facing page)

FAJITAS

Preparation time: 30–40 minutes

Marinating time: 4 hours or until next day

Grilling time: 15–20 minutes

Now popular in restaurants all over the country, *fajitas*—make-it-yourself burritos filled with grilled steak—are just as good at home.

       3 **pounds skirt steaks, trimmed of excess fat**
       ½ **cup lime juice**
       ⅓ **cup salad oil**
       ⅓ **cup tequila or lime juice**
       4 **cloves garlic, minced or pressed**
    1½ **teaspoons ground cumin**
       1 **teaspoon oregano leaves**
       ½ **teaspoon pepper**
       4 **or 5 small onions (unpeeled), cut in half lengthwise**
       8 **to 10 green onions, rinsed well and drained**
       3 **cans (about 1 lb. *each*) refried beans**
          Salsa Fresca (recipe follows)
          Guacamole (page 201)
     16 **to 20 flour tortillas, *each* about 8 inches in diameter**
          Sour cream
          Fresh cilantro (coriander) sprigs

Cut steaks crosswise into about 12-inch lengths, then arrange in a 9- by 13-inch dish. Mix lime juice, oil, tequila, garlic, cumin, oregano, and pepper. Pour over meat; turn meat to coat. Place onion halves, cut side down, in marinade alongside meat. Cover and refrigerate for at least 4 hours or until next day, turning meat occasionally.

Tie green onions together 3 inches from roots to form a brush. Heat beans in a large pan; keep warm. Prepare Salsa Fresca and Guacamole.

Place onion halves on a lightly greased grill 4 to 6 inches above a solid bed of hot coals. Cook for about 7 minutes; turn over. Lift meat from marinade and drain briefly (reserve marinade). Place on grill. Baste meat and onion halves with marinade, using green onion roots as a brush. Continue to cook onion halves until soft and browned (5 to 9 more minutes). Cook meat, turning once, until done to your liking; cut to test (about 6 minutes for rare). Transfer meat and onions to a carving board; keep warm. Roll green onion brush in marinade and lay on grill; turn often until tops are wilted (3 to 5 minutes). Place brush on board; remove string. Thinly slice meat across the grain.

Heat tortillas on grill as needed, turning often with tongs, just until softened (15 to 30 seconds). Place a few meat slices down center of each tortilla; top with some beans, a few pieces of onion from onion halves, Salsa Fresca, Guacamole, sour cream, and cilantro. Fold to enclose. Eat green onions alongside. Makes 8 to 10 servings.

Per serving: 695 calories, 41 g protein, 76 g carbohydrates, 24 g total fat, 70 mg cholesterol, 1082 mg sodium

Salsa Fresca. Mix 3 large ripe **tomatoes,** diced, ½ cup chopped **fresh cilantro (coriander),** and 1 small **onion,** chopped. Season to taste with 5 to 7 tablespoons seeded, minced **fresh hot chiles,** 3 to 4 tablespoons **lime juice,** and **salt.** Makes 3 cups.

Per tablespoon: 3 calories, .09 g protein, .6 g carbohydrates, .01 g total fat, 0 mg cholesterol, 399 mg sodium

FLANK STEAK ITALIANO

Preparation time: About 10 minutes

Grilling time: About 14 minutes

Slicing this steak reveals savory ribbons of salami, onion, and cheese inside the meat.

    1½ **pounds flank steak, trimmed of excess fat**
       1 **teaspoon dry basil**
       1 **package (6 oz.) sliced dry salami**
       1 **small white onion, thinly sliced**
       1 **package (6 oz.) sliced provolone cheese**

Lay steak flat. With a sharp knife, cut a deep, long slit in center of a long edge, making a pocket almost as big as steak; do not cut through at sides or back. Sprinkle basil inside pocket; top with half the salami, then with onion, cheese, and remaining salami. Close with metal skewers.

Place steak on a lightly greased grill 4 to 6 inches above a solid bed of medium coals. Cook, turning once, until steak is done to your liking; cut to test (about 14 minutes for medium-rare). To serve, let stand for 5 minutes; then remove skewers and cut steak across the grain into ½-inch-thick slanting slices. Makes 4 to 6 servings.

Per serving: 424 calories, 35 g protein, 2 g carbohydrates, 30 g total fat, 100 mg cholesterol, 846 mg sodium

Colors of the Southwest are captured in this meal. The main attraction: Fajitas (facing page), tender strips of grilled beef to top with fresh tomato salsa and wrap up in warm flour tortillas.

FLANK STEAK WITH LEMON-MUSTARD BASTE

Preparation time: 5–10 minutes

Grilling time: 10–14 minutes

A flavorful baste complements the natural good taste of lean flank steak—and eliminates the need for marinating.

> About 1½ pounds flank steak, trimmed of excess fat
> ¼ cup *each* lemon juice and firmly packed brown sugar
> 2 tablespoons *each* Dijon mustard and soy sauce
> 2 tablespoons olive oil or salad oil
> 1 clove garlic, minced or pressed
> ¼ teaspoon pepper

Score steak about ¼ inch deep on both sides, cutting diagonal slashes about 1 inch apart. Set steak aside.

In a small bowl, whisk together lemon juice, sugar, mustard, soy, oil, garlic, and pepper. Brush steak all over with some of the mustard mixture, then place on a lightly greased grill 4 to 6 inches above a solid bed of hot coals. Cook, turning once and basting several times with mustard mixture, until done to your liking; cut to test (10 to 14 minutes for medium-rare).

To serve, let steak stand for 5 minutes, then cut across the grain into thin slanting slices. Makes about 4 servings.

Per serving: 433 calories, 32 g protein, 16 g carbohydrates, 26 g total fat, 87 mg cholesterol, 850 mg sodium

FLANK STEAK & ORANGE SLICES

Preparation time: 5–10 minutes

Marinating time: 8 hours or until next day

Grilling time: 10–14 minutes

In Brazil, barbecued beef is often marinated in orange juice before grilling, then served with sliced fresh oranges.

> About 1½ pounds flank steak, trimmed of excess fat
> ½ cup orange juice
> 2 tablespoons instant minced onion
> 2 cloves garlic, minced or pressed
> ¼ teaspoon pepper
> 3 tablespoons salad oil
> 2 tablespoons red wine vinegar
> ¾ teaspoon ground cumin
> 2 or 3 large oranges, peeled and sliced

Place steak in a 9- by 13-inch dish. In a bowl, stir together orange juice, onion, garlic, pepper, oil, vinegar, and cumin. Pour over steak and turn steak to coat. Cover and refrigerate for at least 8 hours or until next day, turning steak occasionally.

Lift steak from marinade and drain briefly (reserve marinade). Place steak on a lightly greased grill 4 to 6 inches above a solid bed of hot coals. Cook, turning once and basting several times with marinade, until done to your liking; cut to test (10 to 14 minutes for medium-rare). To serve, let steak stand for 5 minutes, then cut across the grain into thin slanting slices. Garnish with oranges. Makes 4 servings.

Per serving: 453 calories, 33 g protein, 14 g carbohydrates, 29 g total fat, 87 mg cholesterol, 105 mg sodium

⊛ FLANK STEAK SANDWICHES OLÉ

Preparation time: About 15 minutes

Marinating time: 6 hours or until next day

Grilling time: 10–14 minutes

Spoon a zesty avocado and tomato dressing over cheese-topped slices of grilled beef piled high on a toasted French roll. If you prefer, substitute warmed flour tortillas for the rolls.

> About 1½ pounds flank steak, trimmed of excess fat
> ½ cup olive oil or salad oil
> ¼ cup *each* red wine vinegar, lime juice, and finely chopped onion
> 1 teaspoon *each* sugar and oregano leaves
> 2 cloves garlic, minced or pressed
> ¼ teaspoon *each* salt and ground cumin
> Avocado-Tomato Dressing (recipe follows)
> 6 French or steak rolls, split
> Prepared taco sauce or jalapeña sauce
> About 12 ounces sliced jack cheese

Place steak in a 9- by 13-inch dish. In a bowl, stir together oil, vinegar, lime juice, onion, sugar, oregano, garlic, salt, and cumin. Pour over steak, cover, and refrigerate for at least 6 hours or until next day, turning steak occasionally.

Prepare Avocado-Tomato Dressing; cover and refrigerate.

Lift steak from marinade and drain briefly (reserve marinade). Place steak on a lightly greased grill 4 to 6 inches above a solid bed of hot coals. Cook, turning once and basting several times with marinade, until done to your liking; cut to test (10 to 14 minutes for medium-rare). When you turn steak, place rolls, cut side down, around outside of grill to toast.

To serve, let steak stand for 5 minutes, then cut across the grain into thin slanting slices; pile slices evenly atop toasted rolls. Top each serving with a small amount of taco sauce, some of the sliced cheese, and several spoonfuls of Avocado-Tomato Dressing. Makes 6 servings.

Per serving: 748 calories, 40 g protein, 34 g carbohydrates, 49 g total fat, 110 mg cholesterol, 794 mg sodium

Avocado-Tomato Dressing. Pit, peel, and mash 1 large ripe **avocado**. Add 1½ teaspoons **lemon juice,** ¼ teaspoon **salt,** a few drops **liquid hot pepper seasoning,** 1 medium-size **tomato** (peeled and diced), ¼ cup chopped **onion,** and ¼ cup chopped **fresh cilantro (coriander).** Mix well. Makes about 1⅓ cups.

Per tablespoon: 21 calories, .3 g protein, 1 g carbohydrates, 2 g total fat, 0 mg cholesterol, 28 mg sodium

⊛ SESAME FLANK STEAK

Preparation time: 10–15 minutes

Marinating time: 4 hours or until next day

Grilling time: 10–14 minutes

Both toasted sesame seeds and sesame oil flavor this marinated steak. To accompany the meat, you might offer steamed rice and a cucumber salad.

> ¼ cup sesame seeds
> ¼ cup sliced green onions (including tops)
> 3 tablespoons soy sauce
> 2 tablespoons sesame oil or salad oil
> 1 tablespoon *each* vinegar, firmly packed brown sugar, minced fresh ginger, and minced garlic
> 1 teaspoon *each* dry mustard and Worcestershire
> 1½ pounds flank steak, trimmed of excess fat

Toast sesame seeds in a wide frying pan over medium heat until golden (about 3 minutes),

shaking pan often. Crush seeds with a mortar and pestle, then place in a bowl and stir in onions, soy, oil, vinegar, sugar, ginger, garlic, mustard, and Worcestershire.

Place steak in a 9- by 13-inch dish. Pour marinade over steak; turn steak to coat. Cover and refrigerate for at least 4 hours or until next day, turning steak several times.

Lift steak from marinade and drain briefly (reserve marinade). Place on a lightly greased grill 4 to 6 inches above a solid bed of hot coals. Cook, turning once and basting several times with marinade, until done to your liking; cut to test (10 to 14 minutes for medium-rare). To serve, let steak stand for 5 minutes, then cut across the grain into thin slanting slices. Makes about 4 servings.

Per serving: 445 calories, 34 g protein, 8 g carbohydrates, 30 g total fat, 87 mg cholesterol, 892 mg sodium

Hibachi-grilled Indonesian Beef Skewers (facing page) star at this Southeast Asian dinner. Alongside, offer peanut sauce, purchased chili sauce, coconut, and rice (colored yellow with turmeric).

(Pictured on facing page)

INDONESIAN BEEF SKEWERS

Preparation time: 20–30 minutes

Marinating time: 2 hours or until next day

Grilling time: 8–10 minutes

Satay is probably the best-known Southeast Asian food: Indonesia, Malaysia, and Singapore all claim it as their national dish. In this version, cubes of beef are grilled and served with a spicy peanut sauce.

> 1½ **pounds boneless top sirloin steak**
> 1 **clove garlic, minced or pressed**
> 2 **tablespoons soy sauce**
> 1 **tablespoon salad oil**
> 1 **teaspoon** *each* **ground cumin and ground coriander**
> **Basting Sauce (recipe follows)**
> **Peanut Sauce (recipe follows)**

Cut meat into 1-inch cubes. In a bowl, combine garlic, soy, oil, cumin, and coriander. Add meat and stir to coat; then cover and refrigerate for at least 2 hours or until next day, stirring occasionally.

Prepare Basting Sauce and Peanut Sauce. Also soak 10 to 12 long bamboo skewers in hot water to cover for at least 30 minutes or until next day.

Lift meat from marinade and drain briefly (discard marinade). Thread 4 or 5 pieces of meat on each skewer.

Arrange skewers on a lightly greased grill 2 to 4 inches above a solid bed of hot coals. Cook, turning often, until well browned and done to your liking; cut to test (8 to 10 minutes for medium-rare). About 3 minutes before meat is done, brush all over with Basting Sauce. Serve with Peanut Sauce. Makes 4 to 6 servings.

Basting Sauce. In a bowl, mix 3 tablespoons **lemon juice**, 2 tablespoons **soy sauce**, and ¼ teaspoon *each* **ground cumin** and **ground coriander**. If made ahead, cover and refrigerate for up to 2 days.

Per serving: 198 calories, 26 g protein, 1 g carbohydrates, 9 g total fat, 76 mg cholesterol, 572 mg sodium

Peanut Sauce. In a 2-quart pan, combine 1 cup **water**, ⅔ cup **creamy peanut butter**, and 2 cloves **garlic** (minced or pressed). Cook over medium-low heat, stirring, until mixture boils and thickens. Remove from heat and stir in 2 tablespoons firmly packed **brown sugar**, 1½ tablespoons **lemon juice**, 1 tablespoon **soy sauce**, and ¼ to ½ teaspoon **crushed red pepper**. Serve hot. If made ahead, cover and refrigerate for up to 2 days. To reheat, stir over low heat until hot; if necessary, add more water to restore to original consistency. Makes about 2 cups.

Per tablespoon: 36 calories, 2 g protein, 2 g carbohydrates, 3 g total fat, 2 mg cholesterol, 58 mg sodium

SIRLOIN STEAK SKEWERS

Preparation time: 10–15 minutes (including time to cut meat)

Marinating time: 4 hours or until next day

Grilling time: About 15 minutes

Cubes of sirloin steak are soaked in a wine-herb marinade, then threaded on skewers and grilled for a simple and delicious main dish.

> 3 **pounds boneless top sirloin steak, cut into 1½-inch cubes**
> ¾ **cup dry red wine**
> 3 **tablespoons olive oil or salad oil**
> 3 **tablespoons lemon juice**
> 2 **cloves garlic, minced or pressed**
> ¼ **teaspoon** *each* **dry rosemary and thyme leaves**

Place meat in a close-fitting bowl. In a small bowl, stir together wine, oil, lemon juice, garlic, rosemary, and thyme. Pour over meat, cover, and refrigerate for at least 4 hours or until next day, stirring occasionally.

Lift meat from marinade and drain briefly (reserve marinade). Thread meat equally on 6 to 8 sturdy metal skewers and place on a lightly greased grill 4 to 6 inches above a solid bed of hot coals. Cook, turning and basting often with marinade, until well browned and done to your liking; cut to test (about 15 minutes for medium-rare). Makes 6 to 8 servings.

Per serving: 265 calories, 30 g protein, 1 g carbohydrates, 15 g total fat, 79 mg cholesterol, 73 mg sodium

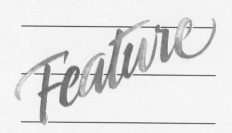

Whether you want to tease before-dinner appetites with just one or two tidbits or stage an all-appetizer patio party, savory morsels hot from the grill are a good choice. Have the ingredients ready in advance; as guests gather, they can tend their own food on the grill.

You'll find five of our favorite grilled appetizers on these two pages. Other recipes in this book work well as hors d'oeuvres, too—for example, Spicy Marinated Shrimp (page 131), Fig & Chicken Skewers (page 147), and Barbecued Shellfish (page 177).

GRILLED CHEESE

Pictured on page 1

24 corn tortillas
   Salad oil
1½ tablespoons olive oil
1 large onion, chopped
2 large tomatoes, seeded and coarsely chopped
¼ teaspoon ground cinnamon
7 to 9 small fresh or canned jalapeño chiles
   Salt
2 pounds mild cheese, such as jack, Münster, teleme, fontina, Edam, or Gouda
1 cup small cooked shrimp

Cut tortillas into quarters. Pour 2 inches salad oil into a deep 2- to 3-quart pan over medium-high heat. Heat oil to 375°F on a deep-frying thermometer. Add tortilla pieces, 6 to 8 at a time, and cook until crisp and golden brown (about 1 minute). Lift out with a slotted spoon; drain on paper towels. If made ahead, let cool, then store airtight at room temperature for up to 2 days. To reheat,

APPETIZERS

FROM THE GRILL

spread in a single layer on 10- by 15-inch baking sheets. Bake in a 400° oven until crisp (about 10 minutes).

Heat olive oil in a wide frying pan over medium-high heat. Add onion and cook, stirring often, until soft (about 10 minutes). Add tomatoes and cinnamon. Increase heat to high; cook, stirring, for 1 minute. Stem, seed, and chop 4 to 6 of the chiles; stir into onion mixture. Season to taste with salt. If made ahead, let cool; cover and refrigerate until next day.

Trim any wax coating from cheese; cut cheese into ¼-inch-thick slices. Arrange in an 8- to 10-inch metal pan or heatproof ceramic dish at least 1½ inches deep, overlapping slices to cover pan bottom and extend up just to edges. (At this point, you may cover and let stand for up to 4 hours.)

Just before heating, spoon tomato mixture over cheese in a 6-inch circle. Top with shrimp and remaining chiles.

Place pan on a grill 4 to 6 inches above a partial bed of medium coals; keep a section of fire grate empty so there's a cool area on grill. Let cheese melt, checking frequently to be sure cheese isn't scorching on bottom by pushing down into center of dish with the tip of a knife. If cheese is getting hot too fast, move it to cool area of grill.

To eat, scoop melted cheese mixture onto tortillas. Makes 12 to 16 servings.

Per serving: 431 calories, 19 g protein, 22 g carbohydrates, 30 g total fat, 65 mg cholesterol, 404 mg sodium

CHICKEN YAKITORI

½ cup soy sauce
½ cup cream sherry, sake, or mirin
3 tablespoons sugar
6 large chicken thighs
½ pound chicken livers
2 bunches green onions

In a pan, combine soy, sherry, and sugar. Bring to a boil over high heat; reduce heat and simmer, uncovered, for 3 minutes. Set aside.

Skin and bone chicken thighs. Rinse meat, pat dry, and cut into bite-size pieces. Also rinse and pat dry chicken livers; cut each liver in half. Trim root ends and any wilted tops from onions; then cut onions into 1½-inch lengths. Thread thigh meat and livers on separate 6-inch metal skewers, including several onion pieces on each skewer. Marinate in soy mixture for 15 minutes.

Lift skewers from marinade and drain briefly (reserve marinade). Place skewers on a lightly greased grill 4 to 6 inches above a solid bed of low coals. Cook, turning as needed to brown evenly and basting with marinade, until browned on all sides. Livers should be firm but still moist in center; cut to test (5 to 7 minutes). Thigh meat should no longer be pink in center; cut to test (8 to 10 minutes). Makes 16 to 20 skewers.

Per skewer: 62 calories, 8 g protein, 4 g carbohydrates, 1 g total fat, 71 mg cholesterol, 444 mg sodium

SAUSAGES WITH MUSTARD CREAM

- 2 egg yolks
- 1 tablespoon sugar
- ¼ cup Dijon mustard
- 2 tablespoons white wine vinegar
- 1 tablespoon water
- 1½ tablespoons prepared horseradish
- 1 tablespoon butter or margarine, at room temperature
- ½ cup whipping cream
- 2 pounds fully cooked sausages, such as knackwurst, kielbasa (Polish sausage), or smoked beef links

In top of a double boiler, beat together egg yolks, sugar, mustard, vinegar, water, horseradish, and butter. Place over simmering water and stir until mixture is thickened (3 to 5 minutes). Then stir over cold water to cool quickly and thoroughly.

Beat whipping cream until it holds stiff peaks. Fold mustard mixture into cream until completely blended. If made ahead, cover and refrigerate for up to 1 week.

Arrange sausages on a lightly greased grill 4 to 6 inches above a solid bed of hot coals. Cook, turning, until well browned on all sides and hot throughout (5 to 10 minutes). Cut sausages into bite-size pieces. Pour mustard cream into a wide bowl; offer as a dip for sausages. Makes 12 to 16 servings.

Per serving: 219 calories, 7 g protein, 3 g carbohydrates, 20 g total fat, 77 mg cholesterol, 698 mg sodium

CHINESE PORK APPETIZERS

- ¼ cup soy sauce
- 2 tablespoons salad oil
- 2 cloves garlic, minced or pressed
- 1 small dried hot red chile, crushed
- ½ teaspoon sugar
- ¼ teaspoon anise seeds
- ⅛ teaspoon *each* ground cinnamon and ground cloves
- 2 pounds lean boneless pork

In a bowl, combine soy, oil, garlic, chile, sugar, anise seeds, cinnamon, and cloves. Cut pork into ¼- to ½-inch-thick strips about 1 inch wide. Stir into soy mixture; cover and refrigerate for 1 to 2 hours, stirring several times.

Thread meat onto small metal skewers, using 1 or 2 strips per skewer. Place on a lightly greased grill 4 to 6 inches above a solid bed of medium coals. Cook, turning occasionally, until browned on outside but no longer pink in center; cut to test (7 to 10 minutes). Makes about 2 dozen appetizers.

Per appetizer: 79 calories, 8 g protein, .46 g carbohydrates, 5 g total fat, 26 mg cholesterol, 191 mg sodium

DILLED SHRIMP

- ¼ cup olive oil or salad oil
- 1½ tablespoons lemon juice
- 1 small clove garlic, minced or pressed
- 1 tablespoon finely chopped parsley
- ¾ teaspoon dill weed
- 1 pound medium-size raw shrimp (30 to 32 per lb.), shelled and deveined

In a bowl, stir together oil, lemon juice, garlic, parsley, and dill weed. Add shrimp and mix well. Cover and refrigerate for 1 to 2 hours.

Lift shrimp from marinade and drain briefly (reserve marinade). Thread shrimp on metal skewers and place on a lightly greased grill 2 to 4 inches above a solid bed of hot coals. Cook, basting several times with marinade and turning once, until shrimp turn pink (about 4 minutes). Makes about 2½ dozen appetizers.

Per appetizer: 29 calories, 2 g protein, .18 g carbohydrates, 2 g total fat, 19 mg cholesterol, 18 mg sodium

(Pictured on facing page)

SKEWERED BEEF & CORN

Preparation time: 30–40 minutes

Marinating time: 6 hours or until next day

Grilling time: About 15 minutes

Tenderized chuck roast, cubed and soaked in a pineapple juice and red wine marinade, is an economical choice for these meat-and-vegetable kebabs.

     4-pound boneless chuck roast
     Unsalted meat tenderizer
     Pineapple-Wine Marinade (recipe follows)
¼   **cup butter or margarine, melted**
¼   **cup salad oil**
     About 5 medium-size ears corn, husked and cut into 2-inch lengths
3   **medium-size green bell peppers, seeded and cut into 1½-inch squares**
2   **large mild red onions, cut into 1½-inch pieces**
1   **medium-size pineapple (about 3½ lbs.), peeled, cored, and cut into 1½-inch cubes**

Cut meat crosswise into steaks about 1½ inches thick. Then apply tenderizer according to package directions. Cut meat into 1½-inch cubes and place in a large bowl.

Prepare Pineapple-Wine Marinade and pour over meat; stir to coat. Cover and refrigerate for at least 6 hours or until next day, stirring occasionally.

In a small bowl, stir together butter, oil, and ⅓ cup of the marinade drained from meat; set aside. Discard remaining marinade.

On long, sturdy metal skewers, thread meat alternately with corn, bell peppers, onions, and pineapple. Brush all over with butter mixture. Place skewers on a lightly greased grill 4 to 6 inches above a solid bed of hot coals. Cook, turning and basting frequently with butter mixture, until meat is done to your liking; cut to test (about 15 minutes for medium-rare). Makes about 8 servings.

Pineapple-Wine Marinade. In a bowl, stir together 1½ cups *each* **canned pineapple juice** and **dry red wine**, 1½ tablespoons **instant minced onion**, 1½ teaspoons *each* **Worcestershire** and **thyme leaves**, ¾ teaspoon **dry mustard**, ¼ cup firmly packed **brown sugar**, ¼ teaspoon **pepper**, and 2 cloves **garlic** (minced or pressed).

Per serving: 578 calories, 39 g protein, 35 g carbohydrates, 32 g total fat, 138 mg cholesterol, 159 mg sodium

SKEWERED BEEF WITH APPLE & LETTUCE

Preparation time: 25–30 minutes (including time to cut meat)

Marinating time: 1–2 hours

Grilling time: About 15 minutes

A soy-based marinade gives a shiny finish to these chunky meat cubes. Wrap the meat and a few crisp apple slices in lettuce leaves, then eat out of hand.

1   **piece fresh ginger (about a 1-inch cube), minced**
¼   **cup soy sauce**
2   **tablespoons *each* dry white wine and firmly packed brown sugar**
1   **tablespoon sesame seeds**
1½ **teaspoons sesame oil**
1   **to 1½ tablespoons chili oil or ½ teaspoon ground red pepper (cayenne)**
2   **pounds boneless beef chuck, trimmed of excess fat and cut into 1½-inch cubes**
1   **large apple, cored and sliced**
     Butter lettuce leaves

In a bowl, stir together ginger, soy, wine, sugar, sesame seeds, sesame oil, and chili oil. Add beef and stir to coat evenly with soy mixture. Cover and refrigerate for 1 to 2 hours.

Lift meat cubes from marinade and drain briefly (reserve marinade); then thread meat equally on 4 sturdy metal skewers. Place skewers on a lightly greased grill 4 to 6 inches above a solid bed of hot coals. Cook, turning as needed and basting often with marinade, until well browned on all sides and done to your liking; cut to test (about 15 minutes for medium-rare).

Push meat off skewers onto a platter. To eat, wrap meat and apple slices in lettuce leaves; eat out of hand. Makes 4 to 6 servings.

Per serving: 292 calories, 25 g protein, 10 g carbohydrates, 16 g total fat, 82 mg cholesterol, 742 mg sodium

Hot off the grill, Skewered Beef & Corn (facing page) makes a colorful outdoor meal. The robust beef cubes and chunks of corn on the cob are threaded on sturdy skewers along with red onion, green pepper squares, and fresh pineapple.

...nutes

...til next day

Sliced bacon, "rippled" over and under beef cubes, apple quarters, and mushrooms, lends its smoky flavor to these festive skewers. Keep a water-filled spray bottle handy to extinguish any flare-ups.

1½ **to 2 pounds tender boneless beef steak (from the rib, loin, or tenderloin), cut about 1½ inches thick**
   Red Wine Marinade (recipe follows)
8 **small white boiling onions**
8 **slices bacon**
8 **large mushrooms**
2 **large Red Delicious apples, cored and quartered**

Cut beef into sixteen 1½-inch cubes; place in a large bowl. Prepare Red Wine Marinade and pour over meat; stir to coat. Cover and refrigerate for at least 4 hours or until next day, stirring several times.

Lift meat from marinade and drain briefly (reserve marinade). Then assemble 4 skewers. For each one, run tip of a long, sturdy metal skewer through one onion, then through one end of a bacon slice. Pierce one mushroom through stem; lap bacon over it and pierce bacon. Thread on one beef cube; lap bacon over and pierce it. Add an apple quarter and one more beef cube, lapping bacon over each; secure bacon end on skewer. Starting with another bacon slice, repeat threading and "rippling" with one more mushroom, another beef cube, an apple quarter, and a final beef cube. Secure bacon end; add one more onion.

Place skewers on a lightly greased grill 4 to 6 inches above a solid bed of medium coals. Cook, turning and basting often with marinade, until bacon is crisp and beef cubes are done to your liking; cut to test (about 15 minutes for medium-rare). Makes 4 servings.

Red Wine Marinade. In a small bowl, stir together ¾ cup **dry red wine**, ½ cup **salad oil**, 1 tablespoon *each* minced **onion** and **Worcestershire**, ⅓ cup **catsup**, 1 teaspoon **dry rosemary**, ¼ teaspoon **pepper**, and 6 drops **liquid hot pepper seasoning**.

Per serving: 642 calories, 36 g protein, 25 g carbohydrates, 44 g total fat, 100 mg cholesterol, 555 mg sodium

 EAST-WEST GRILLED STEAK

Preparation time: 5–10 minutes

Marinating time: 2–4 hours

Grilling time: About 20 minutes

Mediterranean herbs—rosemary, thyme, and sage —blend with Chinese oyster and soy sauces in a distinctively flavored marinade for tenderloin steaks.

1 **to 2 tablespoons salad oil**
4 **beef tenderloin steaks (8 to 10 oz. *each*), cut about 1½ inches thick**
¼ **teaspoon coarsely ground pepper**
1 **tablespoon minced parsley**
1 **teaspoon *each* rubbed sage, dry rosemary, and thyme leaves**
2 **tablespoons soy sauce**
1 **tablespoon oyster sauce**
2 **teaspoons *each* sugar and brandy**

Rub oil on both sides of each steak to coat evenly. In a small bowl, combine pepper, parsley, sage, rosemary, and thyme; rub mixture into both sides of each steak.

In a 9-inch square pan, stir together soy, oyster sauce, sugar, and brandy until sugar is dissolved. Turn steaks in soy mixture, one at a time, coating evenly. Set steaks side by side in pan; cover and refrigerate for at least 2 hours or up to 4 hours.

Place steaks on a lightly greased grill 4 to 6 inches above a solid bed of medium coals. Cook, turning as needed, until browned on both sides and done to your liking; cut to test (about 20 minutes for rare). Brush any remaining soy mixture over steaks as they cook. Makes 4 servings.

Per serving: 344 calories, 41 g protein, 4 g carbohydrates, 17 g total fat, 119 mg cholesterol, 783 mg sodium

⊚ STEAK, POTATO & ONION GRILL

Preparation time: 10–15 minutes

Grilling time: 20–30 minutes

Thick steak, potato wedges, and whole green onions all barbecue together in this satisfying meal. The grilled onions are quite a treat—toasty in spots, and sweeter and chewier than when raw.

    18 green onions
     8 cups cold water
     2 teaspoons salt
     6 medium-size thin-skinned potatoes
        Mustard Butter (recipe follows)
        2½- to 3-pound porterhouse steak,
        cut 2 inches thick

Cut root ends from onions, peel off outer layer, and trim tops, leaving about 4 inches of green leaves. Rinse well. Pour water into a bowl and stir in salt; immerse onions in salted water. Set aside. Scrub potatoes, but do not peel. Cut each potato lengthwise into eighths and immerse in salted water with onions. Also prepare Mustard Butter.

Cook steak and potatoes at the same time. Place steak on a lightly greased grill 4 to 6 inches above a solid bed of medium coals. Cook, turning several times, until richly browned and done to your liking; cut to test (20 to 30 minutes for medium-rare).

Also lift potatoes from water, drain, and mix with ¼ cup of the Mustard Butter; arrange about half the potatoes over coals without overlapping. Cook potatoes, turning as needed, until well browned and tender when pierced (about 10 minutes). As potatoes are cooked, push them to a cooler section of grill and set remaining potatoes over coals.

Just before steak is ready, lift onions from water and lay on grill; cook until white part is tinged with brown and tops are limp (about 5 minutes).

To serve, let steak stand for 5 minutes, then cut into slices. Accompany steak, potatoes, and onions with Mustard Butter. Makes 4 to 6 servings.

Per serving: 347 calories, 30 g protein, 33 g carbohydrates, 10 g total fat, 74 mg cholesterol, 440 mg sodium

Mustard Butter. Blend 1 cup (½ lb.) **butter** or margarine, melted, with 3 tablespoons **Dijon mustard** and ¼ cup minced **shallots.** Serve hot.

Per tablespoon: 81 calories, .13 g protein, .6 g carbohydrates, 9 g total fat, 24 mg cholesterol, 154 mg sodium

⊚ SWISS MUSTARD STEAK

Preparation time: 3–5 minutes

Grilling time: 20–30 minutes

While the steak is on the grill, you assemble a mustard-wine sauce in a rimmed platter. As you slice the meat on the platter, its juices blend into the sauce.

        3½- to 4-pound boneless top sirloin or top
        round steak, cut 2 inches thick
     1 clove garlic
     ¼ cup dry vermouth or dry white wine
     1 tablespoon Dijon mustard
     ¼ teaspoon Worcestershire
     ⅛ teaspoon *each* dry rosemary, dry basil,
        oregano leaves, and dry tarragon
        Salt and pepper

Place steak on a lightly greased grill 4 to 6 inches above a solid bed of medium coals. Cook, turning once, until done to your liking; cut to test (20 to 30 minutes for medium-rare).

While steak is grilling, prepare sauce. Crush garlic in bottom of a warm rimmed platter. Stir in vermouth, mustard, and Worcestershire. Sprinkle in rosemary, basil, oregano, and tarragon and stir again. Place hot cooked steak on platter, setting it in sauce. Season to taste with salt and pepper. Cut meat across the grain into thin slanting slices. Swirl each piece in sauce before transferring to individual plates. Makes 8 to 10 servings.

Per serving: 207 calories, 28 g protein, 1 g carbohydrates, 9 g total fat, 74 mg cholesterol, 113 mg sodium

*For an elegant party entrée, try these tender little Grilled
Orange-Coriander Steaks (facing page). Fresh seasonal
vegetables such as summer squash and sugar snap peas
complement the juicy rare beef.*

⬤ PEPPER STEAK

Preparation time: 5–10 minutes

Marinating time: 30 minutes

Grilling time: 10–12 minutes

Hot, herb-scented tomato slices adorn this classic pepper steak. Just before serving, ignite warmed brandy and spoon it over the grilled meat.

    2 tablespoons cracked pepper
    4 small New York or club steaks (6 to 8 oz. *each*),
       cut 1 inch thick
    3 tablespoons butter or margarine
    2 large firm tomatoes, cut into ½-inch-thick
       slices
    ⅛ teaspoon *each* dry basil and garlic salt
    ¼ cup brandy

Sprinkle pepper over both sides of each steak; press into surfaces. Let stand at room temperature for 30 minutes.

Melt butter in a wide frying pan over medium heat. Add tomatoes and cook just until heated through. Transfer to a platter, sprinkle with basil and garlic salt, and keep warm.

Place steaks on a lightly greased grill 4 to 6 inches above a solid bed of hot coals. Cook, turning once, until done to your liking; cut to test (10 to 12 minutes for rare). Arrange steaks on platter with tomatoes. Warm and ignite brandy; spoon over steaks. Makes 4 servings.

Per serving: 363 calories, 38 g protein, 5 g carbohydrates, 21 g total fat, 120 mg cholesterol, 240 mg sodium

⬤ *(Pictured on facing page)* GRILLED ORANGE-CORIANDER STEAKS

Preparation time: 5–10 minutes

Marinating time: 4 hours or until next day

Grilling time: 10–12 minutes

Meat marinades can often double as bastes or sauces, and this tangy orange juice marinade is no exception. Brush some of it over tender New York steaks on the grill; offer more to spoon over the meat at the table.

    1   teaspoon grated orange peel
    ¾   cup orange juice
    1   small onion, minced
    3   cloves garlic, minced or pressed
    ¼   cup white wine vinegar
    1½   tablespoons ground coriander
    1   teaspoon *each* cracked pepper and dry basil
    4   small New York or beef tenderloin steaks
         (6 to 8 oz. *each*), cut 1 inch thick
         Finely shredded orange peel (optional)
         Salt

In a bowl, stir together grated orange peel, orange juice, onion, garlic, vinegar, coriander, pepper, and basil. Cover and refrigerate ½ cup of the mixture

until serving time. Place steaks in a heavy-duty plastic bag; pour in remaining marinade. Seal bag securely and rotate to distribute marinade. Place in a shallow baking pan and refrigerate for at least 4 hours or until next day, turning bag over several times.

Lift steaks from marinade and drain briefly (reserve marinade). Place on a lightly greased grill 4 to 6 inches above a solid bed of hot coals. Cook, turning once and basting often with marinade, until browned on both sides and done to your liking; cut to test (10 to 12 minutes for rare). While steaks are grilling, pour the ½ cup chilled marinade into a small pan. Place over low heat until hot.

Place steaks on warm plates; garnish with shredded orange peel, if desired. Offer heated marinade to spoon over each steak. Let guests season steaks to taste with salt. Makes 4 servings.

Per serving: 298 calories, 37 g protein, 8 g carbohydrates, 12 g total fat, 97 mg cholesterol, 89 mg sodium

BARBECUED STEAK WESTERN

Preparation time: About 10 minutes

Marinating time: 8 hours or until next day

Grilling time: 20–30 minutes

A spicy barbecue sauce like this one is excellent on any cut of beef. For a special occasion, try it on a thick sirloin steak.

- **3½-pound boneless top sirloin steak, cut 2 inches thick**
- ½ **cup** *each* **salad oil and finely chopped onion**
- ⅓ **cup lemon juice**
- 2 **tablespoons catsup**
- 1 **tablespoon** *each* **Worcestershire and prepared horseradish**
- 1 **teaspoon paprika**
- ¼ **teaspoon pepper**
- 1 **clove garlic, minced or pressed**
- 2 **bay leaves**

Trim excess fat from steak. Place steak in a heavy-duty plastic bag. In a small bowl, stir together oil, onion, lemon juice, catsup, Worcestershire, horse-radish, paprika, pepper, garlic, and bay leaves. Pour marinade over steak, then seal bag securely and rotate to distribute marinade. Place in a shallow baking pan and refrigerate for at least 8 hours or until next day, turning bag over several times.

Lift steak from marinade and drain briefly (reserve marinade). Place steak on a lightly greased grill 4 to 6 inches above a solid bed of medium coals. Cook, turning once and basting often with marinade, until done to your liking; cut to test (20 to 30 minutes for medium-rare).

To serve, let steak stand for 5 minutes, then cut across the grain into thin slanting slices. Makes 6 to 8 servings.

Per serving: 387 calories, 35 g protein, 4 g carbohydrates, 25 g total fat, 92 mg cholesterol, 152 mg sodium

STEAK & ONIONS

Preparation time: 5–10 minutes

Marinating time: 8 hours or until next day

Grilling time: 40–50 minutes

If you like your steak medium-rare, start grilling the onions about 15 minutes before putting on the steak (as we've done here). If you prefer more well-done meat, you can start onions and steak at about the same time.

- **3-pound top round steak, cut 2 inches thick**
- ⅓ **cup** *each* **red wine vinegar and salad oil**
- 2 **tablespoons honey**
- 1 **tablespoon Worcestershire**
- 1 **teaspoon** *each* **dry mustard and oregano leaves**
- ½ **teaspoon pepper**
- 3 **green onions (including tops), finely chopped**
- 2 **cloves garlic, minced or pressed**
- 8 **small onions (unpeeled),** *each* **about 2 inches in diameter**

Place steak in a heavy-duty plastic bag. In a bowl, stir together vinegar, oil, honey, Worcestershire, mustard, oregano, pepper, green onions, and garlic; pour over meat in bag. Seal bag securely and rotate to distribute marinade. Place in a shallow baking pan and refrigerate for at least 8 hours or until next day, turning bag over several times.

Place onions on a lightly greased grill 4 to 6 inches above a solid bed of medium coals. Cook for 15 minutes, turning every 5 minutes. Lift steak from marinade and drain briefly (reserve mari-nade). Place steak on grill. Cook, turning steak and onions every 5 to 10 minutes and brushing steak often with marinade, until onions are soft when squeezed (25 to 35 more minutes) and steak is done to your liking; cut to test (20 to 30 minutes for medium-rare).

If steak is done before onions, remove from grill and keep warm.

To serve, cut steak across the grain into thin slanting slices; cut onions in half lengthwise and eat from skins. Makes 6 to 8 servings.

Per serving: 363 calories, 39 g protein, 12 g carbohydrates, 17 g total fat, 101 mg cholesterol, 96 mg sodium

◉ VEGETABLE-STUFFED BARBECUED STEAK

Preparation time: 20–30 minutes

Marinating time: 4 hours or until next day

Grilling time: About 30 minutes

Each thick slice of this savory marinated steak holds a generous portion of herbed onion and mushroom stuffing.

          3-pound top round steak, cut 2 inches thick
          Garlic Marinade (recipe follows)
 ½ cup (¼ lb.) butter or margarine
 1 stalk celery, chopped
 1 medium-size onion, chopped
 ½ pound mushrooms, sliced
 1 teaspoon thyme leaves
 ½ teaspoon oregano leaves
 1½ cups croutons, slightly crushed

Cut a deep, long slit in center of a long edge of steak to make a pocket; be careful not to cut through meat at sides or back. Place steak in a heavy-duty plastic bag, then prepare Garlic Marinade and pour over steak. Seal bag securely and rotate to distribute marinade. Place in a shallow baking pan and refrigerate for at least 4 hours or until next day, turning bag over occasionally.

Melt butter in a wide frying pan over medium heat; add celery, onion, and mushrooms. Cook, stirring often, until onion is soft. Stir in thyme, oregano, and croutons. Remove from heat.

Lift steak from marinade and drain briefly (reserve marinade). Stuff pocket with mushroom mixture; close pocket and secure with metal skewers.

Place steak on a lightly greased grill 4 to 6 inches above a solid bed of medium coals. Cook, turning and basting with marinade, until done to your liking; cut to test (about 30 minutes for medium-rare). To serve, let steak stand for 5 minutes; then remove skewers and cut steak crosswise into ½-inch-thick slices. Makes about 6 servings.

Garlic Marinade. Mix ½ cup **salad oil,** ¼ cup *each* **red wine vinegar** and **lemon juice,** 1 tablespoon **instant minced onion,** 2 cloves **garlic** (minced or pressed), and ½ teaspoon **pepper.**

Per serving: 680 calories, 53 g protein, 11 g carbohydrates, 46 g total fat, 176 mg cholesterol, 436 mg sodium

◉ SANTA FE SHORT RIBS

Preparation time: 5–10 minutes

Marinating time: 4 hours or until next day

Grilling time: 30–40 minutes

Soaked in chile salsa, these meaty beef short ribs cook on a covered barbecue in less than an hour. For the marinade, use your favorite brand of bottled salsa—mild, medium, or spicy-hot, as you prefer.

          Unsalted meat tenderizer
 6 pounds lean beef short ribs, cracked
 1½ cups dry red wine
 3 tablespoons olive oil or salad oil
 1 small onion, chopped
 2 cloves garlic, minced or pressed
 ½ teaspoon *each* salt and pepper
 1 bay leaf
 ½ cup prepared red chile salsa

Apply tenderizer to ribs according to package directions; then place ribs in a large heavy-duty plastic bag. In a bowl, stir together wine, oil, onion, garlic, salt, pepper, bay leaf, and salsa. Pour over meat in bag; seal bag securely and rotate to distribute marinade. Place in a shallow baking pan. Refrigerate for at least 4 hours or until next day, turning bag over occasionally.

Lift ribs from marinade and drain briefly (reserve marinade). Place on a lightly greased grill 4 to 6 inches above a solid bed of medium coals. Cover barbecue and adjust dampers (or cover with a tent of heavy-duty foil). Cook, turning and basting occasionally with marinade, until meat near bone is done to your liking; cut to test (30 to 40 minutes for medium-rare). Makes 6 servings.

Per serving: 455 calories, 39 g protein, 8 g carbohydrates, 29 g total fat, 114 mg cholesterol, 561 mg sodium

⬤ ASIAN SHORT RIBS

Preparation time: About 20 minutes

Marinating time: About 4 hours

Grilling time: About 30 minutes

Typical teriyaki seasonings—soy, garlic, ginger, and onion—flavor these meaty ribs. The marinade can also be used on standing rib bones.

> 2 tablespoons sesame seeds
> ⅓ cup *each* sugar, soy sauce, and regular-strength chicken broth
> 3 tablespoons bourbon
> 1 teaspoon chopped fresh ginger
> 1 clove garlic, quartered
> 1 small onion, cut into 8 wedges
> 2 tablespoons sesame oil or salad oil
> 1 green onion (including top), finely chopped
> Unsalted meat tenderizer
> 4 pounds lean beef short ribs, cut into 3- to 4-inch lengths

Toast sesame seeds in a small frying pan over medium heat until golden (about 3 minutes), shaking pan often. Pour seeds into a blender and add

sugar, soy, broth, bourbon, ginger, garlic, onion wedges, and oil. Whirl until well blended, then stir in green onion and set aside.

Apply tenderizer to ribs according to package directions. Place each rib with bone side down and score meat in a crisscross pattern. Make one set of parallel cuts ½ inch apart, cutting through meat halfway to bone. Then make a second series of cuts at right angles to the first set, making cuts ½ inch deep and ½ inch apart. Place ribs in a large heavy-duty plastic bag. Pour marinade over meat in bag; seal bag securely and rotate to distribute marinade. Place in a shallow baking pan. Refrigerate for about 4 hours, turning bag over occasionally.

Lift ribs from marinade and drain briefly (reserve marinade). Place on a lightly greased grill 4 to 6 inches above a solid bed of medium coals. Cook, turning and basting often with marinade, until ribs are well browned on all sides and meat near bone is done to your liking; cut to test (about 30 minutes for medium-rare). Makes 4 servings.

Per serving: 533 calories, 40 g protein, 21 g carbohydrates, 32 g total fat, 114 mg cholesterol, 1513 mg sodium

---

(Pictured on facing page)

⬤ BARBECUED PRIME RIB BONES

Preparation time: About 5 minutes

Marinating time: About 2 hours

Grilling time: 20–25 minutes

If you relish the sweet meat that clings to bones, you'll enjoy these hearty standing ribs. To serve, just pile the ribs on a big platter; garnish with cherry peppers and watercress, if you like.

> **About 6 pounds standing rib bones**
> **Mustard Marinade (recipe follows)**

Arrange bones in a large, shallow pan. Prepare Mustard Marinade and pour over ribs; turn to coat. Cover and let stand for about 2 hours.

Lift bones from marinade and drain briefly (reserve marinade). Place on a lightly greased grill 4 to 6 inches above a solid bed of hot coals. Cook, turning and basting frequently with marinade, until done to your liking; cut to test (20 to 25 minutes for medium-rare). Makes 6 servings.

Mustard Marinade. In a small bowl, combine ⅓ cup **Dijon mustard** and 2 tablespoons **red wine vinegar**. Beating constantly with a wire whisk, add ¼ cup **olive oil** or salad oil, a few drops at a time. Then beat in 1 clove **garlic** (minced or pressed), ½ teaspoon *each* **thyme leaves** and **Worcestershire**, and ¼ teaspoon **pepper**.

Per serving: 608 calories, 32 g protein, 2 g carbohydrates, 51 g total fat, 120 mg cholesterol, 491 mg sodium

Always a favorite with family and friends: Barbecued Prime Rib Bones (facing page), soaked in a tangy mustard marinade. Serve with roasted potatoes, fresh peas, and cold beer.

NEW YORK STRIP WITH GARLIC PEPPER

Preparation time: 5–10 minutes

Marinating time: 1 hour or until next day

Grilling time: 35–40 minutes

From time to time, many supermarkets offer good buys on big boneless cuts of beef such as a New York strip. Simply seasoned, it's an ideal choice for your next crowd-size barbecue.

⅓ **cup minced garlic (about 20 large cloves)**
⅓ **cup cracked pepper**
8- to 10-pound trimmed New York strip (boneless loin)

Combine garlic and pepper; rub over both sides of beef. Cover and let stand at room temperature for 1 hour or refrigerate until next day.

Place beef on a lightly greased grill 4 to 6 inches above a solid bed of hot coals. Cook, turning as needed to brown evenly, until a meat thermometer inserted in thickest part registers 135° to 140°F for rare (35 to 40 minutes). To serve, let meat stand for 10 minutes; then cut across the grain into thin slanting slices. Makes 16 to 20 servings.

Per serving: 290 calories, 39 g protein, 2 g carbohydrates, 13 g total fat, 104 mg cholesterol, 94 mg sodium

BEEF TENDERLOIN IN RED WINE MARINADE

Preparation time: 5–10 minutes

Marinating time: 3 hours or until next day

Grilling time: About 50 minutes

For a special dinner, consider barbecuing a whole beef tenderloin. This handsome cut is quite expensive, but keep in mind that it will serve a dozen generously—and there's no waste. Plan well ahead for this entrée; you'll probably need to special-order the tenderloin from your meat market.

5- to 6-pound whole beef tenderloin (fillet of beef), trimmed of excess fat
2 **cups dry red wine**
½ **cup olive oil**
1 **large onion, chopped**
½ **cup chopped parsley**
2 **cloves garlic, minced or pressed**
2 **bay leaves**
1 **teaspoon pepper**

Place beef in a 4- to 6-gallon heavy-duty plastic bag set in a rimmed baking pan (at least 10 by 15 inches). In a bowl, stir together wine, oil, onion, parsley, garlic, bay leaves, and pepper. Pour over meat in bag; seal bag securely. Let stand at room temperature for at least 3 hours or refrigerate until next day, turning bag over several times.

Lift meat from marinade and drain briefly (reserve marinade). Fold thin end of fillet under; tie securely with string to make fillet as evenly thick as possible. Place meat on a lightly greased grill 4 to 6 inches above a solid bed of medium coals. Cook, basting frequently with marinade and turning every 5 minutes for even browning, until a meat thermometer inserted in thickest part registers 135° to 140°F for rare (about 50 minutes).

To serve, let meat stand for 10 minutes; then cut across the grain on a slight diagonal into ½-inch-thick slices. Makes about 12 servings.

Per serving: 334 calories, 34 g protein, 2 g carbohydrates, 20 g total fat, 99 mg cholesterol, 78 mg sodium

CHUCK STEAK WITH LEMON-ANCHOVY BUTTER

Preparation time: About 10 minutes

Grilling time: About 20 minutes

Form a flavorful lemon-anchovy butter into a ring and serve it alongside tender barbecued steak—then let guests cut slices from the ring to top each portion of meat.

  ½ **cup (¼ lb.) butter or margarine,**
     at room temperature
  1 **teaspoon lemon juice**
  1 **can (2 oz.) anchovy fillets, drained**
     Chopped parsley
     Unsalted meat tenderizer (optional)
  3½- **to 4-pound bone-in chuck steak,**
     cut 1½ inches thick

In a small bowl, beat together butter, lemon juice, and anchovies until thoroughly blended. Blend in about 1 teaspoon parsley. Shape mixture into a ring, ball, or loaf, place on a bed of parsley, cover, and refrigerate.

If using tenderizer, apply it to steak according to package directions. Place steak on a lightly greased grill 4 to 6 inches above a solid bed of medium coals. Cook, turning once, until done to your liking; cut to test (about 20 minutes for rare). To serve, let meat stand for 5 minutes, then cut across the grain into thin slanting slices. Pass lemon-anchovy butter at the table to top individual portions. Makes 4 to 6 servings.

Per serving: 445 calories, 35 g protein, .06 g carbohydrates, 33 g total fat, 159 mg cholesterol, 507 mg sodium

GRILLED PEPPERED ROAST

Preparation time: About 10 minutes

Marinating time: 4 hours or until next day

Grilling time: About 30 minutes

Marinated and peppered chuck roast is an economical choice for grilling. Corn on the cob, tossed salad, and crusty bread make good accompaniments.

     5-pound bone-in chuck roast,
     cut 2 inches thick
  ½ **cup *each* salad oil and red wine vinegar**
  2 **tablespoons Worcestershire**
  2 **large cloves garlic, minced or pressed**
  1 **teaspoon dry basil**
     Unsalted meat tenderizer
  4 **to 5 tablespoons whole black peppercorns,**
     coarsely crushed

With a fork, pierce roast deeply all over; place in a heavy-duty plastic bag set in a shallow baking pan. In a bowl, stir together oil, vinegar, Worcestershire, garlic, and basil; pour over meat. Seal bag securely and rotate to distribute marinade. Refrigerate for at least 4 hours or until next day, turning bag over several times.

Lift meat from marinade and drain briefly (reserve marinade). Apply tenderizer to meat according to package directions. Spread crushed peppercorns out on a flat surface and press meat into pepper, coating both sides.

Place meat on a lightly greased grill 4 to 6 inches above a solid bed of medium coals. Cook, turning once and basting with marinade, until meat is browned on all sides and done to your liking; cut to test (about 30 minutes for rare).

To serve, let meat stand for 10 minutes; then cut on a slight diagonal into thin slices. Makes about 6 servings.

Per serving: 602 calories, 48 g protein, 5 g carbohydrates, 42 g total fat, 162 mg cholesterol, 166 mg sodium

A barbecued boneless beef roast makes an almost effortless main dish for eight to ten lucky diners. A simple soy marinade, crunchy with sesame seeds, gives our Sesame Beef Roast (facing page) its distinctive flavor.

SAVORY CHUCK ROAST

Preparation time: About 50 minutes

Grilling time: About 30 minutes

Sliced celery, onion rings, and plenty of seasonings go into this full-flavored barbecue sauce. It's a wonderful baste for a thick chuck roast.

- ¼ cup olive oil or salad oil
- 1 medium-size onion, thinly sliced and separated into rings
- 1 clove garlic, minced or pressed
- ½ cup thinly sliced celery
- ¾ cup *each* catsup and tomato-based chili sauce
- ½ cup water
- 2 tablespoons *each* Worcestershire, wine vinegar, and lemon juice
- 1 teaspoon *each* prepared horseradish and prepared mustard
- ½ teaspoon hickory-smoked salt
  Few drops liquid hot pepper seasoning
- ½ teaspoon pepper
- 3 tablespoons firmly packed brown sugar
- ½ cup dry sherry
  Unsalted meat tenderizer
  5-pound chuck roast, cut 2 inches thick

Heat oil in a wide frying pan over medium heat. Add onion and cook, stirring often, until soft (about 10 minutes). Add garlic, celery, catsup, chili sauce, water, Worcestershire, vinegar, lemon juice, horseradish, mustard, hickory-smoked salt, hot pepper seasoning, pepper, sugar, and sherry. Bring to a boil; then reduce heat and simmer, uncovered, for 30 minutes. Remove from heat.

Apply tenderizer to meat according to package directions. Brush meat on both sides with sauce, then place on a lightly greased grill 4 to 6 inches above a solid bed of medium coals. Cover barbecue and adjust dampers (or cover with a tent of heavy-duty foil). Cook, turning and basting occasionally with sauce, until done to your liking; cut to test (about 30 minutes for rare). To serve, let meat stand for 10 minutes; then cut on a slight diagonal into thin slices. Pass any remaining sauce at the table. Makes about 6 servings.

Per serving: 622 calories, 50 g protein, 29 g carbohydrates, 33 g total fat, 162 mg cholesterol, 1186 mg sodium

---

(Pictured on facing page)

SESAME BEEF ROAST

Preparation time: About 10 minutes

Marinating time: 8 hours or until next day

Grilling time: 1½–1¾ hours

This delicious beef roast benefits from marinating for a full day. If you enjoy the flavor of sesame with beef, you might also try Sesame Flank Steak (page 39) and Korean Barbecued Beef Strips (page 191).

- ⅓ cup sesame seeds
- ½ cup *each* salad oil and soy sauce
- ⅓ cup lemon juice
- 2 tablespoons white wine vinegar
- 1 tablespoon sugar
- 2 cloves garlic, minced or pressed
- 1 medium-size onion, sliced
  4-pound crossrib or sirloin tip roast

Toast sesame seeds in a wide frying pan over medium heat until golden (about 3 minutes), shaking pan often. Remove from heat and add oil, soy, lemon juice, vinegar, sugar, garlic, and onion. Place meat in a close-fitting bowl; pour marinade over meat, cover, and refrigerate for at least 8 hours or until next day, turning meat occasionally.

Barbecue meat by indirect heat (see page 10). Lift meat from marinade and drain briefly (reserve marinade); then place on a lightly greased grill directly above drip pan. Cover barbecue and adjust dampers as necessary to maintain an even heat. Cook, basting occasionally with marinade, until a meat thermometer inserted in thickest part registers 135° to 140°F for rare (1½ to 1¾ hours). Let meat stand for 10 minutes; then cut across the grain into thin slices. Makes 6 to 8 servings.

Per serving: 575 calories, 47 g protein, 6 g carbohydrates, 39 g total fat, 153 mg cholesterol, 1135 mg sodium

CRUSTY CROSSRIB ROAST

Preparation time: About 5 minutes

Marinating time: 2 hours

Grilling time: About 2 hours

A crossrib roast is simply a boned, rolled chuck roast. Cooked rare and cut into thin slices, it's tender and juicy.

      5-pound crossrib roast
  ¼ **cup** *each* **salad oil and apple juice**
  ½ **cup strong black coffee**
  1 **tablespoon fennel seeds**
  ½ **teaspoon onion powder**
  ⅛ **teaspoon pepper**

Place meat in a close-fitting bowl. In another bowl, mix oil, apple juice, coffee, fennel seeds, onion powder, and pepper. Pour over meat, cover, and refrigerate for 2 hours, turning meat often.

Barbecue meat by indirect heat (see page 10). Lift meat from marinade and drain briefly (reserve marinade); then place on a lightly greased grill directly above drip pan. Cover barbecue and adjust dampers as necessary to maintain an even heat. Cook, basting occasionally with marinade, until a meat thermometer inserted in thickest part registers 135° to 140°F for rare (about 2 hours). Let meat stand for 10 minutes; then cut across the grain into thin slices. Makes 8 to 10 servings.

Per serving: 372 calories, 36 g protein, 1 g carbohydrates, 24 g total fat, 123 mg cholesterol, 83 mg sodium

BRISKET OF BEEF

Preparation time: About 10 minutes

Marinating time: 4 hours or until next day

Grilling time: About 25 minutes

Marinated in a simple, spicy barbecue sauce and cooked rare, beef brisket is juicy and tender—deserving of the starring role at your next patio party.

      4- to 5-pound beef brisket
  2 **tablespoons** *each* **chili powder, vinegar, and Worcestershire**
  ¼ **teaspoon pepper**
  1 **large onion, chopped**
  2 **cloves garlic, minced or pressed**
  ¾ **cup catsup**
  1 **cup water**
      Unsalted meat tenderizer

Place beef in a large heavy-duty plastic bag. In a bowl, stir together chili powder, vinegar, Worcestershire, pepper, onion, garlic, catsup, and water. Pour over meat in bag; seal bag securely and rotate to distribute marinade. Place in a shallow baking pan. Refrigerate for at least 4 hours or until next day, turning bag over several times.

Lift meat from marinade; scrape off excess (reserve marinade). Pat meat dry and apply tenderizer according to package directions. Place meat on a lightly greased grill 4 to 6 inches above a solid bed of low coals. Cook, turning frequently, until a meat thermometer inserted in thickest part registers 135° to 140°F for rare (about 25 minutes). Remove from grill; let stand for 10 minutes.

Bring marinade to a boil; pour into a bowl. Cut meat across the grain into thin slanting slices. Serve with marinade. Makes 10 to 12 servings.

Per serving: 202 calories, 22 g protein, 7 g carbohydrates, 9 g total fat, 66 mg cholesterol, 270 mg sodium

POUNDED VEAL CHOPS

Preparation time: 10–15 minutes

Grilling time: 4–5 minutes

Pounding with a mallet is a time-honored way to tenderize meat. Here, the technique also serves two other purposes: it works in the seasonings and reduces cooking time on the grill.

> 3 tablespoons minced fresh thyme or 1½ tablespoons dry thyme leaves
> 2 teaspoons grated lemon peel
> ½ cup minced parsley
> 2 tablespoons olive oil or salad oil
> 4 veal rib or loin chops (1 to 1¼ lbs. *total*), cut ¾ to 1 inch thick
> Lemon wedges

In a small bowl, stir together thyme, lemon peel, parsley, and oil. Slash connective tissue around veal chops at about 1-inch intervals. Rub about 1 tablespoon of the thyme mixture on each side of each chop.

Place each chop between 2 sheets of plastic wrap and pound with a flat-surfaced mallet until about ¼ inch thick. (At this point, you may cover and refrigerate for up to 6 hours.)

Place meat on a lightly greased grill 4 to 6 inches above a solid bed of hot coals. Cook, turning as needed to cook evenly, until done to your liking; cut to test (4 to 5 minutes for medium).

To serve, garnish with lemon wedges; squeeze juice over individual chops before eating. Makes 2 to 4 servings.

Per serving: 229 calories, 17 g protein, 2 g carbohydrates, 17 g total fat, 61 mg cholesterol, 44 mg sodium

BARBECUED VENISON RIB CHOPS

Preparation time: 10–15 minutes

Grilling time: 4–6 minutes

Tender cuts of venison, such as rib chops cut from the loin, grill well. Chops from one deer will vary in size—but if cut to the same thickness, they'll cook at about the same rate.

> 8 venison rib chops (2 to 2½ lbs. *total*), cut ¾ to 1 inch thick
> ¼ cup fresh rosemary leaves
> About 2 tablespoons olive oil
> Salt and pepper

Rinse venison and pat dry. Trim off and discard most of the rim fat from chops. Sprinkle half the rosemary evenly over one side of chops; firmly pound meat with a flat-surfaced mallet to hold rosemary in place. Turn chops over, sprinkle with remaining rosemary, and pound again. Lightly brush chops all over with oil.

Place chops on a lightly greased grill 4 to 6 inches above a solid bed of hot coals. Arrange smaller chops near outside edge of coals, larger ones in center. Cook, turning as needed, until browned on both sides and done to your liking; cut to test. Allow about 4 minutes for medium-rare, about 6 minutes for medium; do not overcook (well-done venison is dry and firm). Let guests season meat to taste with salt and pepper. Makes 4 to 6 servings, depending on size of chops.

Per serving: 188 calories, 24 g protein, .35 g carbohydrates, 9 g total fat, 76 mg cholesterol, 105 mg sodium

Starring at our Turkish Lamb Sandwich Buffet (page 62) is a garlic-studded leg of lamb. Guests tuck thin slices of barbecued meat into pocket bread along with lettuce leaves, chunky vegetable relish, and cool yogurt sauce.

Lamb

CHOPS ■ ROASTS ■ KEBABS

Middle Eastern nomads may have been the first cooks to barbecue lamb, spit-roasting the whole animal over an open fire. Today, with the advent of modern barbecue equipment, it's easy to grill all cuts of lamb—from large bone-in or boneless legs to smaller chops and steaks to ground meat patties.

This chapter begins with a selection of recipes you might cook for a crowd, including a fancy fruit-stuffed lamb shoulder and a garlicky leg of lamb to slice and serve in pocket bread with yogurt-mint sauce, tomatoes, and cucumbers. Throughout the rest of the chapter, you'll find many recipes for smaller groups: grilled chops stuffed with pine nuts, sauced with spicy peaches, or pounded and seasoned with rosemary; chunks of lamb threaded on skewers with fresh fruits or vegetables; and grilled ground lamb, formed into logs or patties.

If you're looking for basic grilling directions for various cuts of lamb, turn to page 15. See page 63 for complementary marinades, sauces, and flavored butters.

🔲 TURKISH LAMB SANDWICH BUFFET

Preparation time: About 45 minutes, plus 4 hours for Cucumber-Tomato Relish to stand

Grilling time: About 1¼ hours

Grilled almost unattended on a covered barbecue, then cut into thin slices, leg of lamb makes a savory filling for pocket bread.

> Basting Sauce (recipe follows)
> Cucumber-Tomato Relish (recipe follows)
> Yogurt Sauce (page 28)
> 5½- to 6½-pound leg of lamb, trimmed of excess fat
> 3 or 4 cloves garlic, cut into small slivers
> 10 to 12 pocket breads, *each* about 7 inches in diameter, cut into halves
> Romaine lettuce leaves

Prepare Basting Sauce, Cucumber-Tomato Relish, and Yogurt Sauce.

Cut small gashes in lamb and insert garlic slivers. Barbecue lamb by indirect heat (see page 10), placing it on a lightly greased grill directly above drip pan. Brush meat with Basting Sauce, then cover barbecue and adjust dampers as necessary to maintain an even heat. Cook, brushing frequently with Basting Sauce, until a meat thermometer inserted in thickest part (not touching bone) registers 145°F for medium-rare (about 1¾ hours). Remove from grill; let stand for 10 minutes.

Cut lamb into thin slices. Let guests fill pocket bread halves with meat, romaine leaves, and spoonfuls of Cucumber-Tomato Relish and Yogurt Sauce. Makes 10 to 12 servings.

Basting Sauce. In a bowl, stir together ⅓ cup **olive oil** or salad oil; ½ cup **red wine vinegar;** 2 tablespoons **lemon juice;** 1 small **onion,** finely chopped; 2 cloves **garlic** (minced or pressed); ½ teaspoon **salt;** ¼ teaspoon *each* **ground nutmeg, ground ginger,** and **pepper;** and ⅛ teaspoon **ground cloves.**

Per serving: 397 calories, 34 g protein, 38 g carbohydrates, 12 g total fat, 104 mg cholesterol, 489 mg sodium

Cucumber-Tomato Relish. In a large bowl, stir together ¼ cup **white wine vinegar,** ½ cup **olive oil,** 1 teaspoon *each* **salt** and **sugar,** ¼ teaspoon *each* **oregano leaves** and **pepper,** and 2 tablespoons finely chopped **parsley.** Peel and seed 4 large **tomatoes;** then cut into 1-inch chunks. Also cut 1 long **English cucumber** and 1 small mild **red onion** into about 1-inch chunks. Add tomatoes, cucumber, and onion to oil mixture; stir gently to mix. Cover and refrigerate for at least 4 hours or until next day, stirring several times. Makes about 6 cups.

Per ½ cup: 97 calories, .68 g protein, 4 g carbohydrates, 9 g total fat, 0 mg cholesterol, 188 mg sodium

🔲 MINT-SMOKED LEG OF LAMB

Preparation time: 15 minutes

Grilling time: About 1¾ hours

A few handfuls of fresh mint sprinkled atop the coals give this slowly grilled leg of lamb a pleasant aroma. Garlic and port further flavor the meat.

> 5-pound leg of lamb, trimmed of excess fat
> 3 cloves garlic, cut into quarters
> Pepper
> 1½ teaspoons dry rosemary
> ½ cup port wine
> 2 cups fresh mint sprigs
> Salt

Cut 12 small slits all around lamb; insert a garlic quarter in each slit. Sprinkle lamb with pepper, rub with rosemary, and brush with port.

Barbecue lamb by indirect heat (see page 10), placing it on a lightly greased grill directly above drip pan. Cover barbecue and adjust dampers as necessary to maintain an even heat. Cook, brushing occasionally with port, until a meat thermometer inserted in thickest part (not touching bone) registers 145°F for medium-rare (about 1¾ hours). After 30 minutes of cooking, drop mint onto coals to smolder; quickly replace barbecue cover.

To serve, transfer meat to a board and let stand for 10 minutes, then cut into slices. Let guests season meat to taste with salt. Makes 6 servings.

Per serving: 355 calories, 53 g protein, 3 g carbohydrates, 13 g total fat, 189 mg cholesterol, 131 mg sodium

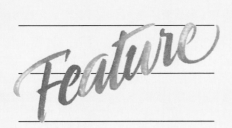

MARINADES, SAUCES & BUTTERS FOR LAMB

A touch of extra flavor is all you need to enhance the mildly wild and distinctive taste of barbecued lamb. Fruity or herbal marinades or bastes—like the choices on this page—best complement the meat.

You'll find basic grilling times and techniques for lamb on page 15.

LAMB MARINADES

Lamb shoulder—one of the tougher cuts—can be tenderized by soaking in a marinade made with an acid such as wine, vinegar, or citrus juice.

Marinate the meat in a close-fitting dish, pan, or bowl, or use a heavy-duty plastic bag. For maximum flavoring and tenderizing, it's usually best to let the meat soak for at least 4 hours—or until next day.

Honey-Wine Marinade. Melt 2 tablespoons **butter** or margarine in a 1- to 2-quart pan over medium heat. Remove from heat and add 1 cup **dry white wine,** 2 tablespoons **white wine vinegar,** ⅓ cup **honey,** 1 teaspoon chopped **fresh mint** or crumbled dry mint, ½ teaspoon **salt,** and 2 cloves **garlic** (minced or pressed). Stir to blend. Makes about 1½ cups.

Sherry-Herb Marinade. In a bowl, combine 1 large **onion** (chopped), ½ cup **dry sherry** or apple juice, ¼ cup **olive oil** or salad oil, 2 teaspoons **oregano leaves,** and ½ teaspoon *each* **salt** and **pepper.** Stir to blend. Makes about 1¼ cups.

SAUCES

Crunchy Carrot & Sweet Pepper Salsa and fragrant Tropical Fruit

Salsa can turn simply grilled lamb chops, steaks, or leg of lamb into special-occasion entrées. Pass the sauces at the table to spoon over individual portions of meat.

Carrot & Sweet Pepper Salsa. Peel and very finely shred 2 medium-size **carrots** and place in a bowl. Seed and dice 1 medium-size **green or red bell pepper;** add to carrots along with ½ cup minced **shallots** or red onion, 6 tablespoons **white wine vinegar,** 2 tablespoons firmly packed **brown sugar,** 1 tablespoon minced **fresh ginger,** and 2 large cloves **garlic** (minced or pressed). Stir until sugar is dissolved. Season to taste with **salt.** Cover and refrigerate for at least 1 hour or up to 2 days. Serve chilled. Makes about 3 cups.

Tropical Fruit Salsa. Peel 1 medium-size firm-ripe **mango** and cut fruit off pit in ½-inch cubes. In a bowl, mix mango, 1 cup diced **fresh pineapple,** 1 cup diced **honeydew melon,** ½ cup diced **red bell pepper,** ⅓ cup **seasoned rice wine vinegar** (or ⅓ cup white wine vinegar and 1 tablespoon sugar), 2 tablespoons minced **fresh cilantro (coriander),** and ½ teaspoon **crushed dried hot red chiles.** (At this point, you may cover and refrigerate for up to 2 days.)

Just before serving, peel 2 large **kiwi fruits;** cut into ¼-inch cubes and add to salsa. Makes about 4 cups.

To give tender cuts of lamb just a hind of added flavor, brush them with a butter-based sauce seasoned with mint, mustard, orange peel, or rosemary and lemon. Use any of these butters melted, as a baste for the meat during cooking; or top the hot grilled meat with spoonfuls of softened Mint Butter or Mustard Butter.

Mint Butter. In a blender or food processor, combine ½ cup (¼ lb.) **butter** or margarine (at room temperature), ½ cup lightly packed **fresh mint leaves,** and 1 teaspoon **lemon juice.** Whirl until well blended; scrape down sides of container often. Makes about ⅔ cup.

Mustard Butter. In a bowl, combine 1 cup (½ lb.) **butter** or margarine (at room temperature), 4 teaspoons **dry mustard,** 1 teaspoon **Worcestershire,** ¼ teaspoon **garlic salt,** ⅛ teaspoon **pepper,** and ⅓ cup chopped **parsley.** Beat until smooth and well blended. Makes about 1 cup.

Parsley-Orange Butter Baste. Melt ½ cup (¼ lb.) **butter** or margarine in a small pan over medium heat; stir in 2 tablespoons *each* grated **orange peel,** finely chopped **parsley,** and **honey.** Remove from heat and stir in ¼ cup **lemon juice.** Makes about 1 cup.

Mediterranean Basting Sauce. Melt ¼ cup **butter** or margarine in a small pan over medium heat; remove from heat and stir in 3 tablespoons **lemon juice,** 4 cloves **garlic** (minced or pressed), and ½ teaspoon chopped **fresh rosemary or oregano leaves.** Makes about ½ cup.

CROSSED-SWORDS LAMB

Preparation time: 20–30 minutes

Marinating time: 2 hours or until next day

Grilling time: About 1¼ hours

If you're looking for an impressive but easy-to-serve company entrée, try this boneless leg of lamb. Have your meatman bone the lamb for you—then simply slash the meat in the thickest parts, set slices of onion in the slashes, and thread the roast onto long, heavy skewers for grilling.

> 5- to 6-pound leg of lamb,
> boned and trimmed of excess fat
> ½   cup medium-dry sherry
> 2   tablespoons olive oil
> 1   medium-size onion
> 8   to 10 fresh rosemary sprigs,
> *each* 3 to 4 inches long
> Salt and pepper

Place lamb in a close-fitting dish. Mix sherry and oil; rub thoroughly over lamb. Cover and refrigerate for at least 2 hours or until next day, turning meat several times.

Lift meat from marinade and drain briefly (reserve marinade); place on a board, boned side up. At 2- to 3-inch intervals, cut about ⅔ of the way through thickest parts of meat. Cut onion into ¼-inch-thick slices, then cut each slice in half crosswise. Fit half-slices, rounded edge up, into meat slashes.

Thread a long, sturdy metal skewer through meat parallel to longest side and about 2 inches in from edge, securing onions. Insert another skewer through opposite side of meat so skewers cross near tips.

Barbecue lamb by indirect heat (see page 10), placing it on a lightly greased grill directly above drip pan. Brush meat with reserved marinade, then cover barbecue and adjust dampers as necessary to maintain an even heat. Cook, brushing occasionally with marinade, until a meat thermometer inserted in thickest part of lamb (not touching skewer) registers 135° to 140°F (about 1¼ hours). Because of the meat's uneven thickness, you will have both rare and well-done portions. About 5 minutes before roast is done, tuck sprigs of rosemary into slashes in lamb.

Transfer lamb to a platter, using skewers to lift it. Let stand for 10 minutes, then pull out skewers and slice meat. Let guests season to taste with salt and pepper. Makes about 8 servings.

Per serving: 301 calories, 40 g protein, 3 g carbohydrates, 13 g total fat, 141 mg cholesterol, 99 mg sodium

LEMON-MUSTARD BUTTERFLIED LAMB

Preparation time: 15–20 minutes

Marinating time: 4 hours or until next day

Grilling time: 40–45 minutes

Though typically barbecued by indirect heat, a boned and butterflied leg of lamb can be grilled directly over the coals, just like a thick steak. This recipe features a penetrating mustard marinade.

> 5- to 6-pound leg of lamb, boned, butterflied,
> and trimmed of excess fat
> ½   cup *each* lemon juice and Dijon mustard
> ¼   cup firmly packed brown sugar
> 3   tablespoons Worcestershire
> 2   cloves garlic, minced or pressed
> 2   tablespoons olive oil or salad oil
> Thin lemon slices
> Fresh cilantro (coriander) or parsley sprigs

Place lamb in a close-fitting dish. Stir together lemon juice, mustard, sugar, Worcestershire, garlic, and oil; rub mixture all over lamb. Cover and refrigerate for at least 4 hours or until next day, turning lamb several times.

Lift lamb from marinade and drain briefly (reserve marinade), then place on a lightly greased grill 4 to 6 inches above a solid bed of medium coals. Cook, turning as needed and brushing occasionally with marinade, until a meat thermometer inserted in thickest part of lamb registers 135° to 140°F (40 to 45 minutes). Thickest portions of meat will be rare; thinner sections will be medium to well done.

To serve, place lamb on a board and let stand for 10 minutes; then cut across the grain into thin slices. Makes about 8 servings.

Per serving: 340 calories, 40 g protein, 10 g carbohydrates, 14 g total fat, 141 mg cholesterol, 614 mg sodium

Wreathed in rosemary and supported on heavy skewers,
tantalizing Crossed-swords Lamb (facing page) is ready
to serve. Thick slices of onion and a sherry marinade flavor
the succulent meat.

GRILLED LAMB WITH CURRANT CHUTNEY

Preparation time: About 1 hour

Marinating time: 2 hours or until next day

Grilling time: 40–45 minutes

Soak this boned and butterflied leg of lamb in a red wine and curry marinade, grill it over a solid bed of coals, and serve with a spicy homemade chutney.

>6- to 7-pound leg of lamb, boned, butterflied, and trimmed of excess fat
>
>½ cup dry red wine
>
>1 teaspoon curry powder
>
>½ teaspoon dry tarragon
>
>¼ teaspoon lemon pepper seasoning
>
>Currant Chutney (recipe follows)

Place lamb in a close-fitting dish. In a small bowl, stir together wine, curry powder, tarragon, and lemon pepper. Pour mixture over lamb and turn to coat; then cover and refrigerate for at least 2 hours or until next day, turning lamb several times. Meanwhile, prepare Currant Chutney; set aside.

Lift lamb from marinade and drain briefly (reserve marinade). Place on a lightly greased grill 4 to 6 inches above a solid bed of medium coals. Cook, turning as needed and basting occasionally with marinade, until a meat thermometer inserted in thickest part of lamb registers 135° to 140°F (40 to 45 minutes). Thickest portions of meat will be rare; thinner sections will be medium to well done.

To serve, place lamb on a board and let stand for 10 minutes; then cut across the grain into thin slices. Offer Currant Chutney to spoon over individual servings. Makes 8 to 10 servings.

Per serving: 251 calories, 38 g protein, 1 g carbohydrates, 9 g total fat, 136 mg cholesterol, 115 mg sodium

Currant Chutney. Melt 3 tablespoons **butter** or margarine in a wide frying pan over medium heat. Add ½ cup finely chopped **onion** and 1 small **red bell pepper,** seeded and diced; cook, stirring, until onion is soft (about 10 minutes). Add ½ cup **dried currants** and 1 teaspoon **curry powder;** stir until currants plump up slightly. Add 1 cup **dry red wine,** ½ teaspoon **dry tarragon,** ¼ cup **black currant liqueur** (crème de cassis), ⅛ teaspoon **ground red pepper** (cayenne), 1 **beef bouillon cube,** and 2 teaspoons **red wine vinegar.** Bring to a boil over high heat; then reduce heat, cover, and simmer until mixture is reduced to about 1¼ cups (about 30 minutes). Makes about 1¼ cups.

Per tablespoon: 31 calories, .23 g protein, 4 g carbohydrates, 2 g total fat, 5 mg cholesterol, 57 mg sodium

FRUIT & HERB-SCENTED LAMB

Preparation time: About 15 minutes

Marinating time: 3 hours or until next day

Grilling time: About 1¼ hours

This butterflied leg of lamb is studded with slivers of garlic and soaked in pomegranate juice and red wine, then grilled on a covered barbecue. (Look for pomegranate juice in a specialty foods shop.)

>5½- to 6½-pound leg of lamb, boned, butterflied, and trimmed of excess fat
>
>3 or 4 cloves garlic, cut into small slivers
>
>1 cup pomegranate juice
>
>2 cups dry red wine
>
>1 large onion, chopped
>
>1 teaspoon *each* dry rosemary and oregano leaves

Cut small gashes in lamb; insert garlic slivers. Place meat in a close-fitting dish. Mix pomegranate juice, wine, onion, rosemary, and oregano; pour over meat. Cover; refrigerate for at least 3 hours or until next day, turning meat several times.

Barbecue lamb by indirect heat (see page 10). Lift meat from marinade and drain briefly (reserve marinade); then place on a lightly greased grill directly above drip pan. Cover barbecue; adjust dampers as necessary to maintain an even heat. Cook until a meat thermometer inserted in thickest part of lamb registers 135° to 140°F (about 1¼ hours). Thickest portions of meat will be rare; thinner sections will be medium to well done.

Meanwhile, pour marinade through a wire strainer into a wide frying pan; discard residue in strainer. Bring marinade to a boil over high heat; continue to boil until reduced to about ¾ cup.

To serve, let meat stand for 10 minutes; then cut across the grain into thin slices. Pass sauce to spoon over meat. Makes about 8 servings.

Per serving: 311 calories, 44 g protein, 7 g carbohydrates, 11 g total fat, 156 mg cholesterol, 111 mg sodium

SALT-BRINED GRILLED LAMB

Preparation time: 15–20 minutes

Marinating time: 2–3 days

Grilling time: About 1½ hours

Salt brine is typically thought of as a preservative—but in this case, it acts more like a flavorful marinade, helping to keep the meat moist and succulent during grilling. (Plan ahead for this roast—it must soak for 2 to 3 days before cooking.)

  8 **cups water**
  ½ **cup sugar**
  ¼ **cup salt**
  3 **tablespoons cardamom seeds, crushed**
  2 **tablespoons whole black peppercorns**
  ½ **cup minced fresh ginger**
    3½- to 4-pound boned and tied leg of lamb

In a 3- to 4-quart pan, combine water, sugar, salt, cardamom seeds, peppercorns, and ginger. Bring to a boil over high heat; then remove from heat and let cool. Set a large heavy-duty plastic bag in a 9- by 13-inch pan. Pour brine into bag, then add lamb; seal bag securely. Refrigerate for 2 to 3 days, turning bag over occasionally.

Barbecue lamb by indirect heat (see page 10). Lift lamb from brine and drain briefly, then place on a lightly greased grill directly above drip pan. Pour brine through a wire strainer; discard liquid and distribute seasonings over coals. Cover barbecue and adjust dampers as necessary to maintain an even heat. Cook until a meat thermometer inserted in thickest part registers 135° to 140°F for rare (about 1½ hours).

To serve, let roast stand for 10 minutes; then cut across the grain into thin slices. Makes 8 to 10 servings.

Per serving: 157 calories, 22 g protein, 3 g carbohydrates, 5 g total fat, 79 mg cholesterol, 714 mg sodium

FRUIT-STUFFED LAMB SHOULDER

Preparation time: 35–45 minutes

Grilling time: 1½–2 hours

A dried-fruit filling scented with lemon and rosemary is tucked inside this boned lamb shoulder; more of the same filling is stirred into the pan drippings to make a flavorful gravy.

  2 **packages (8 oz.** *each***) mixed dried fruit, pitted (if necessary) and cut into pieces**
  ½ **cup chopped onion**
  1 **teaspoon** *each* **grated lemon peel and dry rosemary**
  ⅔ **cup water**
    3- to 4-pound boned and tied lamb shoulder
    Salt and pepper
    About 2 cups regular-strength chicken broth
  1 **tablespoon cornstarch mixed with 2 tablespoons water**

In a small pan, combine fruit, onion, lemon peel, rosemary, and the ⅔ cup water. Cook over medium heat, uncovered, stirring often, until liquid is absorbed (about 8 minutes). Remove from heat; let cool.

Untie lamb and lay out flat. Sprinkle with salt and pepper, then spread with half the fruit mixture. Roll roast and tie securely at 2-inch intervals. Then tuck in ends of roast; tie around length of roll in several places.

Barbecue lamb by indirect heat (see page 10), placing it on a lightly greased grill directly above drip pan. Cover barbecue and adjust dampers as necessary to maintain an even heat. Cook until a meat thermometer inserted in thickest part registers 150°F for medium (1½ to 2 hours).

Let meat stand while you prepare gravy. To make gravy, skim and discard fat from pan drippings. Measure drippings and add enough broth to make 2 cups liquid; pour into a small pan and add remaining fruit mixture. Stir cornstarch mixture, then add to pan. Cook over high heat, stirring constantly, until sauce boils and thickens. Season to taste with salt and pepper. Cut lamb into thick slices, cutting long ties but leaving short ones intact. Pass gravy at the table to accompany meat. Makes 6 to 8 servings.

Per serving: 334 calories, 26 g protein, 39 g carbohydrates, 10 g total fat, 88 mg cholesterol, 320 mg sodium

This simply savory barbecue meal features Rosemary Lamb Chops (facing page) with grilled pattypan squash and bell peppers. Small rosemary sprigs garnish each chop; if you like, use a larger sprig to brush on the lemony basting sauce.

(Pictured on facing page)

ROSEMARY LAMB CHOPS

Preparation time: 5–10 minutes

Grilling time: About 10 minutes

Fragrant rosemary adds just the right accent to a simple lemon-butter basting sauce. Before serving, garnish each lamb chop with rosemary sprigs.

- ¼ **cup butter or margarine**
- 3 **tablespoons lemon juice**
- 4 **cloves garlic, minced or pressed**
- ½ **teaspoon chopped fresh rosemary leaves**
- 6 **lamb rib or loin chops, cut about 1 inch thick**
  Fresh rosemary sprigs

Melt butter in a small pan, then remove from heat and stir in lemon juice, garlic, and chopped rosemary. Trim excess fat from chops; then place chops on a lightly greased grill 4 to 6 inches above a solid bed of hot coals. Cook, turning once and basting often with butter mixture, until chops are well browned on outside but still pink in center; cut to test (about 10 minutes). Garnish with rosemary sprigs. Makes 3 to 6 servings.

Per 2-chop serving: 370 calories, 30 g protein, 2 g carbohydrates, 26 g total fat, 148 mg cholesterol, 232 mg sodium

INDIAN LAMB CHOPS

Preparation time: About 15 minutes

Marinating time: 4 hours or until next day

Grilling time: About 10 minutes

Plain yogurt sparked with onions, lemon juice, cilantro, and eight spices makes the Indian-style marinade and sauce for these round-bone lamb chops.

- 2 **medium-size onions, cut into chunks**
  About 2 tablespoons chopped fresh cilantro (coriander)
- 1 **tablespoon ground coriander**
- 2 **teaspoons ground cumin**
- 1½ **teaspoons *each* pepper, ground cloves, and ground cardamom**
- 1 **teaspoon *each* ground ginger, poppy seeds, and ground cinnamon**
- 2½ **tablespoons butter or margarine, melted**
- 2 **cups plain yogurt**
- 6 **tablespoons lemon juice**
- 12 **round-bone lamb chops, cut about 1 inch thick**

In a food processor or blender, combine onions, cilantro, ground coriander, cumin, pepper, cloves, cardamom, ginger, poppy seeds, cinnamon, butter, yogurt, and lemon juice. Whirl until smoothly puréed.

Trim excess fat from lamb chops, then place chops in a 9- by 13-inch dish. Pour yogurt marinade over chops and turn to coat. Cover and refrigerate for at least 4 hours or until next day, turning chops several times.

Lift chops from marinade and drain briefly (reserve marinade). Place chops on a lightly greased grill 4 to 6 inches above a solid bed of hot coals. Cook, turning once, until chops are well browned on outside but still pink in center; cut to test (about 10 minutes).

Warm reserved marinade in a small pan on grill; offer to spoon over individual servings. Makes 6 to 12 servings.

Per serving: 313 calories, 36 g protein, 5 g carbohydrates, 16 g total fat, 134 mg cholesterol, 136 mg sodium

⊕ GRILLED LAMB CHOPS WITH SPICED PEACHES

Preparation time: 10–15 minutes

Grilling time: About 10 minutes

Sliced fresh peaches spiced with cinnamon and ginger cook alongside these lamb chops to make a sweet, flavorful topping.

8 to 10 lamb rib chops, cut about 1 inch thick

¼ cup *each* sugar and cider vinegar

1 small onion, minced

½ cup raisins

1 teaspoon *each* ground cinnamon and ground ginger

3 medium-size ripe peaches, peeled, pitted, and cut into ¼-inch-thick slices
   Salt and pepper

Trim excess fat from lamb chops, then place chops to one side of a lightly greased grill 4 to 6 inches above a solid bed of hot coals. Cook, turning once, until well browned on outside but still pink in center; cut to test (about 10 minutes).

While chops are cooking, combine sugar, vinegar, onion, raisins, cinnamon, and ginger in an 8- to 10-inch frying pan. Place pan on grill next to lamb chops. Cook, stirring frequently, for 5 minutes. Add peaches and stir gently just until hot (about 3 more minutes). If spiced peaches are done before chops (or vice versa), move cooked food to a cooler part of grill to keep warm until both foods are ready.

To serve, let guests season chops to taste with salt and pepper; offer peaches to spoon over meat. Makes 4 servings.

Per serving: 378 calories, 30 g protein, 40 g carbohydrates, 11 g total fat, 106 mg cholesterol, 74 mg sodium

⊕ POUNDED LAMB CHOPS

Preparation time: About 20 minutes

Grilling time: About 4 minutes

Pounded flat before grilling, rosemary-fragrant lamb rib chops cook in just a few minutes. You can use the same technique for veal chops—see page 59.

4 cloves garlic, minced or pressed

2 tablespoons minced fresh rosemary leaves or 1 tablespoon dry rosemary

½ cup minced parsley

2 tablespoons olive oil or salad oil

4 lamb rib or loin chops (about 1¼ lbs. *total*), cut 1 inch thick
   Fresh rosemary sprigs

Combine garlic, minced rosemary, parsley, and oil. Slash fat around lamb chops at about 1-inch intervals. Rub about 1 tablespoon of the rosemary mixture on both sides of each chop. Place each chop between 2 sheets of plastic wrap; pound around bone with a flat-surfaced mallet until meat is about ¼ inch thick.

Place chops on a lightly greased grill 4 to 6 inches above a solid bed of hot coals. Cook, turning as needed, until chops are well browned on outside but still pink in center; cut to test (about 4 minutes). Garnish with rosemary sprigs. Makes 2 generous or 4 smaller servings.

Per 2-chop serving: 363 calories, 30 g protein, 4 g carbohydrates, 25 g total fat, 106 mg cholesterol, 79 mg sodium

⊕ PINE NUT–STUFFED LAMB CHOPS

Preparation time: 20–30 minutes

Grilling time: About 10 minutes

Before grilling these lamb chops, you cut a pocket in each one and fill it with a rich, lemon-scented pine nut stuffing. Depending on appetites, allow one or two chops per serving.

- 8 **lamb rib or loin chops, cut 1 inch thick**
- 2 **tablespoons butter or margarine**
- 3 **tablespoons lemon juice**
- ¼ **teaspoon** *each* **oregano leaves, salt, and pepper**
- ½ **cup pine nuts**
- 1 **clove garlic, minced or pressed**
- 1 **teaspoon grated lemon peel**
- 3 **tablespoons** *each* **finely minced green onions (including tops) and finely minced parsley**

With a sharp knife, cut a horizontal pocket in each lamb chop, starting at fat edge and cutting to bone. Set chops aside.

Melt butter in a small frying pan. Transfer 1 tablespoon of the melted butter to a small bowl and stir in lemon juice, oregano, salt, and pepper; set aside. Add pine nuts and garlic to remaining melted butter in pan. Cook over medium heat, stirring frequently, until nuts are golden brown. Remove from heat; stir in lemon peel, onions, and parsley.

Stuff ⅛ of the pine nut mixture (about one rounded tablespoon) into pocket of each chop. Lightly brush both sides of chops with some of the lemon juice mixture. Place chops on a lightly greased grill 4 to 6 inches above a solid bed of hot coals. Cook, turning once, until chops are well browned on outside but still pink in center; cut to test (about 10 minutes).

To serve, drizzle chops with any remaining lemon juice mixture. Makes 4 to 8 servings.

Per 2-chop serving: 375 calories, 34 g protein, 4 g carbohydrates, 26 g total fat, 122 mg cholesterol, 269 mg sodium

⊕ PORTUGUESE LAMB SHOULDER CHOPS

Preparation time: 10–15 minutes

Marinating time: 8 hours or until next day

Grilling time: About 10 minutes

Take your pick of two spicy Portuguese-style marinades to enhance the flavor of thick lamb shoulder chops. Both marinades are based on red wine, but one is flavored with cinnamon and cumin, while the other features whole pickling spice and cloves.

- **Cumin-Cinnamon Marinade or Pickling Spice Marinade (recipes follow)**
- 6 **lamb shoulder chops, cut 1 inch thick**

Prepare your choice of marinade. Trim excess fat from lamb chops, then add chops to marinade; turn to coat. Cover and refrigerate for at least 8 hours or until next day, turning several times.

Lift chops from marinade and drain briefly (reserve marinade). Place chops on a lightly greased grill 4 to 6 inches above a solid bed of hot coals. Cook, turning once and basting frequently with marinade, until chops are well browned on outside but still pink in center; cut to test (about 10 minutes). Makes 6 servings.

Cumin-Cinnamon Marinade. In a large bowl, stir together 1 cup **dry red wine**, ½ cup **olive oil** or salad oil, 3 cloves **garlic** (minced or pressed), ½ teaspoon **salt**, 1 teaspoon **ground cumin**, ¾ teaspoon **ground cinnamon**, ⅓ cup chopped **onion**, and 1 tablespoon **cumin seeds.**

Pickling Spice Marinade. In a large bowl, stir together 1 cup **dry red wine**, ¼ cup *each* **salad oil** and **red wine vinegar**, 2 cloves **garlic** (minced or pressed), ½ teaspoon **salt**, ½ cup chopped **onion**, 1 tablespoon **whole mixed pickling spice**, 4 **whole cloves**, and ¼ teaspoon **ground cloves.**

Per serving with Cumin-Cinnamon Marinade: 429 calories, 34 g protein, 3 g carbohydrates, 31 g total fat, 125 mg cholesterol, 269 mg sodium

Per serving with Pickling Spice Marinade: 347 calories, 34 g protein, 2 g carbohydrates, 22 g total fat, 125 mg cholesterol, 267 mg sodium

LEMON LAMB STEAKS

Preparation time: *About 10 minutes*

Marinating time: *4 hours or until next day*

Grilling time: *8–10 minutes*

Steaks cut from the broad end of a leg of lamb are an excellent choice for grilling. Here, the steaks are soaked in a lemon-oregano marinade before cooking.

- **4 lamb leg steaks (about 10 oz.** *each*)**, cut ¾ to 1 inch thick**
- **⅔ cup salad oil**
- **⅓ cup lemon juice**
- **1 medium-size onion, chopped**
- **1 teaspoon** *each* **salt and oregano leaves**
- **¼ teaspoon pepper**
  Lemon slices
  Parsley sprigs

Place lamb steaks in a close-fitting dish. In a bowl, stir together oil, lemon juice, onion, salt, oregano, and pepper; pour over meat. Turn meat to coat; then cover and refrigerate for at least 4 hours or until next day, turning meat several times.

Lift meat from marinade and drain briefly (reserve marinade). Place on a lightly greased grill 4 to 6 inches above a solid bed of hot coals. Cook, turning once and basting occasionally with marinade, until meat is well browned on outside but still pink in center; cut to test (8 to 10 minutes). Garnish meat with lemon slices and parsley. Makes 4 servings.

Per serving: 592 calories, 40 g protein, 3 g carbohydrates, 46 g total fat, 141 mg cholesterol, 652 mg sodium

---

(Pictured on facing page)

SHISH KEBAB WITH APRICOTS

Preparation time: *About 1 hour (including time to cut meat)*

Marinating time: *4 hours or until next day*

Grilling time: *12–15 minutes*

For pretty, bright-colored kebabs, thread chunks of onion and red bell pepper on skewers along with lamb and dried apricots soaked in a fresh-tasting orange juice marinade.

- **Orange-Rosemary Sauce (recipe follows)**
- **3 pounds lean boneless lamb (leg or shoulder), cut into 1½-inch cubes**
- **24 to 30 dried apricots**
- **1 large onion, cut into 1½-inch squares**
- **3 medium-size red bell peppers, seeded and cut into 1½-inch squares**

Prepare Orange-Rosemary Sauce. Add lamb and apricots to sauce; stir to coat. Cover and refrigerate for at least 4 hours or until next day, stirring several times.

Lift meat and apricots from sauce and drain briefly (reserve sauce). On 8 sturdy metal skewers, thread meat alternately with apricots, onion, and bell peppers.

Place skewers on a lightly greased grill 4 to 6 inches above a solid bed of medium coals. Cook, turning occasionally and basting frequently with sauce, until meat is well browned on outside but still pink in center; cut to test (12 to 15 minutes). Makes about 8 servings.

Orange-Rosemary Sauce. In a large bowl, stir together 1 teaspoon grated **orange peel,** ⅔ cup **orange juice,** ½ cup **olive oil** or salad oil, 3 tablespoons **white wine vinegar,** 2 tablespoons **soy sauce,** 1¼ teaspoons crushed **dry rosemary,** ½ cup minced **shallots,** 2 cloves **garlic** (minced or pressed), and ⅛ teaspoon **pepper.** If made ahead, cover and refrigerate until next day.

Per serving: 442 calories, 39 g protein, 21 g carbohydrates, 23 g total fat, 128 mg cholesterol, 352 mg sodium

Lamb cubes and plump dried apricots soak in a citrusy
marinade, then team up with red peppers and onion in
Shish Kebab with Apricots (facing page). Serve with fluffy
couscous pilaf and a salad of orange slices, onions,
and romaine.

GREEK SHISH KEBAB

Preparation time: About 40 minutes (including time to cut meat)

Marinating time: 4 hours or until next day

Grilling time: 12–15 minutes

In the Middle East, *shish kebab* (literally, "meat on a stick") describes any skewered, grilled meat. But to most American cooks, *shish kebab* means this Greek-style recipe: cubes of lamb marinated in lemon juice, olive oil, and oregano, then skewered with vegetables.

- ⅓ **cup olive oil or salad oil**
- 3 **tablespoons lemon juice**
- 1 **large onion, finely chopped**
- 2 **bay leaves**
- 2 **teaspoons oregano leaves**
- ½ **teaspoon pepper**
- 2 **pounds lean boneless lamb (leg or shoulder), cut into 1½-inch cubes**
- 1 **large mild red onion, cut into 1-inch pieces**
- 1 **large green or red bell pepper, seeded and cut into 1½-inch squares**
- ½ **pound medium-size mushrooms**
  About 1 cup cherry tomatoes

In a large bowl, stir together oil, lemon juice, chopped onion, bay leaves, oregano, and pepper. Add lamb; stir to coat. Cover and refrigerate for at least 4 hours or until next day, stirring several times.

Lift meat from marinade and drain briefly. Add red onion, bell pepper, and mushrooms to marinade; turn to coat, then lift out (reserve marinade). On 6 sturdy metal skewers, thread meat alternately with vegetables.

Place skewers on a lightly greased grill 4 to 6 inches above a solid bed of medium coals. Cook, turning and basting frequently with marinade, until meat and vegetables are well browned but meat is still pink in center; cut to test (12 to 15 minutes). Garnish with tomatoes. Makes 6 servings.

Per serving: 356 calories, 34 g protein, 8 g carbohydrates, 20 g total fat, 114 mg cholesterol, 86 mg sodium

PINEAPPLE-GLAZED KEBABS

Preparation time: About 1 hour (including time to cut meat)

Marinating time: 4 hours or until next day

Grilling time: 12–15 minutes

Crushed pineapple, herbs, and white wine combine in a tangy two-way marinade for these kebabs—after marinating the lamb, you whirl the pineapple mixture in a blender to make a thick coating sauce.

- 1 **can (8 oz.) crushed pineapple packed in its own juice**
- 1 **teaspoon dry rosemary**
- ½ **teaspoon *each* pepper and dill weed**
- ¼ **cup dry white wine**
- 3 **tablespoons white wine vinegar**
- 2 **tablespoons salad oil**
- 1 **clove garlic, minced or pressed**
  5- to 6-pound leg of lamb, cut into 1½-inch cubes
  Salt

In a large bowl, stir together pineapple and its juice, rosemary, pepper, dill weed, wine, vinegar, oil, and garlic. Add lamb; stir to coat. Cover and refrigerate for at least 4 hours or until next day, stirring meat several times.

Lift meat from pineapple marinade and drain briefly (reserve marinade). Thread meat equally on 6 to 8 sturdy metal skewers. Whirl reserved marinade in a blender or food processor until coarsely puréed. With a brush, dab purée evenly onto meat.

Place skewers on a lightly greased grill 4 to 6 inches above a solid bed of medium coals. Cook, turning occasionally and basting frequently with pineapple purée, until meat is well browned on outside but still pink in center; cut to test (12 to 15 minutes). Let guests season meat to taste with salt. Makes 6 to 8 servings.

Per serving: 409 calories, 53 g protein, 7 g carbohydrates, 17 g total fat, 189 mg cholesterol, 130 mg sodium

 AFRICAN GRILLED LAMB

Preparation time: About 40 minutes (including time to cut meat)

Marinating time: 4 hours or until next day

Grilling time: 12–15 minutes

Reserve some of the ginger and garlic marinade to mix with tomatoes and serve alongside this lamb entrée. Grilled zucchini makes a nice side dish (directions for grilling vegetables are on page 155).

- ¾ **cup lime or lemon juice**
- 3 **tablespoons** *each* **salad oil, tomato paste, and minced fresh ginger**
- 3 **cloves garlic, minced or pressed**
- ¼ **teaspoon pepper**
- 2 **pounds lean boneless lamb (leg or shoulder), cut into 1½-inch cubes**
- 2 **large ripe tomatoes, chopped**

In a large bowl, stir together lime juice, oil, tomato paste, ginger, garlic, and pepper. Remove ⅓ of the marinade from bowl and reserve to use for sauce.

Add lamb to remaining marinade in bowl; stir to coat. Cover and refrigerate for at least 4 hours or until next day, stirring several times.

Lift meat from marinade and drain briefly (discard marinade left in bowl). Thread equally on 6 sturdy metal skewers. Place skewers on a lightly greased grill 4 to 6 inches above a solid bed of medium coals. Cook, turning several times, until meat is well browned on outside but still pink in center; cut to test (12 to 15 minutes).

Stir tomatoes into reserved marinade; offer at the table to spoon over individual servings of meat. Makes 6 servings.

Per serving: 299 calories, 34 g protein, 7 g carbohydrates, 15 g total fat, 114 mg cholesterol, 154 mg sodium

PLUM-SAUCED LAMB KEBABS

Preparation time: About 1 hour (including time to cut meat)

Marinating time: 4 hours or until next day

Grilling time: 12–15 minutes

Tangy purple plums, puréed and seasoned, make a sweet-sour marinade and baste for skewered lamb chunks and mushrooms.

- 1 **can (1 lb.) whole purple plums**
- 2 **tablespoons butter or margarine**
- 1 **medium-size onion, chopped**
- ⅓ **cup firmly packed brown sugar**
- ¼ **cup tomato-based chili sauce**
- 2 **tablespoons soy sauce**
- 1 **teaspoon ground ginger**
- 2 **teaspoons lemon juice**
- 2 **pounds lean boneless lamb (leg or shoulder), cut into 1½-inch cubes**
- ½ **pound medium-size mushrooms**

Drain plums, reserving syrup. Pit plums, then place plums and syrup in a food processor or blender and whirl until puréed. Set aside.

Melt butter in a 2- to 3-quart pan over medium heat; add onion and cook, stirring frequently, until soft (about 10 minutes). Stir in sugar, chili sauce, soy, ginger, lemon juice, and plum purée. Bring to a boil over high heat; then reduce heat and simmer, uncovered, stirring occasionally, until sauce is thickened (about 30 minutes). Pour into a large bowl; let cool. Add lamb and stir to coat. Cover and refrigerate for at least 4 hours or until next day, stirring several times.

Lift out meat; let drain. Turn mushrooms in sauce; lift out (reserve sauce). On 6 sturdy metal skewers, thread meat alternately with mushrooms. Place skewers on a lightly greased grill 4 to 6 inches above a solid bed of medium coals. Cook, turning occasionally, until meat is well browned but still pink in center; cut to test (12 to 15 minutes). Brush with sauce during last 5 minutes of cooking. Makes 6 servings.

Per serving: 388 calories, 34 g protein, 36 g carbohydrates, 12 g total fat, 124 mg cholesterol, 634 mg sodium

A fruitful idea for a summer meal: minted, almond-studded
ground lamb patties grilled along with sweet cantaloupe
slices. Juicy orange wedges and fresh mint leaves garnish
Lamb Patties with Mint & Melon (page 78).

CALCUTTA KEBABS

Preparation time: About 45 minutes (including time to cut meat)

Marinating time: 4 hours or until next day

Grilling time: 12–15 minutes

Robustly seasoned with garlic and cumin, these kebabs go well with Indian-style chutney and cooling slices of cantaloupe or honeydew melon.

- ¼ **cup lemon juice**
- ½ **cup salad oil**
- 3 **cloves garlic, minced or pressed**
- 1 **tablespoon ground cumin**
- 2 **pounds lean boneless lamb (leg or shoulder), cut into 1½-inch cubes**
- 2 *each* **medium-size green, red, and yellow bell peppers (or 6 of one color), seeded and cut into 1½-inch pieces**

In a large bowl, stir together lemon juice, oil, garlic, and cumin. Add lamb and stir to coat. Cover and refrigerate for at least 4 hours or until next day, stirring several times.

Lift meat from marinade and drain briefly (reserve marinade), then thread equally on 6 sturdy metal skewers. Thread equal portions of bell peppers, alternating colors, on 6 more skewers. Brush peppers all over with marinade.

Place meat and pepper skewers on a lightly greased grill 4 to 6 inches above a solid bed of medium coals. Cook, turning occasionally and basting once with marinade, until peppers are tender and meat is well browned on outside but still pink in center; cut to test (12 to 15 minutes). Allow one skewer of meat and one of peppers for each serving. Makes 6 servings.

Per serving: 398 calories, 33 g protein, 5 g carbohydrates, 27 g total fat, 114 mg cholesterol, 86 mg sodium

BLACKBERRY SHISH KEBAB

Preparation time: About 45 minutes (including time to cut meat)

Marinating time: 4 hours or until next day

Grilling time: About 8 minutes

Blackberry syrup combines with fresh mint leaves, soy, and vinegar to give kebabs of lamb and water chestnuts a subtle, fruity sweetness. Serve them as an appetizer or main course.

- ½ **cup blackberry syrup**
- ¼ **cup red wine vinegar**
- 2 **tablespoons** *each* **soy sauce and chopped fresh mint**
- 2 **cloves garlic, minced or pressed**
- ½ **teaspoon pepper**
- 2 **cans (about 8 oz.** *each***) whole water chestnuts, drained**
- 1½ **pounds lean boneless lamb (leg or shoulder), cut into 1-inch cubes**

In a large bowl, stir together syrup, vinegar, soy, mint, garlic, and pepper. Add water chestnuts and lamb; stir to coat. Cover and refrigerate for at least 4 hours or until next day, stirring several times.

If using bamboo skewers, soak 12 to 18 skewers in hot water to cover for 30 minutes.

Lift meat and water chestnuts from marinade and drain briefly (discard marinade). Thread meat and water chestnuts alternately on thin bamboo or metal skewers. To avoid splitting water chestnuts, rotate skewer as you pierce them.

Place skewers on a lightly greased grill 4 to 6 inches above a solid bed of medium coals. Cook, turning occasionally, until meat is well browned on outside but still pink in center; cut to test (about 8 minutes). Makes 4 or 5 main-dish servings or about 8 appetizer servings.

Per main-dish serving: 274 calories, 30 g protein, 21 g carbohydrates, 7 g total fat, 103 mg cholesterol, 284 mg sodium

⬤ LAMB SOSATIES

Preparation time: About 30 minutes (including time to cut meat)

Marinating time: 4 hours or until next day

Grilling time: 12–15 minutes

A chile-sparked curry marinade complements the robust flavor of lamb. Serve the kebabs with grilled apricots or nectarines (see page 154).

   4 **pounds lean boneless lamb (leg or shoulder), cut into 1½-inch cubes**
1½ **cups cider vinegar**
   3 **tablespoons apricot or pineapple jam**
1½ **tablespoons *each* curry powder and firmly packed brown sugar**
   4 **small dried hot red chiles, crushed**
   2 **medium-size onions, thinly sliced**
   3 **cloves garlic, minced or pressed**
   2 **bay leaves**

Place lamb in a large bowl; set aside. In a small pan, stir together vinegar, jam, curry powder, sugar, chiles, onions, garlic, and bay leaves. Bring to a boil over high heat, then remove from heat and let cool. Pour vinegar mixture through a strainer over meat in bowl; discard residue in strainer. Stir meat to coat. Cover and refrigerate for at least 4 hours or until next day, stirring several times.

Lift meat from marinade and drain briefly (reserve marinade). Thread meat equally on about 10 sturdy metal skewers. Place skewers on a lightly greased grill 4 to 6 inches above a solid bed of medium coals. Cook, turning often and basting with marinade, until meat is well browned on outside but still pink in center; cut to test (12 to 15 minutes). Makes about 10 servings.

Per serving: 295 calories, 40 g protein, 11 g carbohydrates, 10 g total fat, 136 mg cholesterol, 99 mg sodium

(Pictured on page 76)

⬤ LAMB PATTIES WITH MINT & MELON

Preparation time: 20–25 minutes

Grilling time: 8–10 minutes

Grilled cantaloupe wedges acccompany mint-seasoned ground lamb patties studded with toasted almonds.

  ¼ **cup slivered almonds**
1½ **pounds lean ground lamb**
   2 **tablespoons fine dry bread crumbs**
   1 **egg, beaten**
   1 **teaspoon salt**
   1 **clove garlic, minced or pressed**
  ¼ **cup minced onion**
  ½ **cup minced fresh mint**
   1 **small cantaloupe, cut into 6 wedges**

Toast almonds in a small frying pan over medium-low heat until golden (about 7 minutes), stirring often. Remove from heat; chop finely. Place in a bowl and add lamb, bread crumbs, egg, salt, garlic, onion, and ¼ cup of the mint. Mix well; shape into 6 patties, each about ¾ inch thick.

Place meat patties and melon wedges on a lightly greased grill 4 to 6 inches above a solid bed of hot coals. Cook melon until hot (about 8 minutes), turning as needed. Cook meat, turning once, until well browned on outside but still pink in center; cut to test (8 to 10 minutes).

Transfer meat patties and melon to a platter; sprinkle both with remaining ¼ cup mint. Makes 6 servings.

Per serving: 265 calories, 26 g protein, 10 g carbohydrates, 13 g total fat, 131 mg cholesterol, 459 mg sodium

LAMB POCKET BURGERS

Preparation time: 20–25 minutes

Grilling time: 8–10 minutes

Slip curry-seasoned lamb patties into pocket bread, then add your choice of condiments—we suggest cucumbers, chutney, and yogurt.

- 1 **pound lean ground lamb**
- 1 **small onion, chopped**
- ¼ **cup fine dry bread crumbs**
- ⅓ **cup finely snipped dried apricots**
- 1 **egg**
- 2 **teaspoons curry powder**
- 3 **pocket breads, *each* about 7 inches in diameter, cut into halves**
  Chopped Major Grey's chutney
  Plain yogurt
  Sliced cucumbers

In a bowl, combine lamb, onion, bread crumbs, apricots, egg, and curry powder. Mix well; then shape into 6 oblong patties, each 3 to 4 inches long. If you wish to heat pocket bread halves, stack them and wrap in heavy-duty foil.

Place lamb patties on a lightly greased grill 4 to 6 inches above a solid bed of hot coals. Cook,

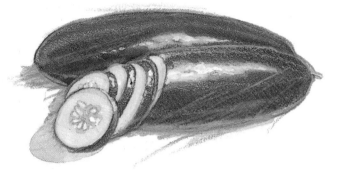

turning once, until well browned on outside but still pink in center; cut to test (8 to 10 minutes). Also heat foil-wrapped pocket bread at side of grill (not directly above coals) until warm, turning several times.

To serve, place each patty in a pocket bread half; top with chutney, yogurt, and cucumbers. Makes 6 servings.

Per serving: 313 calories, 28 g protein, 27 g carbohydrates, 10 g total fat, 131 mg cholesterol, 282 mg sodium

GRILLED LAMB LOGS IN TORTILLAS

Preparation time: About 25 minutes

Grilling time: 10–15 minutes

For these hearty dinner sandwiches, you wrap cylinders of seasoned ground lamb in bacon and cook them quickly on the grill.

- 1½ **pounds lean ground lamb**
- ⅓ **cup finely chopped onion**
- ¼ **cup fine dry bread crumbs**
- ¼ **cup pine nuts or slivered almonds**
- 1 **clove garlic, minced or pressed**
- 1 **egg, beaten**
- 1 **teaspoon salt**
- ½ **teaspoon dry rosemary**
- ¼ **teaspoon pepper**
- 12 **slices bacon**
- 6 **flour tortillas, *each* about 8 inches in diameter**

In a bowl, combine lamb, onion, bread crumbs, pine nuts, garlic, egg, salt, rosemary, and pepper. Mix well; then shape into 6 logs, each about 5 inches long.

Cook bacon, a portion at a time, in a wide frying pan over medium heat until it is partially cooked but still limp (about 3 minutes). Wind 2 bacon slices around each log, securing ends with wooden picks. Also sprinkle a few drops of water over each tortilla; then stack tortillas and wrap in heavy-duty foil.

Place lamb logs on a lightly greased grill 4 to 6 inches above a solid bed of medium coals. Cook, turning frequently, until bacon is crisp and meat is well browned on outside but still pink in center; cut to test (10 to 15 minutes). Also heat foil-wrapped tortillas at side of grill (not directly above coals) until warm (about 10 minutes); turn several times. To serve, wrap each lamb log in a tortilla. Makes 6 servings.

Per serving: 427 calories, 33 g protein, 29 g carbohydrates, 19 g total fat, 142 mg cholesterol, 878 mg sodium

*The smoky flavor of Spicy Ham Steak (page 82) is enhanced
by a sherry-pineapple marinade and baste. Good go-alongs:
steamed broccoli, grilled crookneck squash, and a basket
of your favorite rolls.*

SPARERIBS ■ HAM ■ CHOPS ■ ROASTS

Barbecued pork spareribs are an all-time favorite, whether basted with sweet fruit purées, hot and spicy chili mixtures, or easy tomato-based sauces. But ribs aren't the only cut of pork enhanced by rich smoke flavor: this chapter includes a whole range of barbecued pork recipes.

If you're planning a special-occasion dinner for a large group, you might choose a handsome pork leg, ham, or loin roast. For smaller affairs, you'll find a selection of savory kebabs as well as boneless tenderloin specialties. Quick-to-grill chops, flavorful Italian sausages, and barbecued pork burgers are good choices for more casual dinners or tailgate picnics. You may want to create your own recipes, too—it's easy when you use the tempting collection of marinades and sauces on page 83.

Basic directions for grilling all pork cuts begin on page 16. *Note the internal temperatures and cooking times for roasts:* the temperatures may be lower (and the times shorter) than those you're used to seeing. For years, we've been told that pork must be cooked to 170°F to eliminate any danger of trichinosis. However, the organism responsible for the disease is destroyed when the meat's internal temperature exceeds just 137°F and is held there for a few minutes— and today's lean pork may be dry and tough if cooked to 170°F. To ensure juicy results, we recommend cooking pork just until a meat thermometer inserted in the thickest portion registers 150° to 155°F.

(Pictured on page 80)

SPICY HAM STEAK

Preparation time: 5–10 minutes

Marinating time: 3 hours or until next day

Grilling time: About 20 minutes

A fruity baste flavored with clove and pineapple penetrates this thick ham steak. You can barbecue it at home or bring it along, still marinating, to your favorite picnic site.

¼ **cup butter or margarine, melted**
1 **cup** *each* **dry sherry and pineapple juice**
2 **teaspoons** *each* **ground cloves and paprika**
1 **teaspoon firmly packed brown sugar**
¼ **teaspoon dry mustard**
1 **clove garlic, minced or pressed**
   1¾-pound center-cut ham slice,
   cut 1 inch thick

In a bowl, stir together butter, sherry, pineapple juice, cloves, paprika, sugar, mustard, and garlic. Place ham in a large heavy-duty plastic bag; pour in sherry mixture. Seal bag securely and rotate to distribute marinade. Place in a shallow baking pan; refrigerate for at least 3 hours or until next day, turning bag over several times.

Lift ham from marinade and drain briefly (reserve marinade). Place ham on a lightly greased grill 4 to 6 inches above a solid bed of low coals. Cook, turning and basting frequently with marinade, until ham is browned on outside and hot throughout (about 20 minutes). Makes 5 or 6 servings.

Per serving: 332 calories, 21 g protein, 15 g carbohydrates, 20 g total fat, 88 mg cholesterol, 1639 mg sodium

SHERRY-FLAVORED HAM

Preparation time: 5–10 minutes

Grilling time: 3–3½ hours

This barbecued bone-in ham is a sure crowd-pleaser. Like our grilled ham steak (above), it's spiced with cloves and basted with sherry.

   12- to 14-pound fully cooked bone-in ham
3 **tablespoons prepared mustard**
2 **teaspoons ground cloves**
1 **cup dry sherry or orange juice**

With a sharp knife, score top of ham in a crisscross pattern, making cuts about ¼ inch deep and 1 to 1½ inches apart. Rub ham all over with mustard; sprinkle with cloves.

Barbecue ham by indirect heat (see page 10). Place ham on a lightly greased grill directly above drip pan. Cover barbecue and adjust dampers as necessary to maintain an even heat. Cook until a meat thermometer inserted in thickest part (not touching bone) registers 135°F (3 to 3½ hours). During last hour of cooking, baste ham often with sherry.

To serve, let ham stand for 10 minutes; then cut into thin slices. Makes 20 to 25 servings.

Per serving: 359 calories, 34 g protein, 7 g carbohydrates, 21 g total fat, 111 mg cholesterol, 2579 mg sodium

MARINADES, SAUCES & BUTTERS FOR PORK

Though the pork sold today is much leaner than that marketed 10 years ago, it still has an exceptionally rich flavor that's complemented by sweet or spicy marinades and sauces.

You'll find basic grilling times and techniques for pork on page 16.

MARINADES

A marinade boosts the flavor of any pork cut; in addition, it helps tenderize cuts from the shoulder or butt. Marinate the meat in a close-fitting dish, pan, or bowl; or enclose both meat and marinade in a large heavy-duty plastic bag. It's usually best to marinate for at least 4 hours—or, if possible, until the next day.

Apple Juice Marinade. In a bowl, stir together ½ cup **apple juice,** ¼ cup *each* **soy sauce** and **honey,** 2 tablespoons **lemon juice,** ½ teaspoon **garlic powder,** and ¼ teaspoon *each* **dry mustard** and **ground ginger.** Makes about 1¼ cups.

Fennel-Chile Marinade. In a bowl, combine 1½ cups **dry white wine,** ¼ cup **olive oil** or salad oil, 4 cloves **garlic** (minced or pressed), 2¼ teaspoons *each* crushed **fennel seeds** and **dry basil,** ¾ to 1 teaspoon **crushed dried hot red chiles,** and ¼ cup **white wine vinegar.** Stir well to blend. Makes about 2 cups.

SAUCES

Thick, richly flavored sauces like our Chinese Plum Sauce and Apricot Baste add just the right touch to any cut of grilled pork. Brush either sauce over the meat during the last 5 to 10 minutes of cooking.

Apricot Baste. In a food processor or blender, whirl 1 small can (about 8 oz.) undrained **apricot halves** or sliced peaches until puréed. Pour into a 1½- to 2-quart pan and stir in ¼ cup **catsup,** 3 tablespoons **lemon juice,** 2 tablespoons **salad oil** (or melted butter or margarine), ¼ teaspoon **salt,** ½ teaspoon **liquid smoke** (optional), and ⅛ teaspoon grated **lemon peel.** Bring to a boil; then reduce heat and simmer, uncovered, for 10 to 15 minutes. Makes 1½ cups.

Chinese Plum Sauce. Drain 2 cans (1 lb. *each*) **whole purple plums,** reserving syrup. Remove pits from plums. In a blender, combine pitted plums, 1¼ cups of the reserved syrup (discard remaining syrup), and ¾ cup **water;** whirl until puréed. Set aside.

Heat 1 tablespoon **salad oil** in a 3- to 4-quart pan over medium high heat. Stir in 1 teaspoon **Chinese five-spice,** ½ teaspoon *each* **dry mustard, ground cumin,** and **ground cinnamon,** and ¼ teaspoon **pepper.** Add plum purée, ½ cup **canned tomato sauce,** 1 medium-size **onion** (chopped), 1 tablespoon *each* **soy sauce** and **Worcestershire,** and ¼ teaspoon **liquid hot pepper seasoning.** Bring to a boil; boil, uncovered, until reduced to 3 cups. Stir in 1 tablespoon **rice wine vinegar.** Makes 3 cups.

BUTTERS & BASTES

Before grilling tender cuts such as loin chops, rib chops, and tenderloins, brush them with a simple orange or sesame butter; or use the sweeter, more complex raisin baste, seasoned with garlic and mustard. (To give the flavors time to blend, prepare butters or baste at least an hour in advance.)

Orange Butter Baste. Melt ¼ cup **butter** or margarine in a small pan over medium heat. Remove from heat and stir in ¼ cup **orange juice.** If desired, add ¼ teaspoon *each* **dry rosemary** and **thyme leaves** or ½ teaspoon dry tarragon. Makes about ½ cup.

Sesame Butter. Toast ¼ cup **sesame seeds** in a wide frying pan over medium heat until golden (about 3 minutes), shaking pan often. Let cool. In a bowl, beat ½ cup (¼ lb.) **butter** or margarine (at room temperature) until fluffy; beat in sesame seeds until well blended. Makes about ¾ cup.

Savory Raisin Baste. In a 1½- to 2-quart pan, combine ½ cup finely chopped **raisins;** ¼ cup chopped **onion;** 1 clove **garlic** (minced or pressed); ½ cup **catsup;** ½ cup **regular-strength beef broth** or dry white wine; 3 tablespoons **salad oil;** 2 tablespoons **wine vinegar;** 1 tablespoon firmly packed **brown sugar;** 1 teaspoon **prepared mustard;** 1 teaspoon **liquid smoke** (optional); ½ teaspoon **salt;** and ⅛ teaspoon **dill weed.** Bring to a boil; then reduce heat and simmer, uncovered, for 10 to 15 minutes. Makes about 1¾ cups.

(Pictured on facing page)

PORK CHOPS GRILLED WITH HERBS

Preparation time: About 5 minutes

Grilling time: 10–14 minutes

Calling the family to dinner is easy when you serve these chops. Topped with fresh bay or sage leaves, they smell wonderful as they grill.

4 pork loin or rib chops (1½ to 1¾ lbs. *total*), cut about 1 inch thick

1 clove garlic, cut in half
Salt and pepper

8 large fresh bay leaves, fresh sage leaves, or fresh sage sprigs
About 2 tablespoons olive oil

Rub both sides of pork chops with cut sides of garlic; then sprinkle chops lightly with salt and pepper. Press one bay leaf on each side of each chop; brush chops lightly with oil on both sides.

Place chops on a lightly greased grill 4 to 6 inches above a solid bed of medium coals. Cook, turning once, until meat is well browned on outside and no longer pink near bone in thickest part; cut to test (10 to 14 minutes). Makes 4 servings.

Per serving: 377 calories, 27 g protein, 2 g carbohydrates, 29 g total fat, 95 mg cholesterol, 69 mg sodium

PORK CHOPS WITH SPICED TOMATO PASTE

Preparation time: About 15 minutes

Marinating time: 4 hours or until next day

Grilling time: 5–7 minutes

Bold Indian spices go into the vivid tomato paste that flavors these grilled pork chops. A cool sauce—easily made by blending some of the seasoning paste with yogurt—tempers the meat's spicy heat.

Spiced Tomato Paste (recipe follows)
1 cup plain yogurt
8 pork loin chops (about 2 lbs. *total*), cut about ½ inch thick

Prepare Spiced Tomato Paste. Mix ¼ cup of the paste with yogurt; cover and refrigerate.

Scrape remaining Spiced Tomato Paste into a 9- by 13-inch pan. Trim and discard fat from chops; then set chops in pan and turn to coat with paste. Cover and refrigerate for at least 4 hours or until next day, turning chops occasionally. Paste will coagulate when cold; before you grill chops, stir paste to soften, then spread evenly over meat.

Place chops on a lightly greased grill 4 to 6 inches above a solid bed of medium coals. Cook, turning often, until meat is browned on outside and no longer pink near bone in thickest part; cut to test (5 to 7 minutes). Pass yogurt sauce at the table. Makes 4 servings.

Spiced Tomato Paste. In a blender, combine 1 large **onion** (chopped); ½ cup **wine vinegar;** 1 can (6 oz.) **tomato paste;** 3 tablespoons **salad oil;** 2 tablespoons chopped **fresh ginger;** 2 teaspoons **ground coriander;** ½ teaspoon *each* **ground red pepper** (cayenne) and **ground cumin;** ¼ teaspoon **ground mace** or ground nutmeg; and ¼ teaspoon *each* **ground cloves** and **ground turmeric.**

Per serving: 598 calories, 41 g protein, 17 g carbohydrates, 41 g total fat, 130 mg cholesterol, 474 mg sodium

Aromatic fresh bay leaves lend tantalizing flavor to Pork Chops Grilled with Herbs (facing page). Simply press a leaf to one side of each chop, brush with oil, and grill until richly browned and tender.

⊙ POUNDED PORK & CHILI CHOPS

Preparation time: About 10 minutes

Grilling time: 5–6 minutes

Pork chops gain extra flavor from a chili-cumin seasoning mixture pounded into the meat before cooking.

    1 **tablespoon chili powder**
   ½ **teaspoon ground cumin**
    2 **cloves garlic, minced or pressed**
    1 **small onion, minced**
    2 **tablespoons salad oil**
    4 **pork loin or rib chops (about 1¼ lbs. *total*), cut about ½ inch thick**
    1 **small orange, cut into wedges**
       Fresh cilantro (coriander) sprigs

Stir together chili powder, cumin, garlic, onion, and oil. Slash fat around edges of chops at about 1-inch intervals. Spread about 1 tablespoon of the chili mixture on each side of each chop. Place each chop between 2 sheets of plastic wrap. With a flat-surfaced mallet, pound meat evenly and firmly around bone until about ¼ inch thick.

Place meat on a lightly greased grill 4 to 6 inches above a solid bed of medium coals. Cook, turning once, until well browned on outside and no longer pink near bone; cut to test (5 to 6 minutes).

Serve chops with orange wedges and cilantro; squeeze orange over meat before eating. Makes 2 to 4 servings.

Per serving: 342 calories, 23 g protein, 5 g carbohydrates, 25 g total fat, 79 mg cholesterol, 77 mg sodium

⊙ GRILLED GINGERED PORK CHOPS

Preparation time: About 10 minutes

Marinating time: 4 hours or until next day

Grilling time: 8–10 minutes

Dry sherry and lots of fresh ginger lend intriguing flavor to pork shoulder chops. You might accompany the meat with grilled pear halves and wedges of grilled cabbage (see pages 154 and 155).

   ¼ **cup minced fresh ginger**
   ¾ **cup dry sherry**
    2 **cloves garlic, minced or pressed**
    3 **tablespoons soy sauce**
    2 **tablespoons salad oil**
    1 **tablespoon sugar**
    4 **pork shoulder chops (about 1½ lbs. *total*), cut about ¾ inch thick**

In a large bowl, stir together ginger, sherry, garlic, soy, oil, and sugar. Add pork chops and turn to coat. Cover and refrigerate for at least 4 hours or until next day, turning several times.

Lift meat from marinade and drain briefly (reserve marinade). Place meat on a lightly greased grill 4 to 6 inches above a solid bed of medium coals. Cook, brushing occasionally with marinade and turning once, until well browned on outside and no longer pink near bone in thickest part; cut to test (8 to 10 minutes). Makes 4 servings.

Per serving: 504 calories, 28 g protein, 11 g carbohydrates, 38 g total fat, 120 mg cholesterol, 860 mg sodium

CURRIED PORK STEAK WITH MELON

Preparation time: 5–10 minutes

Grilling time: 15–20 minutes

Steaks cut from the broad end of a leg of pork take nicely to cooking on the grill. This thick steak is basted with a curry-chutney butter; cantaloupe rings grill alongside.

½ cup (¼ lb.) butter or margarine

2 teaspoons curry powder

2 tablespoons *each* lemon juice and finely chopped Major Grey's chutney

2½- to 3-pound pork leg steak, cut 1½ inches thick

1 large cantaloupe, peeled, cut crosswise into ½-inch-thick rings, and seeded

Melt butter in a small pan over medium heat; stir in curry powder, lemon juice, and chutney. Brush pork steak and cantaloupe with part of the butter mixture.

Place meat on a lightly greased grill 4 to 6 inches above a solid bed of medium coals. Cook, basting occasionally with butter mixture and turning several times, until meat is well browned on outside and no longer pink near bone; cut to test (15 to 20 minutes). During last 5 minutes of cooking, arrange cantaloupe rings on grill. Cook, brushing occasionally with butter mixture and turning once, until heated through (about 5 minutes).

To serve, cut steak into ½-inch-thick slices; accompany with cantaloupe. Makes 4 to 6 servings.

Per serving: 494 calories, 27 g protein, 14 g carbohydrates, 37 g total fat, 137 mg cholesterol, 240 mg sodium

ORIENTAL-STYLE PORK TENDERLOINS

Preparation time: About 5 minutes

Marinating time: 8 hours or until next day

Grilling time: 18–22 minutes

Pork tenderloins are the strips of tender meat found beneath the loin. Here, the strips marinate in a sweet soy mixture before grilling.

2 pork tenderloins (¾ to 1 lb. *each*)

½ cup *each* soy sauce and regular-strength chicken broth

¼ cup sake or dry sherry

6 tablespoons sugar

1 teaspoon minced garlic

1 teaspoon red food coloring (optional)

With a small, sharp knife, trim surface fat and thin, silvery membrane from tenderloins. Fold and tie thin end of each tenderloin under to give meat an even thickness.

In a large bowl, stir together soy, broth, sake, sugar, garlic, and, if desired, food coloring. Add tenderloins and turn to coat. Cover and refrigerate for at least 8 hours or until next day, turning tenderloins several times.

Barbecue meat by indirect heat (see page 10). Lift meat from marinade and drain briefly (discard marinade). Place meat on a lightly greased grill directly above drip pan. Cover barbecue and adjust dampers as necessary to maintain an even heat. Cook until meat is no longer pink in thickest part (cut to test) or until a meat thermometer inserted in thickest part (not folded end) and set parallel to length registers 150° to 155°F. Cooking will take 18 to 22 minutes.

To serve, let meat stand for 10 minutes; then cut across the grain into thin slanting slices. Makes about 4 servings.

Per serving: 328 calories, 41 g protein, 24 g carbohydrates, 7 g total fat, 126 mg cholesterol, 2275 mg sodium

Quickly grilled, then sliced, Spicy Pork Tenderloins (facing page) are an easy-to-handle entrée for four. If you like, nest each serving of meat in saffron-tinted rice and accompany with grilled vegetables.

(Pictured on facing page)

SPICY PORK TENDERLOINS

Preparation time: About 5 minutes

Marinating time: 4 hours or until next day

Grilling time: 18–22 minutes

Use your favorite prepared mustard in the marinade for these tender, hot-sweet pork strips. You might serve them with grilled peppers and slim Oriental eggplants (see page 155).

    2 pork tenderloins (¾ to 1 lb. *each*)
    ¼ cup *each* honey and prepared mustard
    ¼ teaspoon *each* salt and chili powder

With a small, sharp knife, trim surface fat and thin, silvery membrane from tenderloins. Fold and tie thin end of each tenderloin under to give meat an even thickness.

    In a large bowl, stir together honey, mustard, salt, and chili powder. Add tenderloins and turn to coat. Cover and refrigerate for at least 4 hours or until next day, turning tenderloins several times.

Barbecue meat by indirect heat (see page 10). Lift meat from marinade and drain briefly (reserve marinade); place on a lightly greased grill directly above drip pan. Cover barbecue and adjust dampers as necessary to maintain an even heat. Cook, brushing once with reserved marinade, until meat is no longer pink in thickest part (cut to test) or until a meat thermometer inserted in thickest part (not folded end) and set parallel to length registers 150° to 155°F. Cooking will take 18 to 22 minutes.

    To serve, let meat stand for 10 minutes; then cut across the grain into thin slanting slices. Makes about 4 servings.

Per serving: 301 calories, 40 g protein, 19 g carbohydrates, 7 g total fat, 126 mg cholesterol, 424 mg sodium

PORK TENDERLOINS CRUSTED WITH MUSTARD SEEDS

Preparation time: About 10 minutes

Marinating time: 4 hours or until next day

Grilling time: 18–22 minutes

Boneless, tender, and very lean, pork tenderloin cooks quickly. The delicate flavor is enhanced by assertive seasonings—here, coarsely ground black pepper and mustard seeds.

    2 pork tenderloins (¾ to 1 lb. *each*)
    1 teaspoon coarsely ground pepper
    5 to 6 tablespoons mustard seeds
    1 tablespoon butter or margarine, melted
       Dijon mustard
       Salt

With a small, sharp knife, trim surface fat and thin, silvery membrane from tenderloins. Sprinkle evenly with pepper. Put mustard seeds in a pan longer than tenderloins; roll meat in seeds until heavily coated. Cover and refrigerate for at least 4 hours or until next day.

Fold and tie thin end of each tenderloin under to give meat an even thickness. Then place seed-coated meat on a lightly greased grill 4 to 6 inches above a solid bed of medium coals. Cook, turning often to brown evenly, until meat is no longer pink in thickest part (cut to test) or until a meat thermometer inserted in thickest part of tenderloin (not folded end) and set parallel to length registers 150° to 155°F. Cooking will take 18 to 22 minutes.

    Transfer meat to a board; brush seeds with butter to make them shiny. Slice meat across the grain and serve with mustard; let guests season meat to taste with salt. Makes about 4 servings.

Per serving: 317 calories, 42 g protein, 5 g carbohydrates, 13 g total fat, 133 mg cholesterol, 121 mg sodium

INDONESIAN PORK ROAST WITH PEANUT SAUCE

Preparation time: About 20 minutes

Marinating time: 8 hours or until next day

Grilling time: 2–2½ hours

Warm and spicy peanut sauce is just as good with soy-marinated pork shoulder as it is with beef *satay* (page 41).

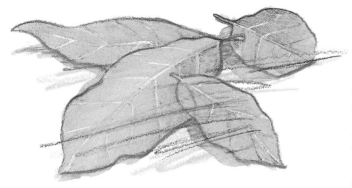

1 cup regular-strength chicken broth
⅓ cup sugar
¼ cup soy sauce
2 tablespoons dry sherry
   4- to 5-pound boned and tied pork shoulder or pork butt roast
   Peanut Sauce (page 41)

In a large bowl, stir together broth, sugar, soy, and sherry. Add pork and turn to coat. Cover and refrigerate for at least 8 hours or until next day, turning several times.

Barbecue meat by indirect heat (see page 10). Lift meat from marinade and drain briefly (discard marinade). Place meat on a lightly greased grill directly above drip pan. Cover barbecue and adjust dampers as necessary to maintain an even heat. Cook until a meat thermometer inserted in thickest part registers 150° to 155°F (1½ to 2¼ hours). Meanwhile, prepare Peanut Sauce.

To serve, let meat stand for 10 minutes; then cut across the grain into thin slanting slices. Serve with sauce. Makes 8 to 10 servings.

Per serving: 442 calories, 28 g protein, 8 g carbohydrates, 32 g total fat, 123 mg cholesterol, 597 mg sodium

PORTUGUESE BARBECUED PORK

Preparation time: About 10 minutes

Marinating time: 1–3 days

Grilling time: About 2 hours

Vindhalos—pork roast soaked in a spicy vinegar and garlic marinade—is a popular traditional dish in Portugal. You might accompany it with grilled new potatoes, zucchini, and tomatoes (see page 155).

  1½ cups red wine vinegar
    1 cup water
    6 cloves garlic, minced or pressed
    1 tablespoon ground allspice
    2 bay leaves
    ½ teaspoon salt
    2 teaspoons *each* ground red pepper (cayenne) and paprika
     4-pound boned and tied pork shoulder or pork butt roast

In a large bowl, stir together vinegar, water, garlic, allspice, bay leaves, salt, red pepper, and paprika. Add pork and turn to coat. Cover and refrigerate for at least 24 hours or up to 3 days, turning pork several times.

Barbecue meat by indirect heat (see page 10). Lift meat from marinade and drain briefly (reserve marinade); then place on a lightly greased grill directly above drip pan. Cover barbecue and adjust dampers as necessary to maintain an even heat. Cook, basting frequently with marinade, until a meat thermometer inserted in thickest part registers 150° to 155°F (about 2 hours). To serve, let meat stand for 10 minutes; then cut across the grain into thin slanting slices. Makes about 8 servings.

Per serving: 525 calories, 35 g protein, 4 g carbohydrates, 40 g total fat, 154 mg cholesterol, 108 mg sodium

SAVORY FLAT BREADS

FOR THE GRILL

Big wheels of bread seasoned with fresh Italian herbs or pungent Indian spices bake in just minutes on the barbecue. You can start from scratch or use purchased frozen dough; either way, you'll get fragrant, chewy breads to enjoy as a first course with cheese and salad or to serve alongside grilled meats or chicken.

GRILLED ITALIAN HERB FLAT BREAD

2⅓ cups warm water (about 110°F)
 1 package active dry yeast
1⅔ cups whole wheat flour
 1 teaspoon salt
   About 1 cup olive oil
   About 4½ cups all-purpose flour
 1 cup chopped fresh basil leaves or ¼ cup dry basil leaves
 ¾ cup chopped fresh oregano leaves or 2 tablespoons dry oregano leaves
 ¾ cup minced parsley
   Kosher or regular salt

In a large bowl, mix 1⅔ cups of the water and yeast; let stand until yeast is softened (about 5 minutes). Stir in whole wheat flour. Cover with plastic wrap and let stand at room temperature for 4 hours or until next day.

Add remaining ⅔ cup water, the 1 teaspoon salt, and 3 tablespoons of the oil to yeast mixture in bowl. Add 1½ cups of the all-purpose flour and mix slowly with an electric mixer until ingredients are moistened. Then beat on high speed until dough is stretchy (about 2 minutes). Add 3 cups more all-purpose flour and stir with a heavy spoon until well moistened.

Scrape dough onto a floured board and knead until smooth and no longer sticky (5 to 10 minutes), adding all-purpose flour as required. Place dough in a greased bowl; turn dough over to grease top. Cover and let rise in a warm place until dough is about doubled in bulk (about 1 hour). Knead on a lightly floured board to expel air bubbles, then divide into 6 equal balls.

Work with one piece of dough at a time, keeping remaining pieces covered. On a floured board, roll each ball into about a 10-inch-diameter round. Drizzle with about 1 tablespoon of the oil, sprinkle with 4 teaspoons of the fresh basil (or 1 teaspoon of the dry basil), 1 tablespoon of the fresh oregano (or ½ teaspoon of the dry oregano), and 1 tablespoon of the parsley. Sprinkle with kosher salt to taste. Roll lightly to press seasonings in.

Turn round over onto a piece of floured foil; repeat seasoning and rolling process on second side. Place foil-supported round on a 12- by 15-inch baking sheet.

Shape and season remaining dough in the same way, stacking each piece on top of the first. (At this point, you may cover and refrigerate for up to 3 hours.)

To cook, pick up one dough round, supporting it with foil; flip dough onto a lightly greased grill 4 to 6 inches above a solid bed of medium coals. Peel off foil. You can cook 2 pieces of dough at a time on a 22- to 24-inch grill. Cook, turning once, until bread is speckled with gold on both sides (5 to 7 minutes).

With a wide metal spatula, remove bread from grill. Cook remaining dough rounds in the same way. Serve hot or cool. Makes 6 rounds (2 or 3 servings per round).

Per serving: 262 calories, 5 g protein, 33 g carbohydrates, 13 g total fat, 0 mg cholesterol, 124 mg sodium

GRILLED INDIAN MINT FLAT BREAD

Follow directions for **Grilled Italian Herb Flat Bread,** but omit basil, oregano, and parsley. Instead, sprinkle each side of each round with ¼ cup chopped **fresh mint leaves,** ½ teaspoon **cumin seeds,** and ¼ teaspoon **ground coriander;** sprinkle with **kosher salt** and **ground red pepper** (cayenne) to taste. Makes 6 rounds (2 or 3 servings per round).

Per serving: 258 calories, 5 g protein, 32 g carbohydrates, 13 g total fat, 0 mg cholesterol, 123 mg sodium

QUICK GRILLED FLAT BREADS

Instead of making dough for Grilled Italian Herb Flat Bread, use 3 loaves (1 lb. *each*) **frozen whole wheat or white bread dough,** thawed. Cut each loaf in half, shape, season (Italian or Indian), and bake as directed. Makes 6 rounds (2 or 3 servings per round).

Per serving: 203 calories, 6 g protein, 36 g carbohydrates, 4 g total fat, 4 mg cholesterol, 365 mg sodium

VENEZUELAN PORK BUTT

Preparation time: About 15 minutes

Marinating time: 4 hours or until next day

Grilling time: About 40 minutes

For this recipe, you butterfly a boneless pork butt roast, slitting it and spreading it flat to make a thick rectangular steak. Before grilling the steak, marinate it in a simple mixture of oil, vinegar, pimentos, and parsley.

       4-pound boneless pork butt roast
   1   **large onion, coarsely chopped**
   1   **can (4 oz.) pimentos, drained and finely chopped**
   2   **cloves garlic, minced or pressed**
   ⅓   **cup chopped parsley**
   ½   **cup distilled white vinegar**
   ¼   **cup salad oil**
   ¼   **teaspoon pepper**

Untie pork butt if necessary; then butterfly (slit at center and spread out flat) to make a 1½-inch-thick steak. With a knife, score meat in a crisscross pattern, making cuts about ½ inch deep and 1½ inches apart. Place meat in a large heavy-duty plastic bag.

In a bowl, stir together onion, pimentos, garlic, parsley, vinegar, oil, and pepper. Pour mixture over meat in bag. Seal bag securely; rotate to distribute marinade. Place in a shallow baking pan; refrigerate for at least 4 hours or until next day, turning bag over several times.

Barbecue meat by indirect heat (see page 10). Lift meat from marinade and drain briefly. Scrape off and discard vegetable bits clinging to meat; reserve remaining marinade. Place meat on a lightly greased grill directly above drip pan. Cover barbecue and adjust dampers as necessary to maintain an even heat. Cook, basting occasionally with marinade, until a meat thermometer inserted in thickest part registers 150° to 155°F (about 40 minutes).

To serve, cut meat across the grain into thin slanting slices. Pour any remaining marinade into a small pan and bring to a boil; pass at the table to spoon over meat. Makes about 8 servings.

Per serving: 673 calories, 41 g protein, 2 g carbohydrates, 54 g total fat, 183 mg cholesterol, 129 mg sodium

(Pictured on facing page)

SALT-BRINED GRILLED PORK

Preparation time: About 10 minutes

Marinating time: 2–3 days

Grilling time: 45–55 minutes

This roast gets its firm, yet very moist texture from several days of soaking in a light fennel-seasoned salt brine.

   8   **cups water**
   ½   **cup sugar**
   ¼   **cup salt**
   3   **tablespoons fennel seeds, crushed**
   2   **tablespoons** *each* **thyme leaves and whole black peppercorns**
       Colored part of peel cut from 1 large orange
       4-pound center-cut boneless pork loin roast

In a 3- to 4-quart pan, combine water, sugar, salt, fennel seeds, thyme, peppercorns, and orange peel. Bring to a boil over high heat; then remove from heat and let cool.

Set a large heavy-duty plastic bag in a 9- by 13-inch pan. Pour brine into bag, then add pork; seal bag securely. Rotate bag to distribute marinade. Refrigerate for 2 to 3 days, turning bag over occasionally.

Barbecue meat by indirect heat (see page 10). Lift meat from brine and drain briefly, then place on a lightly greased grill directly above drip pan. Pour brine through a wire strainer; discard liquid and distribute seasonings over coals. Cover barbecue and adjust dampers as necessary to maintain an even heat. Cook until a meat thermometer inserted in thickest part registers 150° to 155°F (45 to 55 minutes).

To serve, let meat stand for 10 minutes; then cut across the grain into thin slanting slices. Makes 8 to 10 servings.

Per serving: 427 calories, 35 g protein, 6 g carbohydrates, 29 g total fat, 124 mg cholesterol, 1460 mg sodium

Salt-brined Grilled Pork (facing page) absorbs subtle flavor as it marinates in fennel-seasoned brine. Accompaniments for this special-occasion entrée include sushi, cucumber salad, oranges, and snow peas.

JELLY-GLAZED PORK LOIN

Preparation time: About 20 minutes

Grilling time: 1¼–1½ hours

When brushed with a sweet-sour baste, grilled pork yields especially flavorful pan drippings you can use in a quick-to-make sauce to pass at the table.

> ½ teaspoon garlic salt
> ¼ teaspoon ground cumin
> 1½ teaspoons chili powder
>   4-pound center-cut boneless pork loin roast
> ½ cup apple jelly
> ½ cup catsup
> 2 tablespoons vinegar
> 1 tablespoon *each* cornstarch and water

In a saucer, combine garlic salt, cumin, and 1 teaspoon of the chili powder; rub into surfaces of pork. Set pork aside.

In a small pan, melt jelly; then stir in catsup, vinegar, and remaining ½ teaspoon chili powder. Bring to a boil; boil, uncovered, for 2 minutes. Set aside.

Barbecue pork by indirect heat (see page 10), placing it on a lightly greased grill directly above drip pan. Cover barbecue and adjust dampers as necessary to maintain an even heat. Cook until a meat thermometer inserted in thickest part of pork registers 150° to 155°F (1¼ to 1½ hours); frequently brush jelly baste over roast during last 30 minutes of cooking, using it all.

Let meat stand while you prepare sauce. To prepare sauce, pour pan drippings into a 2-cup glass measure; skim and discard fat, then add enough water to make 1 cup total. Pour into a small pan. Blend cornstarch and 1 tablespoon water; pour into pan. Bring to a boil over high heat, stirring; continue to boil, stirring, until thickened.

To serve, cut meat across the grain into thin slanting slices. Pass sauce at the table to spoon over individual portions. Makes about 8 servings.

Per serving: 578 calories, 44 g protein, 19 g carbohydrates, 35 g total fat, 154 mg cholesterol, 411 mg sodium

APPLE-GLAZED PORK LOIN

Preparation time: About 15 minutes

Grilling time: 1½–2 hours

To serve this apple-flavored bone-in roast, just cut it into individual chops.

>   4-pound bone-in pork loin roast
> 1 cup apple juice
> 3 tablespoons soy sauce
> 1 clove garlic, minced or pressed
> ¼ teaspoon ground ginger
> 1½ teaspoons *each* cornstarch and water

Barbecue pork by indirect heat (see page 10), placing pork on a lightly greased grill directly above drip pan. Cover barbecue and adjust dampers as necessary to maintain an even heat. Cook for 1 hour.

Meanwhile, in a bowl, stir together apple juice, soy, garlic, and ginger. After meat has cooked for 1 hour, baste with apple juice mixture. Continue to cook, basting frequently, until a meat thermometer inserted in thickest part (not touching bone) registers 150° to 155°F (30 to 60 more minutes).

Let meat stand while you prepare sauce. To make sauce, skim and discard fat from pan drippings. In a small pan, combine drippings and remaining apple juice mixture. Stir together cornstarch and water; pour into pan. Bring to a boil over high heat; boil, stirring, until thickened.

To serve, cut roast into individual chops. Offer sauce to spoon over meat. Makes 6 servings.

Per serving: 577 calories, 38 g protein, 6 g carbohydrates, 43 g total fat, 149 mg cholesterol, 621 mg sodium

⬤ PLUM GOOD SPARERIBS

Preparation time: 20–30 minutes

Grilling time: 1–1¼ hours

Fruit and pork are natural partners, as you'll see from many of the recipes in this chapter. Here, a tangy plum purée is brushed over spareribs to make a finger-licking good entrée.

  1 **can (1 lb.) whole purple plums**
  ⅔ **cup orange juice**
  ¼ **cup** *each* **lemon juice, soy sauce, tomato-based chili sauce, and orange marmalade**
  2 **tablespoons firmly packed brown sugar**
  1 **tablespoon Dijon mustard**
  ½ **teaspoon** *each* **grated orange peel, grated lemon peel, dry rosemary, ground cloves, and ground ginger**
  1 **tablespoon instant minced onion**
  6 **to 7 pounds pork spareribs, trimmed of excess fat and cut into 2- to 3-rib portions**

Drain plums, reserving syrup. Pit plums, then place plums and syrup in a food processor or blender and whirl until puréed. Add orange juice, lemon juice, soy, chili sauce, marmalade, sugar, mustard, orange peel, lemon peel, rosemary, cloves, ginger, and onion. Whirl until puréed. Brush ribs with some of the plum sauce.

Barbecue ribs by indirect heat (see page 10). Place ribs, meat side up, on a lightly greased grill directly above drip pan. Cover barbecue and adjust dampers as necessary to maintain an even heat. Cook ribs, brushing occasionally with plum sauce, until meat near bone is no longer pink; cut to test (1 to 1¼ hours).

To serve, pour remaining plum sauce into a pan; bring to a boil. Pass sauce at the table to spoon over ribs. Makes 6 to 8 servings.

Per serving: 631 calories, 40 g protein, 26 g carbohydrates, 40 g total fat, 161 mg cholesterol, 824 mg sodium

⬤ GINGERED COUNTRY RIBS

Preparation time: About 30 minutes

Grilling time: About 1½ hours

Baste these ribs with a spicy tomato sauce as they cook slowly on an open grill, then sprinkle with chopped candied ginger just before serving.

  1 **can (8 oz.) tomato sauce**
  1 **can (about 1 lb.) tomato purée**
  ¼ **cup** *each* **wine vinegar and firmly packed brown sugar**
  1 **tablespoon Worcestershire**
  1 **or 2 lemon slices**
  1 **medium-size onion, finely chopped**
  1 **clove garlic, minced or pressed**
  ½ **teaspoon** *each* **chili powder, celery salt, and dry mustard**
  ⅛ **teaspoon pepper**
  6 **pounds lean country-style spareribs, trimmed of excess fat**
  2 **tablespoons very finely chopped candied or crystallized ginger**

In a 2-quart pan, combine tomato sauce, tomato purée, vinegar, sugar, Worcestershire, lemon slices, onion, garlic, chili powder, celery salt, mustard, and pepper. Bring to a boil over high heat; then reduce heat, cover, and simmer for 20 minutes, stirring occasionally.

Arrange ribs on a lightly greased grill 4 to 6 inches above a solid bed of low coals. Cook, turning and basting often with sauce, until meat near bone is no longer pink; cut to test (about 1½ hours). Every 30 minutes, add 5 or 6 briquets to fire, spacing them evenly to maintain a constant temperature.

To serve, sprinkle ribs evenly with ginger. Makes about 8 servings.

Per serving: 548 calories, 26 g protein, 20 g carbohydrates, 40 g total fat, 117 mg cholesterol, 595 mg sodium

Juicy Roasted Salsa Spareribs (facing page) are paired with corn on the cob for a casual dinner. The sauce is based on grilled tomatoes and mild green chiles; you might grill a few extra to serve with the ribs.

(Pictured on facing page)

ROASTED SALSA SPARERIBS

Preparation time: About 30 minutes

Grilling time: 1¼–1½ hours

The barbecue does double duty when you prepare these succulent pork ribs from Mexico's Yucatán peninsula. Start by charring tomatoes and green chiles for a piquant salsa. Then grill the ribs, using the salsa as a basting sauce. Let diners embellish individual servings of ribs with extra salsa, sour cream, and a squeeze of lime.

- 6 **large firm-ripe tomatoes**
- 8 **large fresh mild green chiles such as Anaheim (California), pasilla, or poblano**
- ¼ **cup** *each* **red wine vinegar and chopped fresh cilantro (coriander)**
- 3 **cloves garlic, minced or pressed**
  Salt
- 2 **slabs (3 to 4 lbs.** *each***) pork spareribs, trimmed of excess fat**
  About 1 cup sour cream
- 3 **or 4 limes, cut into wedges**

To prepare fire, mound and ignite 50 charcoal briquets (see page 10). When coals are heavily spotted with gray ash, spread to make an even layer.

Set tomatoes and chiles on a lightly greased grill 4 to 6 inches above prepared coals. Cook, turning as needed, until chiles are charred on all sides (7 to 10 minutes) and tomatoes are hot and streaked with brown (about 15 minutes).

Using long tongs, mound hot charcoal for indirect cooking (see page 10), adding 5 fresh briquets to each side.

To make the salsa, chop tomatoes and chiles; discard stems and seeds. Place chopped tomatoes and chiles and their juices in a bowl. Stir in vinegar, cilantro, and garlic; season to taste with salt. Spread some of the salsa evenly over both sides of ribs.

Place ribs, meat side up, on grill directly above drip pan (overlap ribs to fit on grill if necessary). Cover barbecue and adjust dampers as necessary to maintain an even heat. Cook, basting occasionally with some of the remaining salsa, until meat near bone is no longer pink; cut to test (1 to 1¼ hours).

To serve, cut ribs into 2- to 3-rib portions. Offer remaining salsa, sour cream, and lime wedges alongside ribs. To eat, top ribs with salsa, sour cream, and a squeeze of lime. Makes 6 to 8 servings.

Per serving: 639 calories, 42 g protein, 14 g carbohydrates, 47 g total fat, 173 mg cholesterol, 154 mg sodium

EASY COUNTRY-STYLE SPARERIBS

Preparation time: About 35 minutes

Grilling time: 1–1¼ hours

The familiar red barbecue sauce based on catsup, sherry, and Worcestershire is always a favorite with meaty pork ribs.

- 1 **cup** *each* **catsup, water, and dry sherry**
- ¼ **cup Worcestershire**
- 1 **medium-size onion, sliced**
- 1 **large lemon, thinly sliced**
- 1 **clove garlic, minced or pressed**
- 2 **tablespoons butter or margarine**
  About 4 pounds lean country-style spareribs, trimmed of excess fat

In a 2- to 3-quart pan, combine catsup, water, sherry, Worcestershire, onion, lemon, garlic, and butter. Bring to a boil over high heat; then reduce heat and simmer, uncovered, stirring occasionally, for 30 minutes. Brush ribs with sauce.

Barbecue ribs by indirect heat (see page 10). Place ribs, fat side up, on a lightly greased grill directly above drip pan. Cover barbecue; adjust dampers as necessary to maintain an even heat. Cook ribs, brushing occasionally with sauce, until meat near bone is no longer pink; cut to test (1 to 1¼ hours).

To serve, pour remaining sauce into a pan; bring to a boil. Pass hot sauce at the table to spoon over ribs. Makes about 6 servings.

Per serving: 537 calories, 24 g protein, 22 g carbohydrates, 40 g total fat, 114 mg cholesterol, 699 mg sodium

INDONESIAN SPARERIBS

Preparation time: 10–15 minutes

Marinating time: 2 hours or until next day

Grilling time: 1–1¼ hours

The peanut is an essential element in Indonesian cuisine, often combined with soy, garlic, and ginger in meat marinades and bastes. This sauce for pork spareribs is made with peanut butter—smooth or crunchy, as you prefer—and includes orange liqueur and sherry in addition to the traditional seasonings.

> 4 **cloves garlic, quartered**
> 1 **piece fresh ginger (about a 1-inch cube), quartered**
> ¼ **cup** *each* **peanut butter, dry sherry, and orange-flavored liqueur**
> 1 **medium-size onion, quartered**
> ½ **cup soy sauce**
> 3 **tablespoons prepared taco sauce or salsa**
> 3 **tablespoons lemon juice**
> 1 **slab (3 to 4 lbs.) pork spareribs, trimmed of excess fat**

In a blender, combine garlic, ginger, peanut butter, sherry, liqueur, onion, soy, taco sauce, and lemon juice. Whirl until smoothly puréed.

Place ribs in a 10- by 15-inch pan; pour soy marinade over ribs. Cover and refrigerate for at least 2 hours or until next day, turning ribs several times.

Barbecue ribs by indirect heat (see page 10). Lift ribs from marinade and drain briefly (reserve marinade); then place ribs, meat side up, on a lightly greased grill directly above drip pan. Cover barbecue and adjust dampers as necessary to maintain an even heat. Cook ribs, brushing occasionally with marinade, until meat near bone is no longer pink; cut to test (1 to 1¼ hours).

To serve, pour remaining marinade into a small pan; bring to a boil over high heat, stirring to prevent scorching. Pass at the table to spoon over individual portions. Makes about 4 servings.

Per serving: 685 calories, 46 g protein, 16 g carbohydrates, 49 g total fat, 161 mg cholesterol, 2344 mg sodium

BEST-EVER BABY BACK RIBS

Preparation time: About 50 minutes

Grilling time: 1–1¼ hours

In case you're wondering, baby back ribs don't come from piglets—"baby" refers to the size of the bones, not the age of the animal. These little bones actually parallel the pork loin. They're increasingly available today, since so much pork loin is now marketed as boneless roasts.

> 1½ **tablespoons butter or margarine**
> 1 **medium-size onion, chopped**
> ½ **cup** *each* **water, catsup, tomato-based chili sauce, dark molasses, and firmly packed brown sugar**
> ¼ **cup cider vinegar**
> 2 **tablespoons** *each* **lemon juice and Worcestershire**
> 2 **teaspoons** *each* **dry mustard and liquid smoke**
> ½ **teaspoon** *each* **pepper and paprika**
> 3 **to 4 pounds pork baby back ribs, trimmed of excess fat**

Melt butter in a wide frying pan over medium heat. Add onion and cook, stirring often, until soft (about 10 minutes). Stir in water, catsup, chili sauce, molasses, sugar, vinegar, lemon juice, Worcestershire, mustard, liquid smoke, pepper, and paprika. Bring to a boil over high heat; then reduce heat and simmer, uncovered, until reduced to about 2¼ cups (about 30 minutes). Remove from heat.

Barbecue ribs by indirect heat (see page 10). Place ribs, meat side up, on a lightly greased grill directly above drip pan. Brush with sauce. Cover barbecue and adjust dampers as necessary to maintain an even heat. Cook ribs, brushing with sauce and turning occasionally, until meat near bone is no longer pink; cut to test (1 to 1¼ hours).

To serve, heat remaining sauce. Pass at the table to spoon over individual portions. (Any unused sauce may be refrigerated for up to 1 week. Serve with hamburgers or brush on chicken as it grills.) Makes 3 or 4 servings.

Per serving: 851 calories, 41 g protein, 71 g carbohydrates, 45 g total fat, 172 mg cholesterol, 1112 mg sodium

CHILES

ON THE BARBECUE

Cooked on the barbecue, these lean and simple *chiles rellenos* (stuffed chiles) are grilled *au naturel*—in their skins. Prepared this way, they're lighter than the typical batter-coated fried version of the dish, with a more pronounced chile flavor.

Both cone-shaped poblano and slender, tapering Anaheim (California) chiles work well in this recipe, though the broader poblanos are easier to fill and often hold more.

GRILLED CHILES RELLENOS WITH SHRIMP

Pictured on page 12

Tomato Salsa (recipe follows)
8 to 12 large fresh mild green chiles such as Anaheim (California), *each* 6 to 6½ inches long; or 8 to 12 fresh poblano chiles, *each* 3 to 5 inches long
1 pound small cooked shrimp
¾ cup thinly sliced green onions (including tops)
Sour cream

Prepare Tomato Salsa; cover and refrigerate.

Using a barbecue with a lid, place chiles on a lightly greased grill 4 to 6 inches above a solid bed of hot coals. Cook, uncovered, without turning, until chiles are blistered and slightly charred on one side (2 to 3 minutes). Remove from grill; peel off any blistered skin that comes off easily. Slit each chile lengthwise down cooked side. Scrape out seeds but leave chiles whole.

Mix shrimp and onions; fill chiles equally. Place chiles, slit side up, on grill 4 to 6 inches above a solid bed of medium coals. Cover barbecue. Cook until shrimp mixture is hot to touch (5 to 7 minutes). Transfer chiles to plates; pass Tomato Salsa and sour cream at the

table. Makes 4 main-dish servings or 8 to 12 side-dish servings.

Tomato Salsa. In a bowl, stir together 1 large **tomato** (coarsely chopped); ¼ cup chopped **onion**; 1 to 1½ tablespoons finely chopped seeded **fresh or canned jalapeño chiles** or drained, seeded canned chipotle chiles in sauce; 1 tablespoon *each* chopped **fresh cilantro (coriander)** and **white wine vinegar;** and 1 clove **garlic** (minced or pressed). Cover and refrigerate for at least 2 hours or until next day.

Per side-dish serving: 51 calories, 9 g protein, 3 g carbohydrates, .5 g total fat, 74 mg cholesterol, 87 mg sodium

GRILLED CHILES RELLENOS WITH ONIONS & CHEESE

Prepare **Tomato Salsa** and **chiles** as for **Grilled Chiles Rellenos with Shrimp.** For the filling, melt 3 tablespoons **butter** or margarine in a wide frying pan over medium heat. Add 3 large **onions,** thinly sliced;

cook, stirring often, until onions are very limp and light gold (about 15 minutes). Stir in ½ cup **golden raisins** and 3 to 4 tablespoons minced drained, seeded **canned chipotle chiles in sauce** (or use minced seeded fresh or canned jalapeños). Let cool. Then stir in 1½ cups (6 oz.) shredded **jack cheese.** (At this point, you may cover and refrigerate filling until next day.)

Evenly fill chiles with onion mixture. Cook as for **Grilled Chiles Rellenos with Shrimp,** increasing grilling time to 7 to 10 minutes. Serve with salsa. Makes 8 to 12 side-dish servings.

Per serving: 129 calories, 5 g protein, 12 g carbohydrates, 8 g total fat, 20 mg cholesterol, 165 mg sodium

GRILLED CHILES RELLENOS WITH CORN

Prepare **Tomato Salsa** and **chiles** as for **Grilled Chiles Rellenos with Shrimp.** For the filling, melt 2 tablespoons **butter** or margarine in a wide frying pan over medium heat. Add 1 large **onion** (chopped) and 1 medium-size **red bell pepper** (seeded and chopped). Cook, stirring often, until onion is soft (10 minutes).

Add 2 cups **fresh or frozen corn kernels** (thawed if frozen); cook, stirring, until corn is hot. Let cool, then stir in 1 cup (4 oz.) shredded **sharp Cheddar cheese.** Evenly spoon corn mixture into chiles.

Cook as for **Grilled Chiles Rellenos with Shrimp,** increasing grilling time to 8 to 10 minutes. Serve with salsa. Makes 8 to 12 side-dish servings.

Per serving: 95 calories, 4 g protein, 9 g carbohydrates, 5 g total fat, 15 mg cholesterol, 85 mg sodium

HOT-SWEET RIBS

Preparation time: 30–40 minutes

Grilling time: 1–1¼ hours

These ribs are double glazed—first rubbed with a mixture of cayenne pepper and brown sugar, then finished off with an assertive sauce.

- ¼ **cup firmly packed brown sugar**
- 1 **teaspoon ground red pepper (cayenne)**
- 1 **slab (3½ to 4 lbs.) pork spareribs, trimmed of excess fat**
  Hot-Sweet Sauce (recipe follows)

Mix sugar and red pepper; rub onto both sides of ribs.

Barbecue ribs by indirect heat (see page 10). Place ribs, meat side up, on a lightly greased grill directly above drip pan. Cover barbecue, adjust dampers as necessary to maintain an even heat, and cook ribs for 30 minutes. Meanwhile, prepare Hot-Sweet Sauce.

Brush ribs with about ⅓ of the sauce; continue to cook for 15 more minutes. Turn ribs over, baste with half the remaining sauce, and cook for 15 more minutes. Turn ribs over again, baste with remaining sauce, and continue to cook until meat near bone is no longer pink; cut to test (5 to 15 more minutes).

To serve, cut between bones. Makes 3 or 4 servings.

Hot-Sweet Sauce. Heat ¼ cup **olive oil** or salad oil in a 2- to 3-quart pan over medium heat. Add 4 cloves **garlic** (minced or pressed); stir until golden (about 4 minutes). Stir in ½ cup *each* firmly packed **brown sugar, red wine vinegar,** and **regular-strength chicken broth;** ¼ cup **tomato paste;** 3 tablespoons **soy sauce;** and 2 teaspoons **dry mustard.** Bring to a boil over medium-high heat; cook, stirring often, until reduced to 1 cup (about 15 minutes).

Per serving: 862 calories, 47 g protein, 38 g carbohydrates, 58 g total fat, 187 mg cholesterol, 925 mg sodium

BARBECUED LEG OF PORK

(Pictured on facing page)

Preparation time: About 10 minutes

Marinating time: 8 hours or until next day

Grilling time: 2½–3 hours

A coating of puréed orange and lime keeps this roast moist. Accompany the handsome entrée with grilled sweet potatoes or yams and grilled fruit such as peaches, pineapple, or papaya. (Directions for grilling fruits and vegetables are on pages 154 and 155.)

- **7- to 8-pound shank-end leg of pork**
- ½ **large orange (unpeeled), cut into pieces**
- ½ **large lime (unpeeled), cut into pieces**
- 1 **clove garlic, quartered**
- 3 **tablespoons salad oil**
- 2 **tablespoons cider vinegar**
- ¼ **teaspoon** *each* **ground ginger and ground nutmeg**

Using a sharp knife, cut leathery skin from pork. Then score through fat just to meat, making diagonal cuts ½ to ¾ inch apart.

In a food processor or blender, combine orange, lime, garlic, oil, vinegar, ginger, and nutmeg. Whirl until puréed. Smear orange mixture over all sides of pork; place pork in a deep container, cover, and refrigerate for at least 8 hours or until next day.

Barbecue pork by indirect heat (see page 10). Lift pork from bowl and place on a lightly greased grill directly above drip pan. Cover barbecue and adjust dampers as necessary to maintain an even heat. Cook until a meat thermometer inserted in thickest part (not touching bone) registers 150° to 155°F (2½ to 3 hours). To serve, let roast stand for 10 minutes; then cut into thin slanting slices. Makes about 10 servings.

Per serving: 554 calories, 41 g protein, 2 g carbohydrates, 41 g total fat, 155 mg cholesterol, 98 mg sodium

Hours of slow cooking on the grill give Barbecued Leg of Pork (facing page) its rich, smoky flavor. Alongside the meat, serve your choice of grilled fruits and vegetables—and fresh Lady apples in season, if you like.

VIETNAMESE SKEWERED PORK & ONION

Preparation time: About 40 minutes

Marinating time: 2 hours

Grilling time: 7–10 minutes

For the most authentic flavor, use fish sauce and lemon grass in these skewers. Both ingredients are available in Asian markets; if you can't find them, substitute soy sauce and grated lemon peel.

>   **Lemon Grass Marinade (recipe follows)**
>   **Seasoning Sauce (recipe follows)**
> 2½ **to 3 pounds boneless pork loin or leg**
> 1 **large onion**

Prepare marinade and sauce. Cut pork across the grain into ¼-inch-thick slices; cut each slice into 2-inch squares. Mix meat with marinade; cover and refrigerate for 2 hours.

Cut onion into 1-inch chunks; separate each chunk into layers. Place an onion piece in center of each marinated meat square. Wrap meat around onion to enclose, then insert a metal skewer through meat and onion. Repeat with remaining onion and meat, threading 4 to 6 bundles on each skewer. Also roll up any meat pieces too small to wrap around onion; thread on skewers.

Place skewers on a lightly greased grill 4 to 6 inches above a solid bed of hot coals. Cook, turning frequently, until meat is no longer pink in center; cut to test (7 to 10 minutes). Serve with Seasoning Sauce. Makes 6 to 8 servings.

Lemon Grass Marinade. Thinly slice enough **fresh lemon grass** to make 3 tablespoons. (Or use 3 tablespoons sliced dry lemon grass, soaked in hot water for 30 minutes; or use 1 teaspoon grated lemon peel.) In a food processor, combine lemon grass or lemon peel; 1 medium-size **onion**, cut into chunks; 3 or 4 cloves **garlic**; 3 tablespoons **sugar**; 2 tablespoons **salted roasted peanuts**; 1 tablespoon **fish sauce** or soy sauce; 1½ teaspoons **pepper**; and 1 teaspoon **Chinese five-spice**. Whirl until smooth.

Per serving: 367 calories, 24 g protein, 4 g carbohydrates, 28 g total fat, 92 mg cholesterol, 164 mg sodium

Seasoning Sauce. In a bowl, mix 2 tablespoons **fish sauce** or soy sauce, 1 tablespoon **lime juice**, 2 cloves **garlic** (minced or pressed), ¼ cup **water**, and 2 tablespoons *each* **sugar** and finely shredded **carrot**. Cover and refrigerate. Makes ⅔ cup.

Per tablespoon: 15 calories, .4 g protein, 4 g carbohydrates, 0 g total fat, 0 mg cholesterol, 144 mg sodium

PORK WITH PEPPERS & PINEAPPLE

Preparation time: 45 minutes (including time to cut meat)

Marinating time: 8 hours or until next day

Grilling time: 15–20 minutes

Large chunks of hoisin-seasoned pork, squares of red bell pepper, and juicy fresh pineapple add up to extra-colorful skewers.

> 1 **can (8 oz.) crushed pineapple packed in its own juice**
> 2 **cloves garlic, cut in half**
> 1 **teaspoon ground ginger**
> 2 **tablespoons red wine vinegar**
> 3 **tablespoons soy sauce**
> ½ **cup *each* hoisin sauce and catsup**
> 3 **to 3½ pounds boneless pork leg or shoulder, cut into 1½-inch cubes**
> 2 **large red or green bell peppers, seeded and cut into 1½-inch squares**
> 1 **large pineapple (4 to 5 lbs.), peeled, cored, and cut into 1½-inch cubes**

In a blender or food processor, combine canned pineapple and its juice, garlic, ginger, vinegar, soy, hoisin, and catsup. Whirl until well blended. Pour pineapple mixture into a large bowl; add pork and stir to coat. Cover and refrigerate for at least 8 hours or until next day, stirring several times.

Lift pork from marinade; drain briefly (reserve marinade). On 8 sturdy metal skewers, thread pork alternately with bell peppers and pineapple cubes.

Place skewers on a lightly greased grill 4 to 6 inches above a solid bed of hot coals. Cook, basting often with reserved marinade and turning frequently, until meat is no longer pink in center; cut to test (15 to 20 minutes). Makes 8 servings.

Per serving: 456 calories, 30 g protein, 30 g carbohydrates, 24 g total fat, 104 mg cholesterol, 1142 mg sodium

⊕ TERIYAKI PORK & SLAW SANDWICHES

Preparation time: About 45 minutes (including time to cut meat)

Marinating time: 4 hours or until next day

Grilling time: About 10 minutes

To assemble these sweet-and-sour sandwiches, you wrap flour tortillas around teriyaki-flavored pork cubes and spoonfuls of crunchy pineapple slaw.

- 1 **can (8 oz.) crushed pineapple packed in its own juice**
- ½ **cup soy sauce**
- 1 **clove garlic, minced or pressed**
- 1 **tablespoon** *each* **honey and salad oil**
- 2 **teaspoons minced fresh ginger**
- 2½ **to 3 pounds boneless pork shoulder, cut into 1-inch cubes**
  Pineapple Slaw (recipe follows)
- 8 **to 10 flour tortillas,** *each* **about 8 inches in diameter**
  Red leaf or butter lettuce leaves

Drain pineapple, reserving juice. Set drained pineapple aside to use in slaw. In a large bowl, stir together pineapple juice, soy, garlic, honey, oil, and ginger. Add pork and stir to coat evenly. Cover and refrigerate for at least 4 hours or until next day.

If using bamboo skewers, soak 8 skewers in hot water to cover for 30 minutes.

Meanwhile, prepare Pineapple Slaw. Also sprinkle a few drops of water over each tortilla; then stack tortillas and wrap in heavy-duty foil. Set aside.

Lift meat from marinade and drain briefly (reserve marinade). Thread 5 or 6 meat cubes on each of 8 bamboo or metal skewers. Place skewers on a lightly greased grill 4 to 6 inches above a solid bed of hot coals. Cook, basting occasionally with marinade and turning often, until meat is well browned on the outside but no longer pink in center; cut to test (7 to 9 minutes). Also heat foil-wrapped tortillas at side of grill (not directly over coals) until warm (about 10 minutes); turn several times.

To serve, offer lettuce leaves and Pineapple Slaw with grilled meat and tortillas. To eat, place a lettuce leaf in center of a tortilla; top with meat and a spoonful of slaw. Roll up and eat out of hand. Makes 8 servings.

Per serving: 473 calories, 26 g protein, 29 g carbohydrates, 27 g total fat, 96 mg cholesterol, 1305 mg sodium

Pineapple Slaw. In a large bowl, combine **reserved drained pineapple,** 8 cups shredded **cabbage,** ½ cup thinly sliced **green onions** (including tops), and 2 large **carrots,** shredded.

In a small bowl, combine 1 cup **mayonnaise,** 1 tablespoon **lemon juice,** 1½ teaspoons **Dijon mustard,** and ½ teaspoon *each* **salt** and **ground coriander.** Just before serving, pour dressing over cabbage mixture; toss until well blended. Makes 7 to 8 cups.

Per ½ cup: 119 calories, .8 g protein, 5 g carbohydrates, 11 g total fat, 8 mg cholesterol, 172 mg sodium

Spirited Italian sausages pair up with bell pepper strips to make colorful Red Bell Pepper & Sausage Loaf (facing page). You can assemble the skewer ahead, then tote it to a park or tailgate picnic for grilling.

⚫ PORK & MELON SKEWERS

Preparation time: 40–50 minutes (including time to cut meat)

Marinating time: 4 hours or until next day

Grilling time: 12–15 minutes

Grilled pork cubes and melon wedges, flavored in a rosemary-citrus marinade, join up in this refreshing entrée.

Rosemary-Citrus Marinade (recipe follows)
½ **large onion**
1 **large cantaloupe, honeydew, casaba, or Crenshaw melon**
1½ **pounds boneless pork leg or shoulder, cut into 1¼-inch cubes**

Prepare Rosemary-Citrus Marinade.

Cut onion into 1-inch chunks; separate each chunk into layers. Cut unpeeled melon into 12 wedges; remove seeds. Place onion, melon, and pork in a large heavy-duty plastic bag, pour in marinade, and seal bag securely. Rotate bag to distribute marinade; then place in a shallow baking pan. Refrigerate for at least 4 hours or until next day, turning bag over several times.

Lift onion, melon, and meat from marinade; drain briefly (reserve marinade). Place 3 melon wedges on a flat surface with flesh of one piece against rind of the next. Push 2 parallel metal skewers through center of melon wedges. Set aside. Repeat with remaining melon wedges, using 3 more pairs of skewers.

On 4 skewers, thread meat alternately with onion. Place meat skewers on a lightly greased grill 4 to 6 inches above a solid bed of hot coals. Cook for 5 minutes, basting with marinade and turning often. Set melon skewers on grill alongside meat skewers. Continue to cook meat until no longer pink in center; cut to test (7 to 10 more minutes). Cook melon until hot and streaked with brown (about 10 minutes). Turn and baste meat and fruit often. Makes 4 servings.

Rosemary-Citrus Marinade. In a bowl, stir together ½ cup *each* **orange, lemon, and lime juice;** ⅓ cup **honey;** ¼ cup chopped **onion;** ¼ cup **olive oil** or salad oil; 2 tablespoons **Dijon mustard;** 2 teaspoons **fresh rosemary leaves** or 1 teaspoon dry rosemary; ½ teaspoon *each* **ground coriander** and **ground nutmeg;** and ¼ teaspoon **pepper.**

Per serving: 639 calories, 30 g protein, 48 g carbohydrates, 38 g total fat, 103 mg cholesterol, 593 mg sodium

(Pictured on facing page)

⚫ RED BELL PEPPER & SAUSAGE LOAF

Preparation time: About 15 minutes

Grilling time: 5–8 minutes

Here's a party-size sandwich that's easy to put together. Just skewer and grill simmered Italian sausages and bright red bell pepper strips, then enclose in a long loaf of French bread.

6 **mild Italian sausages (1¼ to 1½ lbs.** *total***)**
¼ **cup butter or margarine**
1 **clove garlic, minced or pressed**
1 **long loaf (1 lb.) French bread, cut in half lengthwise**
2 **large red bell peppers, seeded and cut lengthwise into 1½-inch-wide strips**
6 **ounces sliced mozzarella or provolone cheese Prepared mustard**

Prick sausages in several places; then place in a wide frying pan and add enough water to cover. Bring to a boil over high heat; reduce heat to low, cover, and simmer for 5 minutes. Drain sausages and set aside.

Melt butter in a small pan over medium heat; stir in garlic. Drizzle garlic butter evenly over cut side of each bread half; set aside.

On a sturdy metal skewer at least 12 inches long, thread sausages alternately with bell pepper strips, running skewer through center of each sausage and pepper strip.

Place skewer on a lightly greased grill 4 to 6 inches above a solid bed of hot coals. Cook, turning occasionally, until sausages are well browned on outside and hot throughout; cut to test (5 to 8 minutes). Then set bread halves, cut side down, on grill. Cook, watching carefully, just until bread is streaked with brown (1 to 2 minutes).

Overlap cheese slices on one bread half. Top with sausage-pepper skewer. Set top of bread in place; pull out skewer. Cut loaf into 6 portions; let guests add mustard to taste. Makes 6 servings.

Per serving: 599 calories, 27 g protein, 46 g carbohydrates, 34 g total fat, 99 mg cholesterol, 1261 mg sodium

⬤ SAUSAGE BURGERS ITALIANO

Preparation time: 20–30 minutes

Grilling time: 10–12 minutes

The flavor of these hearty Italian sausage sandwiches may remind you of pizza. Embellish individual servings with shredded cheese, marinated artichokes, onions, and bell pepper strips.

> 1 **pound mild Italian sausages**
> ¼ **cup fine dry bread crumbs**
> 1 **small onion, finely chopped**
> 1 **egg, beaten**
> ½ **teaspoon oregano leaves**
> 12 **slices French bread, buttered**
> **Condiments (suggestions follow)**

Remove casings from sausages; crumble meat into a large bowl. Add bread crumbs, onion, egg, and oregano. Mix well. Shape sausage mixture into 6 oblong patties, each about the size of a slice of French bread.

Place patties on a lightly greased grill 4 to 6 inches above a solid bed of medium coals. Cook, turning once, until meat is no longer pink in center; cut to test (10 to 12 minutes). Watch carefully for flare-ups during grilling. When meat is nearly done, grill bread just until streaked with brown (1 to 2 minutes per side).

To serve, place each patty between 2 slices of toasted bread. Pass condiments for guests to add to sandwiches. Makes 6 servings.

Condiments. Set out in separate bowls: shredded **mozzarella cheese; marinated artichoke hearts,** thinly sliced lengthwise; thinly sliced **mild onion;** and thin **red bell pepper** strips.

Per serving: 482 calories, 19 g protein, 43 g carbohydrates, 25 g total fat, 112 mg cholesterol, 1036 mg sodium

⬤ COMBINATION GRILL

Preparation time: 10–15 minutes

Grilling time: About 15 minutes

Threaded on skewers, fresh figs and cheese are warmed on the grill along with Italian sausages and toast for an enticing entrée.

> **Rosemary Butter (recipe follows)**
> 4 **or 8 hot or mild Italian sausages (about ¼ lb. *each*)**
> 12 **small or 6 large fresh figs, stems trimmed (cut large figs in half)**
> 6 **ounces Jarlsberg cheese, cut into 1-inch chunks**
> 8 **thin slices French bread**

Prepare Rosemary Butter; set aside.

Place sausages on a lightly greased grill 4 to 6 inches above a solid bed of medium coals. Cook, turning often, until no longer pink in center; cut to test (about 15 minutes).

Meanwhile, alternate whole or cut figs and cheese chunks on 4 sturdy metal skewers. Place on grill and cook, turning once and basting with Rosemary Butter, until figs are warm and cheese is soft (2 to 4 minutes).

At the same time, brush bread with Rosemary Butter. Place on grill and lightly toast (1 to 2 minutes per side).

Transfer hot skewers of figs and cheese to a serving dish and accompany with toast and sausages. Makes 4 servings.

Rosemary Butter. Melt ¼ cup **butter** or margarine in a small pan; stir in 1 tablespoon chopped **fresh rosemary leaves** or 1 teaspoon dry rosemary.

Per serving: 812 calories, 34 g protein, 65 g carbohydrates, 44 g total fat, 111 mg cholesterol, 1477 mg sodium

SAVORY PORK BALLS WITH APPLES

Preparation time: About 25 minutes

Grilling time: 15–20 minutes

Skewered sweet apple quarters, savory ground pork balls, and crisp bacon offer a winning combination for the barbecue.

- 1½ **pounds lean ground pork**
- 1 **egg**
- ⅓ **cup** *each* **fine dry bread crumbs and finely chopped onion**
- 2 **tablespoons apple juice**
- ½ **teaspoon** *each* **salt and ground ginger**
- ¼ **teaspoon** *each* **ground sage and pepper**
- 8 **slices bacon**
- 2 **large Golden Delicious apples, cored and quartered**

Combine pork, egg, bread crumbs, onion, apple juice, salt, ginger, sage, and pepper. Divide into 16 equal portions; shape each into a ball.

Have ready 4 sturdy metal skewers. To assemble each skewer, pierce one end of a bacon slice with a skewer. Push on a pork ball, pierce bacon again, and add an apple quarter. Pierce bacon again, push on another pork ball, and then pierce bacon end; the bacon forms S-curves around the meat and apple. Repeat until each skewer has 2 bacon slices, 4 pork balls, and 2 apple quarters, all spaced loosely so bacon will brown evenly.

Place skewers on a lightly greased grill 4 to 6 inches above a solid bed of low coals. Cook, turning gently as needed to brown evenly, until bacon is crisp and pork is no longer pink in center; cut to test (15 to 20 minutes). Makes 4 servings.

Per serving: 484 calories, 41 g protein, 22 g carbohydrates, 25 g total fat, 199 mg cholesterol, 643 mg sodium

MU SHU BURGERS

Preparation time: About 25 minutes

Grilling time: 12–14 minutes

Here's a barbecue adaptation of a popular Peking dish—*mu shu* pork. Ground pork patties are tucked into tortillas along with hoisin sauce, green onion, fresh cilantro, and bean sprouts.

- 8 **flour tortillas,** *each* **about 8 inches in diameter**
- 1 **pound lean ground pork**
- 1 **small onion, chopped**
- ¼ **cup fine dry bread crumbs**
- 1 **egg, beaten**
- ½ **cup finely chopped water chestnuts or celery**
- 1 **clove garlic, minced or pressed**
- 2 **tablespoons soy sauce**
- ½ **teaspoon ground ginger**
  Hoisin sauce
- 1 **bunch green onions (including tops), cut into slivers**
- 1½ **to 2 cups bean sprouts**
  Fresh cilantro (coriander) sprigs

Sprinkle a few drops of water over each tortilla; then stack tortillas and wrap in heavy-duty foil.

In a large bowl, combine pork, chopped onion, bread crumbs, egg, water chestnuts, garlic, soy, and ginger. Mix well. Shape mixture into 8 logs, each about 3 inches long.

Place pork logs on a lightly greased grill 4 to 6 inches above a solid bed of hot coals. Cook, turning frequently, until meat is no longer pink in center; cut to test (12 to 14 minutes). Also heat foil-wrapped tortillas at side of grill (not directly over coals) until warm (about 10 minutes); turn several times.

To serve, spread some hoisin on a tortilla. Place a pork log horizontally near lower edge; top with green onions, bean sprouts, and cilantro. Fold tortilla edge up over filling; then fold in sides and roll up to enclose meat and vegetables. Eat out of hand. Makes 8 servings.

Per serving: 258 calories, 17 g protein, 31 g carbohydrates, 7 g total fat, 74 mg cholesterol, 530 mg sodium

Baked on a covered grill and basted with butter sauce, boneless
Barbecued Salmon Fillets (page 110) are simple to serve and
delicious to eat. For a pretty presentation, set each fillet on
a plain white platter; garnish with watercress sprigs
and wedges of lime.

FILLETS ▪ WHOLE FISH ▪ SKEWERS

A hint of smoky flavor from the barbecue enhances just about any fresh fish or shellfish. In this chapter, we've gathered recipes for all types of seafood—from delicate halibut, snapper, and scallops to more assertive salmon and tuna—in recipes for both casual and elegant occasions. You'll also find ideas for cooking fish in all sizes: steaks, fillets, large or small whole fish, skewered chunks. Grilling techniques vary, too; some of these dishes cook on an open grill, while others are best barbecued covered.

If you'd like to add even more recipes to your file, just choose a marinade or sauce from the selection on page 111, match it up with your favorite seafood, and follow the general grilling times and techniques on page 17.

(Pictured on page 108)

BARBECUED SALMON FILLETS

Preparation time: About 15 minutes

Grilling time: 15–18 minutes

A pungent soy-sherry butter sauce flavors these big boneless salmon fillets. Brush some of the sauce over the fish before grilling; offer the rest at the table.

> **6- to 8-pound whole salmon, cleaned, head and tail removed, and cut lengthwise into 2 boneless fillets**
>
> ¾ **cup (¼ lb. plus ¼ cup) butter or margarine**
>
> 2 **cloves garlic, minced or pressed**
>
> 1½ **tablespoons *each* dry mustard and soy sauce**
>
> ⅓ **cup dry sherry**
>
> 3 **tablespoons catsup**

Rinse fish and pat dry; then place each fillet, skin side down, on a piece of heavy-duty foil. Cut foil to follow outlines of fish, leaving a 1- to 2-inch border. Crimp edges of foil.

In a pan, combine butter, garlic, mustard, soy, sherry, and catsup. Stir over medium heat until butter is melted. Brush fish with part of the butter mixture; reserve remaining butter mixture.

Barbecue fish by indirect heat (see page 10), placing foil-supported fish on grill directly above drip pan. Cover barbecue and adjust dampers as necessary to maintain an even heat. Cook until fish flakes when prodded in thickest part (15 to 18 minutes).

Supporting fish with foil, transfer to a warm platter. To serve, cut through flesh of each fillet to skin; slide a wide metal spatula between skin and flesh and lift off each portion. Pass remaining butter mixture to accompany each serving. Makes about 8 servings.

Per serving: 225 calories, 24 g protein, 1.2 g carbohydrates, 14 g total fat, 81 mg cholesterol, 198 mg sodium

GRILLED SALMON ON WILTED CHICORY SALAD

Preparation time: 25–30 minutes

Grilling time: 8–10 minutes

Seasoned with fresh thyme and fragrant olive oil, these grilled salmon steaks are served on a bed of wilted chicory mixed with sautéed mushrooms. We used delicate-tasting chanterelles, sold in specialty markets and some grocery stores; if you can't find them, just substitute regular button mushrooms. (You can start the salmon grilling while the mushrooms are sautéing.)

> ½ **cup extra-virgin olive oil**
>
> ½ **pound chanterelles or regular button mushrooms, cut into ½-inch cubes**
>
> ¼ **cup thinly sliced green onions (including tops)**
>
> 2 **tablespoons red wine vinegar**
>
> 4 **cloves garlic, minced or pressed**
>
> 6 **tablespoons minced fresh thyme leaves or 2 tablespoons dry thyme leaves**
>
> 9 **cups bite-size pieces chicory (curly endive)**
>
> 6 **large salmon steaks or fillets (about 2½ lbs. *total*), cut 1 inch thick**
>
> **Salt and pepper**

Heat 2 tablespoons of the oil in a wide frying pan over high heat. Add mushrooms and cook, stirring frequently, until lightly browned (10 to 12 minutes). Stir in ¼ cup more oil; then mix in onions, vinegar, garlic, and 3 tablespoons of the fresh thyme (or 1 tablespoon of the dry thyme). Remove from heat and add chicory (half at a time, if it doesn't all fit at once); mix and turn until all greens are coated with dressing. Divide salad evenly among 6 dinner plates.

Rinse salmon and pat dry. Coat both sides of each piece of fish with remaining 2 tablespoons oil; then sprinkle both sides with remaining 3 tablespoons fresh thyme (or remaining 1 tablespoon dry thyme).

Place fish on a well-greased grill 4 to 6 inches above a solid bed of hot coals. Cook, turning once with a wide metal spatula, until fish flakes when prodded in thickest part (8 to 10 minutes). Using spatula, set one piece of fish on each serving of salad. Let guests season fish to taste with salt and pepper. Makes 6 servings.

Per serving: 477 calories, 39 g protein, 16 g carbohydrates, 30 g total fat, 92 mg cholesterol, 198 mg sodium

The marinade, baste, or sauce you choose for fish depends upon the particular variety you're grilling. Delicate-tasting types such as scallops and flounder are best when brushed with a simple butter baste or arranged after cooking in a pool of rich, creamy sauce. The same treatment is fine for more intense-flavored fish and shellfish—salmon, tuna, swordfish, shrimp, trout—but these kinds also benefit from soaking in an assertive herb or soy marinade before grilling.

You'll find basic grilling times and techniques for fish on page 17.

MARINADES

Small whole fish as well as fish steaks, fillets, and chunks can all be marinated in a close-fitting dish, pan, or bowl, or enclosed with the marinade in a heavy-duty plastic bag. Usually, you'll need to marinate for just a short time (see suggested times in the recipes below), since seafood soaks up flavor faster than meats and poultry do. Save any marinade the fish doesn't absorb— it's good as a baste.

Basil-Parmesan Marinade. In a food processor or blender, combine ⅔ cup chopped **fresh basil leaves** (or 2 tablespoons dry basil leaves and ¼ cup chopped parsley); ¼ cup **salad oil;** ⅓ cup **white wine vinegar;** 3 tablespoons grated **Parmesan cheese;** 2 cloves **garlic;** and ⅛ teaspoon **pepper.** Whirl until puréed. Soak fish in marinade for 20 to 30 minutes, turning several times. Makes about 1 cup.

Italian-style Marinade. Stir together 2 tablespoons **olive oil;** ½ cup **white wine vinegar;** 1 clove

MARINADES, SAUCES &

BUTTERS FOR FISH

garlic (minced or pressed); ¼ cup chopped **parsley;** and ¼ teaspoon **oregano leaves.** Soak fish in marinade for 15 to 30 minutes, turning several times. Makes about ¾ cup.

SAUCES

Present grilled fish or shellfish in a pool of creamy saffron sauce or Mustard-Dill Beurre Blanc.

Saffron Cream. In a 10- to 12-inch frying pan, combine ½ cup *each* **dry white wine** and **regular-strength chicken broth;** 2 tablespoons minced **shallots** or onion; and a small pinch of **ground saffron** (about ⅟₃₂ teaspoon). Bring to a boil; boil, uncovered, until reduced by half. Add ½ cup **whipping cream,** return to a boil, and boil until reduced to about 1 cup.

To keep sauce warm for up to 2 hours, pour into a 2-cup glass measure set in hot-to-touch water. Stir occasionally and replace water as needed. Makes about 1 cup.

Mustard-Dill Beurre Blanc. In a 10- to 12-inch frying pan, combine 2 tablespoons chopped **shallots,** ⅓ cup **dry white wine,** and 1½ teaspoons **tarragon vinegar.** Bring to a boil; boil, uncovered, until reduced to about ¼ cup. Add 1 cup **whipping cream,** return to a boil, and boil until reduced by half (you should have about ⅔ cup). Turn heat to low. Add ½ cup (¼ lb.) **butter** or margarine in one piece; stir constantly until butter is completely blended

into sauce. Remove from heat and stir in 1½ tablespoons chopped **fresh dill** (or ½ teaspoon dry dill weed) and 1 tablespoon **Dijon mustard.**

To keep warm for up to 2 hours, pour into a 2-cup glass measure set in hot-to-touch water. Stir occasionally and replace water as needed. Makes about 1 cup.

SEASONED BUTTERS & BASTES

The Lemon Butter Baste below is delicious on delicate-flavored fish; stronger-flavored types take well to Sesame-Soy Baste and Nut Butter. (To give the flavors time to blend, prepare butters or baste at least an hour in advance.)

Lemon Butter Baste. Melt ¼ cup **butter** or margarine in a small pan over medium heat. Remove from heat and stir in ¼ cup **lemon juice,** dry sherry, or dry vermouth. If desired, stir in ¼ teaspoon *each* **dry rosemary** and **thyme leaves** or ½ teaspoon dry tarragon. Makes about ½ cup.

Sesame-Soy Baste. Stir together ½ cup **soy sauce;** 3 tablespoons *each* **sesame oil** and minced **green onions** (including tops); 1 tablespoon *each* **vinegar** and minced **fresh ginger;** 2 teaspoons **sugar;** 2 cloves **garlic** (minced or pressed); and a dash of **ground red pepper** (cayenne). Makes about 1 cup.

Nut Butter. Place ¼ cup **butter** or margarine and ½ cup chopped salted **macadamia nuts** or hazelnuts (filberts) in a small, heavy pan. Stir over medium heat until butter is melted. Makes about ¾ cup.

SALMON GRILL DIABLE

Preparation time: 10–15 minutes

Grilling time: 8–10 minutes

While these salmon steaks are still hot from the grill, you top each one with a scoop of mustard butter and let it melt into a piquant sauce.

- ⅓ **cup butter or margarine, at room temperature**
- 2 **tablespoons lemon juice**
- 2 **teaspoons Dijon mustard**
- ⅛ **teaspoon ground red pepper (cayenne)**
- 1 **tablespoon finely chopped parsley**
- 6 **large salmon steaks (about 2½ lbs.** *total*), **cut 1 inch thick**
  About 2 tablespoons olive oil
  Salt and black pepper

In small bowl of an electric mixer, beat butter until creamy; gradually add lemon juice, beating until mixture is fluffy. Beat in mustard, red pepper, and parsley until well blended. If made ahead, cover and refrigerate for up to 2 days; bring to room temperature before using.

Rinse salmon steaks and pat dry. Brush both sides of each steak with oil and lightly sprinkle with salt and black pepper.

Place fish on a well-greased grill 4 to 6 inches above a solid bed of hot coals. Cook, turning once with a wide metal spatula, until fish flakes when prodded in thickest part (8 to 10 minutes).

Using spatula, transfer steaks to a warm platter; top with butter mixture. Makes 6 servings.

Per serving: 369 calories, 33 g protein, .6 g carbohydrates, 25 g total fat, 119 mg cholesterol, 228 mg sodium

SMOKED POACHED SALMON

Preparation time: About 30 minutes

Grilling time: 20–30 minutes

Smoldering hickory chips impart a delicate smoke flavor to salmon fillet as it poaches in white wine seasoned with dill.

- 2 **cups hickory or alder chips**
  3- to 3½-pound salmon fillet (half of a 7- to 8-lb. salmon)
- 6 **tablespoons butter or margarine**
- 1 **cup dry white wine**
- 3 **or 4 fresh dill sprigs or 1 teaspoon dry dill weed**
- 2 **teaspoons mustard seeds**

Soak wood chips in water to cover for 10 to 15 minutes.

Meanwhile, rinse fish and pat dry. Melt 2 tablespoons of the butter in a small pan; generously brush over fish flesh. Using several thicknesses of heavy-duty foil, make a "boat" big enough to accommodate fish. Lay fish in foil boat, skin side up. Pour in wine, then arrange dill sprigs evenly atop fish (or sprinkle fish with dill weed). Sprinkle with mustard seeds.

Prepare barbecue fire for cooking by indirect heat (see page 10). When coals are hot, briefly drain wood chips and sprinkle 1 cup of them over each pile of coals. Place foil boat on grill directly above drip pan. Cover barbecue and adjust dampers as necessary to maintain an even heat. Cook until fish flakes when prodded in thickest part (20 to 30 minutes).

With a wide metal spatula, lift fish from foil boat and place on a warm rimmed platter. Drain wine mixture from foil boat into a small pan; place over high heat and boil until reduced by half. Remove from heat and quickly stir in remaining 4 tablespoons butter until melted. Pour sauce into a bowl; pass at the table to spoon over fish. Makes about 6 servings.

Per serving: 432 calories, 46 g protein, .8 g carbohydrates, 26 g total fat, 156 mg cholesterol, 219 mg sodium

A zesty relish lifts these Yugoslavian Fish Skewers (page 114) out of the ordinary. Chunks of white fish are coated with garlic-seasoned olive oil, quickly grilled, and served with a bright and zippy blend of fresh tomatoes, chiles, and onion.

(Pictured on page 113)
YUGOSLAVIAN FISH SKEWERS

Preparation time: About 30 minutes (including time to cut fish), plus 30 minutes for relish to stand

Grilling time: 10–12 minutes

This recipe from the Adriatic coast features garlicky grilled fish kebabs topped with a chile-seasoned tomato relish.

>   **Serbian Tomato Relish (recipe follows)**
> 3 **tablespoons olive oil**
> 2 **cloves garlic, minced or pressed**
> ¼ **teaspoon pepper**
> 2 **pounds firm-textured fish steaks such as swordfish, halibut, turbot, or ling cod, skinned (if needed) and cut into 1- by 1½-inch chunks**
>   **Salt**

Prepare Serbian Tomato Relish; refrigerate.

In a large bowl, combine oil, garlic, and pepper; add fish chunks and turn to coat. Thread fish chunks equally on 6 sturdy metal skewers.

Place skewers on a well-greased grill 4 to 6 inches above a solid bed of hot coals. Cook, turning several times, until fish flakes when prodded in thickest part (10 to 12 minutes). Season to taste with salt and serve with relish. Makes 6 servings.

Per serving: 224 calories, 27 g protein, .4 g carbohydrates, 12 g total fat, 53 mg cholesterol, 121 mg sodium

Serbian Tomato Relish. Stem, seed, and finely chop 1 *each* **small fresh or canned hot red, green, and yellow chile.** Place chopped chiles in a bowl and add 2 large **tomatoes** (peeled and diced); 1 medium-size **onion** (finely chopped); ¼ teaspoon **salt;** 1 teaspoon **sugar;** and 1 tablespoon **red wine vinegar.** Stir until well blended. Cover and refrigerate for at least 30 minutes or until next day. Makes about 3 cups.

Per ½ cup: 18 calories, .6 g protein, 4 g carbohydrates, .1 g total fat, 0 mg cholesterol, 94 mg sodium

GREEK-STYLE FISH WITH MUSHROOMS

Preparation time: 25–30 minutes (including time to cut fish)

Marinating time: 10 minutes

Grilling time: About 10 minutes

In the Greek seaport of Piraeus, you might dine on pungently seasoned skewers like these. To top the chunks of fish and mushrooms, offer a tart lemon mayonnaise flecked with chopped fresh oregano and green onions.

>   **Lemon-Oregano Sauce (recipe follows)**
>   **About 1¼ pounds firm-textured fish steaks such as swordfish, halibut, or shark, skinned (if needed) and cut into 1- by 1¼-inch chunks**
> 16 **fresh bay leaves (or dry bay leaves soaked in hot water for 1 hour)**
> 16 **large mushrooms**

Prepare Lemon-Oregano Sauce and set aside.

On each of 4 metal skewers, alternate fish chunks with 4 bay leaves and 4 mushrooms. Brush skewered foods lightly with about 2 tablespoons of the sauce; let stand for 10 minutes.

Place skewers on a well-greased grill 4 to 6 inches above a solid bed of hot coals. Cook, turning frequently, until fish flakes when prodded in thickest part (about 10 minutes). Offer remaining Lemon-Oregano Sauce to spoon over individual portions. Makes 4 servings.

Per serving: 187 calories, 28 g protein, 7 g carbohydrates, 6 g total fat, 49 mg cholesterol, 119 mg sodium

Lemon-Oregano Sauce. In a food processor or blender, combine ¼ cup **lemon juice,** 1 clove **garlic** (minced or pressed), ¾ teaspoon **salt,** ¼ teaspoon **pepper,** and 1 **egg.** Whirl until frothy and lemon-colored. With motor running, slowly add ¾ cup **olive oil** or salad oil in a thin stream; continue to whirl until sauce is thick and creamy. Stir in 2 tablespoons minced **green onion** (including top) and 1 tablespoon chopped **fresh oregano** or 1 teaspoon dry oregano leaves. Makes about 1¼ cups.

Per tablespoon: 77 calories, .3 g protein, .3 g carbohydrates, 8 g total fat, 14 mg cholesterol, 87 mg sodium

LEMONY SKEWERED FISH & VEGETABLES

Preparation time: About 20 minutes (including time to cut fish)

Marinating time: 3 hours or until next day

Grilling time: 10–12 minutes

Chunks of firm-textured white fish are soaked in a lemony marinade, then threaded on skewers with vegetables in this colorful, easy-to-assemble entrée.

Lemon Marinade (recipe follows)
1½ **to 2 pounds firm-textured fish steaks such as swordfish, halibut, or shark, skinned (if needed) and cut into 1- by 1½-inch chunks**
2 **small zucchini, cut into ¼-inch-thick slices**
1 **large mild red onion, cut into 1-inch chunks**
2 **large red or green bell peppers, seeded and cut into 1-inch squares**
12 **to 18 large mushrooms**
Salt

Prepare Lemon Marinade. Add fish chunks to marinade in bowl; stir to coat. Cover and refrigerate for at least 3 hours or until next day, mixing gently once or twice.

Lift fish from marinade. Add zucchini, onion, bell peppers, and mushrooms to marinade; stir to coat. Lift vegetables from marinade (discard marinade). Thread fish chunks alternately with vegetables on 6 long, sturdy metal skewers.

Place skewers on a well-greased grill 4 to 6 inches above a solid bed of hot coals. Cook, turning several times, until fish flakes when prodded in thickest part (10 to 12 minutes). Let guests season fish and vegetables to taste with salt. Makes 6 servings.

Lemon Marinade. In a large bowl, stir together ¾ cup **salad oil**, ½ cup **lemon juice**, 2 tablespoons minced **fresh ginger**, 1 teaspoon **soy sauce**, ¼ teaspoon **pepper**, and 1 clove **garlic** (minced or pressed).

Per serving: 285 calories, 22 g protein, 9 g carbohydrates, 18 g total fat, 40 mg cholesterol, 127 mg sodium

JAPANESE SWIMMING FISH

Preparation time: About 30 minutes

Marinating time: 10 minutes

Grilling time: 7–10 minutes

Threaded on pairs of parallel bamboo skewers, these fish fillets look "rippled"—as if they're swimming on the platter.

4 **serving-size pieces firm-textured white fish fillets such as red snapper, sea bass, or ling cod (1 to 1½ lbs. *total*), cut ¾ to 1 inch thick**
3 **tablespoons soy sauce**
2 **tablespoons mirin or cream sherry**
1 **tablespoon lemon juice**
1½ **teaspoons salad oil**

Soak 8 bamboo skewers in hot water to cover for 30 minutes.

Rinse fish and pat dry. Thread 2 skewers lengthwise through each piece of fish, weaving skewers in and out of fish so fish looks slightly "rippled"; space skewers 1 inch apart.

In a small bowl, mix soy, mirin, lemon juice, and oil. Brush some of the soy mixture on both sides of fish pieces; let stand for 10 minutes.

Place fish on a well-greased grill 4 to 6 inches above a solid bed of hot coals. Cook, basting occasionally with remaining soy mixture and turning once, until fish flakes when prodded in thickest part (7 to 10 minutes). Makes 4 servings.

Per serving: 156 calories, 24 g protein, 4 g carbohydrates, 3 g total fat, 42 mg cholesterol, 845 mg sodium

For an especially good-looking entrée, serve Grilled Halibut with Basil-Garlic Butter (facing page). As the butter melts, it forms a garlicky sauce for the fish and accompanying vegetables.

⊚ GRILLED FISH STEAKS WITH MUSTARD SAUCE

Preparation time: About 15 minutes

Grilling time: 8–10 minutes

Just a small amount of buttery mustard sauce enhances the delicate smokiness of grilled fish steaks.

> 6 **firm-textured fish steaks such as swordfish, halibut, sea bass, salmon, or sturgeon (1½ to 2 lbs.** *total***), cut 1 inch thick**
> **About 1½ tablespoons olive oil or salad oil**
> ¼ **cup** *each* **dry white wine and whipping cream**
> 1 **tablespoon Dijon mustard**
> 2 **tablespoons firm butter or margarine, cut into 2 pieces**
> **Salt and pepper**

Rinse fish steaks and pat dry; brush both sides of each steak with oil. Place fish on a well-greased grill 4 to 6 inches above a solid bed of hot coals. Cook, turning once with a wide metal spatula, until fish flakes when prodded in thickest part (8 to 10 minutes). Using spatula, transfer fish to a warm platter and keep warm.

Combine wine, cream, and mustard in a small pan. Bring to a boil over high heat; then boil rapidly until reduced to about ¼ cup. Remove from heat. With a wire whisk or wooden spoon, beat in butter until sauce is smooth and creamy. Season to taste with salt and pepper. Spoon sauce evenly over grilled fish. Makes 6 servings.

Per serving: 255 calories, 21 g protein, .7 g carbohydrates, 15 g total fat, 61 mg cholesterol, 209 mg sodium

⊚ *(Pictured on facing page)*
GRILLED HALIBUT WITH BASIL-GARLIC BUTTER

Preparation time: About 20 minutes

Grilling time: 8–10 minutes

Let shapely pats of basil-fragrant butter melt on top of hot fish fillets to form a rich, intensely flavorful sauce.

> **Basil-Garlic Butter (recipe follows)**
> 6 **halibut steaks (1½ to 2 lbs.** *total***), cut 1 inch thick**
> 2 **tablespoons olive oil**

Prepare Basil-Garlic Butter and set aside.

Rinse fish steaks and pat dry; brush both sides of each steak with oil. Place fish on a well-greased grill 4 to 6 inches above a solid bed of hot coals. Cook, turning once with a wide metal spatula, until fish flakes when prodded in thickest part (8 to 10 minutes).

Using spatula, transfer fish to a warm platter. Top each piece of hot fish with about ⅙ of the Basil-Garlic Butter. Makes 6 servings.

Per serving: 141 calories, 19 g protein, 0 g carbohydrates, 7 g total fat, 30 mg cholesterol, 50 mg sodium

Basil-Garlic Butter. In small bowl of an electric mixer, combine ½ cup minced **fresh basil,** 2 cloves **garlic** (minced or pressed), and ½ cup (¼ lb.) **butter** or margarine (at room temperature). Beat until blended. Season to taste with **pepper.** Use at room temperature; or cover and refrigerate for up to 1 day. If desired, press soft butter mixture into butter molds; refrigerate until firm, then unmold to use. Or spread soft butter mixture into a thin rectangle on a piece of wax paper; refrigerate until firm. Then cut into shapes with a small decorative cutter. Makes about ¾ cup.

Per tablespoon: 70 calories, .2 g protein, .6 g carbohydrates, 8 g total fat, 21 mg cholesterol, 78 mg sodium

GRILLED SOY-LEMON HALIBUT

Preparation time: About 10 minutes

Marinating time: 1–2 hours

Grilling time: 8–10 minutes

A ginger-spiked marinade adds lots of extra flavor but very few calories to naturally low-calorie grilled halibut.

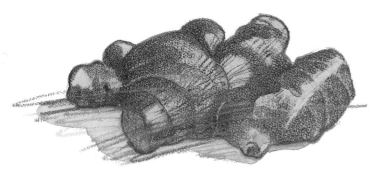

2 tablespoons butter or margarine, melted
3 tablespoons soy sauce
2 tablespoons lemon juice
1 tablespoon *each* sugar and Worcestershire
1 tablespoon minced fresh ginger or ½ teaspoon ground ginger
1 clove garlic, minced or pressed
⅛ teaspoon pepper
6 halibut, shark, or sea bass steaks or fillets (about 2 lbs. *total*), cut about 1 inch thick
Lemon wedges

In a shallow dish, stir together butter, soy, lemon juice, sugar, Worcestershire, ginger, garlic, and pepper. Rinse fish and pat dry; then add to soy marinade in dish and turn to coat. Cover and refrigerate for 1 to 2 hours, turning fish several times.

Lift fish from marinade and drain briefly (reserve marinade). Place fish on a well-greased grill 4 to 6 inches above a solid bed of hot coals. Cook, turning once with a wide metal spatula and basting with marinade several times, until fish flakes when prodded in thickest part (8 to 10 minutes). Using spatula, transfer fish to a warm platter. Serve with lemon wedges. Makes 6 servings.

Per serving: 187 calories, 26 g protein, 4 g carbohydrates, 7 g total fat, 50 mg cholesterol, 648 mg sodium

GRILLED SWORDFISH WITH TOMATO-OLIVE CONFETTI

Preparation time: About 20 minutes

Grilling time: 8–10 minutes

This colorful entrée is just right for a springtime dinner. Warm-from-the-grill swordfish steaks are nested on a bed of watercress, then embellished with a piquant mixture of lime, tomato, olives, and capers.

Tomato-Olive Confetti (recipe follows)
4 swordfish steaks (1¼ to 1½ lbs. *total*), cut 1 inch thick
1 tablespoon olive oil or salad oil
3 cups lightly packed watercress sprigs

Prepare Tomato-Olive Confetti and set aside.

Rinse fish steaks and pat dry; then brush both sides of each steak with oil. Place fish on a well-greased grill 4 to 6 inches above a solid bed of hot coals. Cook, turning once with a wide metal spat-ula, until fish flakes when prodded in thickest part (8 to 10 minutes).

Place an equal portion of watercress on each of 4 dinner plates. Set one fish steak on each portion of watercress; top each with an equal amount of Tomato-Olive Confetti. Makes 4 servings.

Per serving: 185 calories, 26 g protein, .4 g carbohydrates, 8 g total fat, 49 mg cholesterol, 125 mg sodium

Tomato-Olive Confetti. In a bowl, stir together 1 medium-size **tomato** (chopped); ½ cup sliced **pimento-stuffed green olives;** 2 tablespoons drained **capers;** 3 tablespoons *each* sliced **green onions** (including tops) and **lime juice;** and 3 table-spoons **olive oil** or salad oil. Makes about 1¼ cups.

Per ¼ cup: 95 calories, .5 g protein, 2 g carbohydrates, 10 g total fat, 0 mg cholesterol, 418 mg sodium

MUSHROOM-TOPPED SWORDFISH STEAKS

Preparation time: About 20 minutes

Marinating time: 1–2 hours

Grilling time: 8–10 minutes

A tangy fennel-seasoned marinade flavors both the fish and the sautéed mushroom topping in this savory entrée.

> 6 swordfish steaks (2 to 2½ lbs. *total*), cut 1 inch thick
> 3 tablespoons lemon juice
> ¼ cup dry white wine
> 1 clove garlic, minced or pressed
> ½ teaspoon *each* oregano leaves, salt, and pepper
> ¼ teaspoon fennel seeds, crushed
> 2 tablespoons olive oil or salad oil
> ½ pound mushrooms, sliced
> 3 green onions (including tops), thinly sliced

Rinse fish steaks and pat dry; then arrange in a close-fitting bowl or dish. In another bowl, stir together lemon juice, wine, garlic, oregano, salt, pepper, and fennel seeds; pour over fish. Turn fish to coat. Cover and refrigerate for 1 to 2 hours, turning occasionally.

Lift fish from marinade and drain briefly (reserve marinade for topping). Place fish on a well-greased grill 4 to 6 inches above a solid bed of hot coals. Cook, turning once with a wide metal spatula, until fish flakes when prodded in thickest part (8 to 10 minutes).

Meanwhile, heat oil in a wide frying pan over medium-high heat. Add mushrooms and cook, stirring, until soft (about 5 minutes). Stir in reserved marinade and simmer for 2 minutes.

Using spatula, transfer fish to a warm platter. Top each piece with an equal amount of the mushroom mixture; sprinkle evenly with onions. Makes 6 servings.

Per serving: 218 calories, 28 g protein, 3 g carbohydrates, 10 g total fat, 53 mg cholesterol, 308 mg sodium

SAVORY SHARK & VEGETABLES

Preparation time: About 20 minutes (including time to cut fish)

Marinating time: 30–60 minutes

Grilling time: 10–12 minutes

Shark tastes much like swordfish or halibut, but it's less expensive. Available all year round, it's sold both fresh and frozen; you may find it labeled as grayfish, thresher, soupfin, leopard, or dogfish. The flesh is white, firm, meaty, low in fat, and free of small bones.

> ⅓ cup olive oil or salad oil
> ¼ cup lemon juice
> 1 clove garlic, minced or pressed
> 2 tablespoons chopped parsley
> ½ teaspoon *each* salt, dry rosemary, and dry mustard
> ¼ teaspoon pepper
> 1½ to 2 pounds shark fillets or steaks, skinned (if needed) and cut into 1- by 1½-inch chunks
> 1 small onion, cut into 1-inch chunks
> 3 small zucchini, cut into 1-inch lengths

In a bowl, stir together oil, lemon juice, garlic, parsley, salt, rosemary, mustard, and pepper. Add fish and stir to coat. Cover and refrigerate for 30 to 60 minutes.

Lift fish from marinade; add onion and zucchini and turn to coat. Lift vegetables from marinade (reserve any marinade). On 6 metal skewers, alternately thread fish chunks, onion, and zucchini. Place skewers on a well-greased grill 4 to 6 inches above a solid bed of hot coals. Cook, turning as needed and brushing with marinade, until fish flakes when prodded in thickest part (10 to 12 minutes). Makes 6 servings.

Per serving: 267 calories, 25 g protein, 3 g carbohydrates, 17 g total fat, 58 mg cholesterol, 277 mg sodium

(Pictured on facing page)

⬤ GRILLED TUNA STEAKS WITH FRUIT & TERIYAKI SAUCE

Preparation time: About 20 minutes

Grilling time: About 4 minutes

Like fine beef, fresh tuna should be barbecued just to the rare stage to bring out its succulent, surprisingly unfishy flavor. If allowed to cook throughout, it will be too dry.

Look for fresh or frozen tuna at Japanese or other well-stocked fish markets; it's usually sold as bluefin, yellowfin, skipjack, or albacore.

> **Teriyaki Sauce (recipe follows)**
> 4 **tuna steaks (1 to 1¼ lbs. *total*), cut 1 inch thick**
> **About 2 tablespoons salad oil**
> **Salt and pepper**
> 8 **to 12 thin slices peeled papaya or mango**
> 2 **teaspoons chopped candied or crystallized ginger**
> 1 **medium-size green bell pepper, seeded and cut lengthwise into thin slivers**

Prepare Teriyaki Sauce and keep warm.

Rinse fish steaks and pat dry; then brush both sides of each steak with oil. Place fish on a well-greased grill 4 to 6 inches above a solid bed of hot coals. Cook, turning once with a wide metal spatula, until outside is firm and opaque but inside is still translucent and moist-looking (about 4 minutes). Remove fish from grill and season to taste with salt and pepper.

To serve, place one steak on each individual plate; top each steak with ¼ of the Teriyaki Sauce, papaya slices, and ginger. Arrange ¼ of the bell pepper alongside each steak. Makes 4 servings.

Teriyaki Sauce. In a 2- to 3-quart pan, combine ¼ cup *each* **sugar** and **soy sauce,** 6 tablespoons **sake** or dry sherry, and 3 thin slices **fresh ginger.** Bring to a boil over high heat; boil, uncovered, until reduced to ⅓ cup. Discard ginger slices; keep sauce warm.

Per serving: 305 calories, 25 g protein, 24 g carbohydrates, 12 g total fat, 38 mg cholesterol, 1073 mg sodium

⬤ BARBECUED ALBACORE LOIN WITH BASIL & CUCUMBERS

Preparation time: About 25 minutes

Marinating time: 3–6 hours

Grilling time: About 15 minutes

In the past, most of the albacore catch was canned. Today, though, the fish is sold fresh in many markets. Here, we soak an albacore loin in a fresh pesto marinade, then grill it just to the rare stage to retain its moist and meatlike texture.

> ¾ **cup lightly packed fresh basil leaves**
> ⅔ **cup olive oil or salad oil**
> ½ **cup white wine vinegar**
> ¼ **cup freshly grated Parmesan cheese**
> 3 **cloves garlic**
> ¼ **teaspoon pepper**
> **2-pound boned albacore loin, skinned or unskinned**
> 1 **medium-size cucumber, peeled, seeded, and thinly sliced**
> **Salt**

In a food processor or blender, whirl basil, oil, vinegar, cheese, garlic, and pepper until puréed; set aside.

Rinse fish and pat dry. Place fish in a close-fitting bowl or dish. Add ⅔ of the basil marinade; roll fish in marinade to coat. In another bowl, mix remaining basil marinade with cucumber. Cover fish and cucumber and refrigerate for 3 to 6 hours, turning fish several times.

Lift fish from marinade and drain briefly (reserve marinade). Place on a well-greased grill 4 to 6 inches above a solid bed of hot coals. Cook, turning as needed with a wide metal spatula and basting several times with marinade, until fish is browned and firm on outside but still moist and translucent ½ inch below the surface; cut to test (about 15 minutes).

Using spatula, lift fish from grill and place it on a warm platter. Arrange cucumber mixture alongside fish. To serve, cut fish crosswise into 1-inch-thick slices. Let guests season fish to taste with salt. Makes 6 servings.

Per serving: 412 calories, 38 g protein, 4 g carbohydrates, 27 g total fat, 71 mg cholesterol, 135 mg sodium

*A tempting trio: teriyaki sauce, tropical fruit, and tuna steaks
(facing page). Top each succulent steak with a spoonful of sauce,
a few papaya slices, and a sprinkle of candied ginger, then fan
out crisp bell pepper slivers alongside.*

BARBECUED BEER-MARINATED ALBACORE

Preparation time: About 5 minutes

Marinating time: 1–3 hours

Grilling time: About 15 minutes for loin, 7 minutes for steaks

A robust beer marinade and a tangy lemon baste complement the flavor of fresh albacore. Use steaks or a whole loin; either way, the cooking time is brief.

> **2-pound boned albacore loin, skinned or unskinned; or 6 albacore steaks (about 2 lbs.** *total*)**, cut about 1½ inches thick**
> 1 **cup beer**
> 2 **tablespoons butter or margarine, melted**
> 2 **tablespoons lemon juice**

Rinse albacore loin or steaks and pat dry; then place in a close-fitting bowl or dish. Pour in beer and turn fish to coat evenly. Cover and refrigerate for 1 to 3 hours, turning fish occasionally.

Lift fish from beer and drain briefly (discard beer). Stir together butter and lemon juice; generously brush over all sides of fish. Place fish on a well-greased grill 4 to 6 inches above a solid bed of hot coals. Cook, turning as needed with a wide metal spatula and basting several times with lemon butter, until fish is browned and firm on outside but still moist and translucent ½ inch below the surface; cut to test (about 15 minutes for loin, 7 minutes for steaks). Makes 6 servings.

Per serving: 200 calories, 35 g protein, .7 g carbohydrates, 5 g total fat, 78 mg cholesterol, 97 mg sodium

SABLEFISH TERIYAKI

Preparation time: About 15 minutes

Marinating time: 30–45 minutes

Grilling time: 15–20 minutes

Often called butterfish or black cod, buttery-textured sablefish really benefits from grilling, especially when you use a potent basting sauce such as this tangy soy mixture. Sablefish has very tender flesh, though, so it's best to barbecue it on a piece of pierced foil in a covered barbecue.

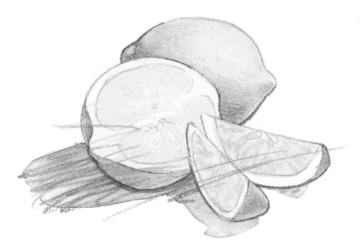

> ¼ **cup soy sauce**
> ½ **cup dry sherry**
> 2 **tablespoons lemon juice**
> ½ **teaspoon grated fresh ginger or ¼ teaspoon ground ginger**
> **2- to 3-pound piece sablefish, cut lengthwise into 2 fillets**

In a small pan, combine soy, sherry, lemon juice, and ginger; simmer for 2 minutes to blend flavors. Set aside.

Rinse fish and pat dry. Place each fillet, skin side down, on a piece of heavy-duty foil; cut foil to follow outlines of fish, leaving a 1- to 2-inch border. Lift fish off foil and pierce each piece of foil in several places with a skewer; set fish back on foil and crimp edges of foil. Brush some of the soy mixture over tops of fish fillets; let stand for 30 to 45 minutes at room temperature.

Barbecue fish by indirect heat (see page 10), placing foil-supported fish on grill directly above drip pan. Cover barbecue and adjust dampers as necessary to maintain an even heat. Cook, basting fish several times with remaining soy mixture, until fish flakes when prodded in thickest part (15 to 20 minutes). Makes about 6 servings.

Per serving: 312 calories, 21 g protein, 4 g carbohydrates, 23 g total fat, 74 mg cholesterol, 773 mg sodium

BARBECUED MACKEREL WITH TWO MARINADES

Preparation time: About 10 minutes

Marinating time: 15–30 minutes

Grilling time: 15–20 minutes

The rich, distinctive flavor of mackerel can be toned down a bit by soaking the fish in an equally authoritative marinade. Here, we offer two choices: a tangy lemon-garlic mixture and a spicy blend of ginger and soy.

> **Lemon-Garlic Marinade or Ginger-Soy Marinade (recipes follow)**
> 6 **to 8 whole mackerel (about ½ lb.** *each***), cleaned**
> **Salt and pepper**

Prepare your choice of marinade and set aside.

Rinse mackerel and pat dry. Slash each fish in several places along backbone. Place fish in a close-fitting bowl or dish and pour in prepared marinade; turn fish to coat. Let stand for 15 to 30 minutes at room temperature, turning fish once.

Lift fish from marinade and drain briefly (reserve marinade). Place fish on a well-greased grill 4 to 6 inches above a solid bed of hot coals. Cook, turning once with a wide metal spatula and basting occasionally with marinade, until fish is well browned and flakes when prodded in thickest part (15 to 20 minutes).

Let guests season fish to taste with salt and pepper. Makes 4 to 6 servings.

Lemon-Garlic Marinade. In a small bowl, stir together ⅓ cup **lemon juice**, 1 large clove **garlic** (minced or pressed), 1 tablespoon **olive oil**, and ½ teaspoon **oregano leaves.**

Ginger-Soy Marinade. In a small bowl, stir together ⅓ cup **soy sauce**, 1 tablespoon **mirin** or cream sherry, 1 clove **garlic** (minced or pressed), and 2 teaspoons grated **fresh ginger.**

Per serving with Lemon-Garlic Marinade: 178 calories, 14 g protein, 1 g carbohydrates, 13 g total fat, 52 mg cholesterol, 70 mg sodium

Per serving with Ginger-Soy Marinade: 170 calories, 15 g protein, 3 g carbohydrates, 10 g total fat, 52 mg cholesterol, 973 mg sodium

BARBECUED CATFISH

Preparation time: 15–20 minutes

Grilling time: 10–15 minutes

Fragile-fleshed catfish are easiest to barbecue in a hinged wire basket (see photo on page 145). In this recipe, they're brushed with a soy and sesame oil baste while they grill.

> 4 **whole catfish (about 13 oz.** *each***), cleaned and skinned, heads removed**
> 2 **tablespoons salad oil**
> ⅓ **cup soy sauce**
> 3 **tablespoons** *each* **sesame oil and minced green onions (including tops)**
> 1 **tablespoon** *each* **vinegar and minced fresh ginger**
> 2 **teaspoons sugar**
> 2 **cloves garlic, minced or pressed**
> ⅛ **teaspoon ground red pepper (cayenne)**

Rinse fish and pat dry. Rub surface of each fish with salad oil, then lay fish on one side of a hinged wire basket with handles. Close basket and secure tightly to hold fish snugly in place; set aside.

In a small bowl, stir together soy, sesame oil, onions, vinegar, ginger, sugar, garlic, and red pepper. Brush over fish.

Place hinged basket with fish on grill 4 to 6 inches above a solid bed of medium coals. Cook, brushing often with soy mixture, until fish flakes when prodded in thickest part (10 to 15 minutes).

Remove hinged basket from barbecue and open carefully, pulling fish free with a fork if they stick. With a wide metal spatula, transfer fish to a warm platter. Makes 4 servings.

Per serving: 325 calories, 25 g protein, 5 g carbohydrates, 23 g total fat, 74 mg cholesterol, 1439 mg sodium

Tangy Citrus Salsa and homemade Jalapeño Mayonnaise enhance these whole Barbecued Trout (facing page). Garnish the fish with grilled green onions and thin orange slices, if you like.

(Pictured on facing page)

BARBECUED TROUT

Preparation time: About 30 minutes

Marinating time: 1–2 hours

Grilling time: 10–12 minutes for whole fish, 6–8 minutes for boned fish

Before grilling, these tender trout soak up flavor in an herb-seasoned marinade. Serve with Citrus Salsa and Jalapeño Mayonnaise.

- **4 whole trout (about ½ lb. *each*), cleaned**
- **⅔ cup salad oil**
- **¼ cup white wine vinegar**
- **½ teaspoon *each* dry basil and oregano leaves**
- **1 clove garlic, minced or pressed**
- **¼ teaspoon *each* salt and pepper**
- **Citrus Salsa and Jalapeño Mayonnaise (recipes follow)**

Rinse fish; pat dry. Leave whole or bone and butterfly.

To bone cleaned trout and keep head and tail in place, open body cavity; insert a sharp knife at head end under backbone and cut between ribs and flesh. Repeat process to free other side. Cut underneath backbone to free. Using kitchen scissors, snip backbone at head and tail; lift out and discard. Cut off and discard fins. Spread fish out flat.

In a shallow pan, stir together oil, vinegar, basil, oregano, garlic, salt, and pepper. Add fish to marinade; turn to coat. Cover and refrigerate for 1 to 2 hours, turning once. Meanwhile, prepare Citrus Salsa and Jalapeño Mayonnaise; cover and refrigerate.

Lift fish from marinade and drain briefly (discard marinade). Barbecue whole fish by indirect heat (see page 10), placing fish on a well-greased grill directly above drip pan; cover barbecue and adjust dampers as necessary to maintain an even heat. Place boned fish on a well-greased grill 4 to 6 inches above a solid bed of hot coals.

Cook whole or boned fish, turning once with a wide metal spatula, just until fish flakes when prodded in thickest part (10 to 12 minutes for whole fish, 6 to 8 minutes for boned fish). Using spatula, transfer cooked trout to a warm platter. Accompany with Citrus Salsa and Jalapeño Mayonnaise. Makes 4 servings.

Per serving: 279 calories, 17 g protein, 1 g carbohydrates, 23 g total fat, 46 mg cholesterol, 111 mg sodium

Citrus Salsa. Cut peel and all white membrane from 2 large **oranges** and 1 large **grapefruit;** lift out sections. Coarsely chop fruit. Also peel and chop 2 medium-size **tomatoes.**

In a bowl, mix oranges, grapefruit, tomatoes, 2 tablespoons *each* **lime juice** and **orange juice,** ¼ cup chopped **fresh cilantro (coriander),** and 1 teaspoon **sugar.** Season to taste with **salt.** If made ahead, cover and refrigerate until next day. Makes 3 cups.

Per ½ cup: 61 calories, 1 g protein, 15 g carbohydrates, .3 g total fat, 0 mg cholesterol, 4 mg sodium

Jalapeño Mayonnaise. In a blender or food processor, combine 3 or 4 **fresh jalapeño or other small hot chiles** (stemmed, seeded, and minced); 1 clove **garlic** (minced or pressed); 1 **egg yolk;** 2 tablespoons **lime juice;** and ½ teaspoon **salt.** Whirl until smoothly puréed. With motor running, slowly add ¾ cup **salad oil**—a drop at a time at first, then in a slow, steady stream. Continue to whirl until mixture is very thick. Before serving, cover and refrigerate for at least 1 hour or up to 3 days. Makes about 1 cup.

Per tablespoon: 96 calories, .2 g protein, .4 g carbohydrates, 11 g total fat, 17 mg cholesterol, 69 mg sodium

YUCATÁN RED SNAPPER

Preparation time: About 30 minutes

Grilling time: 35–45 minutes

Inspired by a technique used in Yucatán, we've coated a whole red snapper in fresh tomato sauce, then baked it with ease in a covered barbecue.

> 2 tablespoons olive oil or salad oil
> 1 large onion, chopped
> 2 cloves garlic, minced or pressed
> 4 teaspoons sugar
> 1 teaspoon salt
> ¼ teaspoon *each* ground cinnamon and ground cloves
> 5 cups peeled, seeded, chopped fresh tomatoes
> 1½ teaspoons *each* lemon juice and water
> 1 tablespoon cornstarch
> 1 or 2 fresh or canned jalapeño chiles, stemmed, seeded, and finely chopped
> 2 tablespoons drained capers
> 5- to 5½-pound whole red snapper, cleaned, scaled, and head removed
> ⅓ cup thinly sliced pimento-stuffed green olives
> 3 tablespoons minced fresh cilantro (coriander)

Heat oil in a wide frying pan over medium heat. Add onion and garlic and cook, stirring often, until onion is soft (about 10 minutes). Stir in sugar, salt, cinnamon, cloves, and tomatoes. Increase heat to high and cook, stirring, until mixture is reduced to a thick sauce (about 8 minutes). Blend lemon juice, water, and cornstarch; stir into tomato mixture. Cook until mixture boils and liquid turns clear; remove from heat. Stir in chiles and capers.

Rinse fish; pat dry. Place a 24-inch length of foil crosswise in a 9- by 13-inch baking pan. Grease foil, then place fish on foil; pour hot sauce over fish.

Barbecue fish by indirect heat (see page 10), placing baking pan directly in center of grill (no need for drip pan below). Cover barbecue and adjust dampers as necessary to maintain an even heat. Cook until fish flakes when prodded in thickest part (35 to 45 minutes).

Skim watery juices off sauce with a spoon; then stir sauce to blend. Lift foil, fish, and clinging sauce and slide onto a warm platter; drizzle with sauce remaining in pan. Garnish with olives and cilantro.

Cut through fish to bone; lift off each serving with a wide metal spatula. Makes 4 to 6 servings.

Per serving: 226 calories, 27 g protein, 13 g carbohydrates, 7 g total fat, 45 mg cholesterol, 711 mg sodium

STRIPED BASS WITH ONION BARBECUE SAUCE

Preparation time: About 30 minutes

Grilling time: About 20 minutes

A delicate hint of smokiness is an excellent flavor accent for moist, mild-flavored striped bass.

> ½ cup salad oil
> ¾ cup chopped onion
> ¾ cup catsup
> ⅓ cup lemon juice
> 3 tablespoons *each* sugar and Worcestershire
> 2 tablespoons prepared mustard
> ½ teaspoon pepper
> Salt
> 7- to 8-pound whole striped bass, cleaned and cut lengthwise into 2 boneless fillets

Heat oil in a 2- to 3-quart pan over medium heat. Add onion and cook, stirring frequently, until soft (about 10 minutes). Add catsup, lemon juice, sugar, Worcestershire, mustard, and pepper.

Reduce heat and simmer, uncovered, until sauce is thickened (10 to 15 minutes). Remove from heat and season to taste with salt.

Rinse fish; pat dry. Place each fillet, skin side down, on a piece of heavy-duty foil; cut foil to follow outlines of fish, leaving a 1- to 2-inch border. Crimp edges of foil. Brush fish with sauce.

Barbecue fillets by indirect heat (see page 10), placing foil-supported fish on grill directly above drip pan. Cover barbecue and adjust dampers as necessary to maintain an even heat. Cook until fish flakes when prodded in thickest part (about 20 minutes). Reheat remaining barbecue sauce.

Supporting fish with foil, transfer to a warm large platter. To serve, cut through flesh of each fillet to skin; slide a wide metal spatula between skin and flesh and lift off each portion. Accompany with sauce. Makes 8 to 10 servings.

Per serving: 253 calories, 21 g protein, 11 g carbohydrates, 14 g total fat, 89 mg cholesterol, 381 mg sodium

SMOKED SALMON

FOR A CROWD

Salmon smoked in a covered barbecue makes a splendid centerpiece for a party buffet. To flavor the fish, you add chips or tiny sticks of aromatic wood to the fire; hickory is a favorite, but you can also use alder, apple, cherry, mountain mahogany, or mesquite.

Besides your barbecue and a supply of wood chips and briquets, you'll need cheesecloth for supporting the fish, a small barbecue or old metal pan for igniting additional coals, and an accurate oven thermometer.

SMOKED SALMON

1 whole salmon (6 to 8 lbs.), cleaned, head and tail removed, and cut lengthwise into 2 boneless fillets
Salt Brine (recipe follows)
Hickory wood chips
Syrup Baste (recipe follows)
Salad oil
Cream cheese and dark bread or miniature bagels

Use tweezers to remove any small bones remaining in salmon fillets; then arrange fillets in a shallow pan. Prepare brine and pour over fish. Cover and let stand at room temperature for 2 to 3 hours (or refrigerate for up to 6 hours). Drain fish, rinse, and pat dry.

Place fillets, skin side down, on several layers of paper towels; let stand for 30 minutes. Then place each fillet, skin side down, on a double thickness of cheesecloth; cut cheesecloth to shape of fish.

Mound 12 charcoal briquets on fire grate of barbecue; ignite. Soak 1 cup hickory chips in warm water to cover for about 30 minutes. Meanwhile, prepare Syrup Baste.

When coals are covered with gray ash (after about 30 minutes), push 6 of them to one side of barbecue, 6 to other side. Drain hickory chips well; sprinkle ½ cup over each group of coals.

Brush cooking grill with oil and set in place 4 to 6 inches above coals.

Place salmon fillets, side by side and cheesecloth side down, in center of grill (no part of fish should be directly above coals). Lightly brush fish with Syrup Baste. Place an oven thermometer in center of grill, cover barbecue, and cook fish for 30 minutes. Meanwhile, in a small barbecue, ignite 6 more briquets; also soak 1 cup more hickory chips in water to cover.

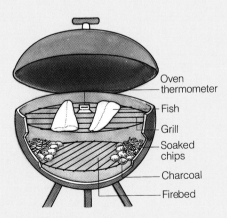

Oven thermometer
Fish
Grill
Soaked chips
Charcoal
Firebed

After 30 minutes, check thermometer; it's important to maintain temperature at 160° to 170°F. Add about 3 more hot coals to each side of barbecue—all 3 if temperature is below 160°F, fewer than 3 if it's above 170°F. Drain hickory chips well and sprinkle ½ cup over each group of coals.

With a paper towel, blot any white juices from fillets so tops remain dry and shiny; lightly brush with baste. Cover and continue to cook. Meanwhile, ignite 6 more briquets in your small barbecue and soak 1 cup more hickory chips.

Continue to add hot coals and soaked, drained hickory chips every 30 minutes or as needed to maintain temperature at 160° to 170°F. Each time you add coals, blot fish and brush with baste. Cook just until fish flakes when prodded in thickest part; total cooking time will be 2 to 3 hours.

Carefully slide fillets onto baking sheets and let cool slightly; then cover and refrigerate until chilled or for up to 2 weeks.

To serve, carefully remove cheesecloth and place fillets on a large serving board. Cut each fillet into slanting slices, cutting each slice away from skin. Serve with cream cheese and dark bread. Makes about 50 servings.

Salt Brine. Dissolve 1 cup **salt** and 1½ cups **sugar** in 8 cups **water;** add 3 tablespoons coarsely ground **pepper** and 3 **bay leaves.**

Syrup Baste. Stir together ¼ cup **maple-flavored syrup,** 1 teaspoon **soy sauce,** ¼ teaspoon *each* **ground ginger** and **pepper,** and 1 clove **garlic** (minced or pressed).

Per serving of salmon: 39 calories, 5 g protein, 1 g carbohydrates, 2 g total fat, 14 mg cholesterol, 150 mg sodium

FISH IN LEAVES

Preparation time: About 20 minutes

Grilling time: About 45 minutes

Wrapped in grape leaves before barbecuing, whole fish turns out moist and juicy. To support the fish during cooking, use a hinged wire basket; these are available at most stores where barbecue equipment is sold. If you can't find a basket, improvise by wrapping the fish first in grape leaves, then in flexible chicken wire.

> **6- to 8-pound whole fish such as salmon, red snapper, rockfish, or striped bass, cleaned and scaled (and head removed, if desired)**
> 2 **lemons, cut into ¼-inch-thick slices**
> 2 **small onions, cut into ¼-inch-thick slices**
> **Salt and pepper**
> **About 24 fresh grape leaves**
> 5 **or 6 fresh or dry bay leaves**

Rinse fish and pat dry. Arrange lemon and onion slices in fish cavity; lightly sprinkle fish all over with salt and pepper. Grease both sides of a hinged wire basket. Line bottom of basket by overlapping about 12 grape leaves. Place fish on top of grape leaves; top evenly with bay leaves, then cover with remaining grape leaves. Fish and leaves should total 4 to 5 inches thick, measured in thickest part. Close basket and secure tightly; then sprinkle grape leaves on both sides of basket with water.

Place basket with fish on a lightly greased grill 4 to 6 inches above a solid bed of medium coals. Cook, turning basket every 15 minutes, until fish flakes when prodded in thickest part (about 45 minutes; push grape leaves away with fork to test). If necessary, add 5 or 6 briquets to the fire after 30 minutes to keep temperature constant.

Open basket; peel off and discard grape leaves, bay leaves, and top layer of fish skin. Slide fish onto a warm platter. To serve, cut down through flesh to backbone, slide a wide metal spatula between flesh and ribs, and lift off each serving. Discard lemon and onion slices. Makes 8 to 10 servings.

Per serving: 142 calories, 19 g protein, 2.4 g carbohydrates, 6 g total fat, 52 mg cholesterol, 42 mg sodium

(Pictured on facing page)

GRILLED SCALLOPS WITH GINGER-LIME SAUCE

Preparation time: About 30 minutes

Grilling time: 5–7 minutes

Grilling scallops quickly over hot coals seals in juices as it adds rich flavor. Serve the tender morsels in a pale green sauce sparked with fresh ginger.

> **Ginger-Lime Sauce (recipe follows)**
> 1½ **pounds scallops, *each* 1 to 1½ inches in diameter**
> **About ¼ cup butter or margarine, melted**

Soak about 8 bamboo skewers in hot water to cover for 30 minutes. Meanwhile, prepare Ginger-Lime Sauce and keep warm.

Rinse scallops to remove any bits of shell or sand; pat dry with paper towels.

Thread scallops on bamboo skewers, piercing them horizontally (through their diameter) so they lie flat. Brush generously with butter. Place scallops on a well-greased grill 4 to 6 inches above a solid bed of hot coals. Cook, turning once, until scallops are opaque throughout; cut to test (5 to 7 minutes).

Pour prepared Ginger-Lime Sauce onto a warm platter. Lay scallops in sauce. Makes about 4 servings.

Per serving: 251 calories, 29 g protein, 4 g carbohydrates, 13 g total fat, 87 mg cholesterol, 391 mg sodium

Ginger-Lime Sauce. In a wide frying pan, combine ½ cup *each* **dry white wine** and **regular-strength chicken broth,** 2 tablespoons minced **shallots** or onion, 1 teaspoon grated **fresh ginger,** and ¼ teaspoon grated **lime peel.** Bring to a boil over high heat; continue to boil, uncovered, until reduced by half. Stir in ½ cup **whipping cream** and boil, uncovered, until reduced to ¾ cup. Reduce heat to medium and add ¼ cup **unsalted butter** all in one chunk; stir constantly until butter is completely blended into sauce. To keep sauce warm for up to 2 hours, pour into a 2-cup glass measure set in hot-to-touch water. Stir occasionally and replace water as needed. Makes about 1 cup sauce.

Per tablespoon: 50 calories, .25 g protein, .5 g carbohydrates, 5 g total fat, 16 mg cholesterol, 35 mg sodium

Dinner for four? Try these skewered grilled scallops served
in a pool of creamy ginger-lime sauce (facing page). Keep the
accompaniments simple: grilled crookneck and tiny pattypan
squash, a radicchio salad, and your favorite rolls.

HAWAII SCALLOP SKEWERS

Preparation time: About 25 minutes

Marinating time: 2–4 hours

Grilling time: 5–7 minutes

Alternate pieces of bacon with marinated scallops, colorful chunks of red bell pepper, and fresh mushrooms to make these teriyaki-flavored skewers.

16 scallops, *each* 1 to 1½ inches in diameter (1¼ to 1½ lbs. *total*)
    Soy Marinade (recipe follows)
16 mushrooms, *each* 1 to 1½ inches in diameter
 4 slices bacon
 2 small red bell peppers, seeded and cut into 1½-inch squares

Rinse scallops to remove any bits of shell or sand.

Prepare Soy Marinade and pour into a deep bowl; add scallops and mushrooms and turn to coat. Cover and refrigerate for 2 to 4 hours, turning several times. Also soak about 8 bamboo skewers in hot water to cover for 30 minutes.

Cook bacon in a wide frying pan over medium heat until it is partially cooked but still limp (about 3 minutes). Drain on paper towels. Cut each bacon slice into 4 pieces.

Lift scallops and mushrooms from marinade and drain briefly (reserve marinade). Thread bacon pieces, scallops, mushrooms, and bell peppers alternately on soaked skewers. Place skewers on a well-greased grill 4 to 6 inches above a solid bed of hot coals. Cook, turning occasionally and basting several times with marinade, until scallops are opaque throughout; cut to test (5 to 7 minutes). Makes 4 servings.

Soy Marinade. In a small bowl, stir together ¼ cup **soy sauce**; 1 tablespoon *each* **lemon juice, dry sherry,** and **salad oil**; 2 cloves **garlic** (minced or pressed); and 1 teaspoon *each* minced **fresh ginger** and **sugar.**

Per serving: 267 calories, 27 g protein, 10 g carbohydrates, 13 g total fat, 57 mg cholesterol, 1388 mg sodium

BARBECUED PRAWNS WRAPPED IN BACON

Preparation time: About 30 minutes

Grilling time: 10–12 minutes

"Colossal" prawns, sometimes called tiger or gulf prawns, are the featured shellfish in this recipe. To prepare the prawns for grilling, wrap them in bacon and thread them onto bamboo skewers, head to head.

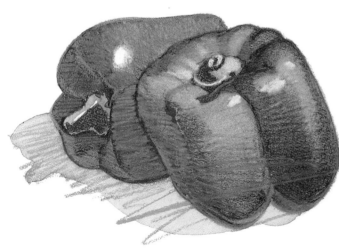

 8 or 16 slices bacon (1 for each prawn)
16 colossal raw prawns or jumbo raw shrimp (10 to 15 per lb.) or 8 extra-colossal raw prawns or shrimp (under 10 per lb.), shelled (leave tails on) and deveined

If using bamboo skewers, soak about 8 skewers in hot water to cover for 30 minutes.

Cook bacon, a portion at a time, in a wide frying pan over medium heat until it is partially cooked but still limp (about 3 minutes). Drain on paper towels.

Wrap each prawn in a slice of bacon. Arrange prawns in pairs on a flat surface, with head ends hooked around one another and tails pointing in opposite directions. On 2 parallel bamboo or metal skewers, thread one pair of extra-colossal or 2 pairs of colossal prawns; prawns should lie flat. Repeat with remaining prawns.

Place skewers on a well-greased grill 4 to 6 inches above a solid bed of hot coals. Cook, turning once, until prawns turn pink and bacon is crisp (10 to 12 minutes). Makes 4 servings.

Per serving: 270 calories, 32 g protein, 1 g carbohydrates, 14 g total fat, 200 mg cholesterol, 578 mg sodium

⬡ MINT-FLAVORED SHRIMP

Preparation time: 20–25 minutes

Marinating time: 2–4 hours

Grilling time: 3–5 minutes

Chopped fresh mint enlivens the well-seasoned marinade for these grilled shrimp. For a summer barbecue party, accompany the shrimp with a pilaf or a cold rice salad.

- ¾ **cup salad oil**
- 1 **tablespoon finely chopped fresh mint or 1 tablespoon dry mint, crumbled**
- 1 **tablespoon white wine vinegar**
- 1 **teaspoon** *each* **chili powder and dry basil**
- ½ **teaspoon salt**
- ¼ **teaspoon pepper**
- 1 **clove garlic, minced or pressed**
- 2 **pounds medium-size raw shrimp (30 to 32 per lb.), shelled and deveined**

In a large bowl, stir together oil, mint, vinegar, chili powder, basil, salt, pepper, and garlic. Add shrimp and stir to coat. Cover and refrigerate for 2 to 4 hours.

If using bamboo skewers, soak about 24 skewers in hot water to cover for 30 minutes.

Lift shrimp from marinade and drain briefly (reserve marinade). Thread about 5 shrimp on a pair of bamboo or thin metal skewers, aligning skewers parallel so shrimp lie flat. Repeat with remaining shrimp. Place shrimp on a well-greased grill 4 to 6 inches above a solid bed of hot coals. Cook, basting with marinade and turning once, until shrimp turn pink (3 to 5 minutes). Makes about 6 servings.

Per serving: 374 calories, 25 g protein, 2 g carbohydrates, 29 g total fat, 186 mg cholesterol, 368 mg sodium

⬡ SPICY MARINATED SHRIMP

Preparation time: 20–25 minutes

Marinating time: 2–4 hours

Grilling time: 3–5 minutes

You season these shrimp in a Creole-style tomato marinade, then grill them on skewers for easy handling.

- ¼ **cup salad oil**
- ½ **teaspoon** *each* **salt and pepper**
- 1 **clove garlic, minced or pressed**
- ⅓ **cup** *each* **white wine vinegar and tomato-based chili sauce**
- 2 **tablespoons Worcestershire**
- ⅛ **teaspoon liquid hot pepper seasoning**
- ½ **cup minced parsley**
- 2 **pounds medium-size raw shrimp (30 to 32 per lb.), shelled and deveined**

In a large bowl, stir together oil, salt, pepper, garlic, vinegar, chili sauce, Worcestershire, hot pepper seasoning, and parsley. Add shrimp and stir to coat. Cover and refrigerate for 2 to 4 hours.

If using bamboo skewers, soak about 24 skewers in hot water to cover for 30 minutes.

Lift shrimp from marinade and drain briefly (reserve marinade). Thread about 5 shrimp on a pair of bamboo or thin metal skewers, aligning skewers parallel so shrimp lie flat. Repeat with remaining shrimp. Place shrimp on a well-greased grill 4 to 6 inches above a solid bed of hot coals. Cook, basting with marinade and turning once, until shrimp turn pink (3 to 5 minutes). Makes about 6 servings.

Per serving: 235 calories, 26 g protein, 7 g carbohydrates, 11 g total fat, 186 mg cholesterol, 624 mg sodium

Crisp, crusty butterflied game hens join up with sweet onion
halves and tender pears and apples on a large barbecue. During
grilling, brush a fennel-seasoned marinade over all the foods.
The recipe for Game Hens or Squab with
Apple Juice is on page 163.

Poultry

CHICKEN ▪ TURKEY ▪ OTHER BIRDS

Poultry cooked over coals takes on a gloriously rich brown color, yet remains succulent and flavorful inside its crisp coat. The most popular bird for the barbecue today is chicken: widely available and versatile, it can be cooked whole, in halves or quarters, or by the piece. And it's easy to flavor in dozens of different ways, using various marinades, sauces, and simple butter bastes.

Other poultry choices for grilling—all as easy to cook as chicken —are turkey, game hens, quail, squab, and duck. All but duck fit today's emphasis on lighter, leaner entrées.

For those who enjoy experimenting, we offer an assortment of marinades and sauces on page 135; you can use these to create your own recipes, following the basic grilling times and techniques on page 18.

GARLIC-ORANGE CHICKEN

Preparation time: About 15 minutes

Marinating time: 2–7 days for marinade; 8 hours or until next day for chicken

Grilling time: 40–50 minutes

You'll need to plan well ahead for this dish. The garlic-orange marinade must stand several days for the flavors to blend, and the chicken marinates overnight in the refrigerator before grilling.

> 3 large cloves garlic, minced or pressed
> ½ cup olive oil or salad oil
> 1½ teaspoons grated orange peel
> ½ teaspoon fresh rosemary leaves or ¼ teaspoon dry rosemary
> 3 small frying chickens (2½ to 3 lbs. *each*)
> Paprika and pepper
> Orange slices and parsley sprigs

In a small jar, combine garlic, oil, orange peel, and rosemary. Stir to blend well, then cover and let stand at room temperature for at least 2 days or up to 1 week.

Remove chicken necks and giblets; reserve for other uses, if desired. Discard lumps of fat. Split each chicken in half; rinse chicken halves and pat dry. Brush chicken all over with garlic oil and arrange in a large baking pan. Cover and refrigerate for at least 8 hours or until next day.

Sprinkle chicken lightly with paprika and pepper. Place chicken, skin side up, on a lightly greased grill 4 to 6 inches above a solid bed of medium coals. Cook, turning as needed, until meat near thighbone is no longer pink; cut to test (40 to 50 minutes). Arrange chicken on a platter; garnish with orange slices and parsley. Makes 6 servings.

Per serving: 678 calories, 68 g protein, .31 g carbohydrates, 43 g total fat, 220 mg cholesterol, 205 mg sodium

CHILI-BASTED CHICKEN WITH PINEAPPLE SALSA

Preparation time: About 30 minutes

Grilling time: 40–50 minutes

Chili-lovers will enjoy this chicken. There's chili powder and cayenne pepper in the baste; liquid hot pepper seasoning heats up the fresh pineapple salsa served alongside the meat.

> 2 frying chickens (about 3½ lbs. *each*)
> 1 teaspoon *each* chili powder and paprika
> ¼ teaspoon ground red pepper (cayenne)
> 2 tablespoons salad oil
> 2 teaspoons Dijon mustard
> Pineapple Salsa (recipe follows)

Remove chicken necks and giblets; reserve for other uses, if desired. Discard lumps of fat. With poultry shears or a knife, cut through each chicken along both sides of backbone. Discard backbones. Place each chicken, skin side up, on a flat surface and press firmly, cracking breastbone slightly, until bird lies reasonably flat. Rinse and pat dry.

In a small bowl, smoothly blend chili powder, paprika, red pepper, oil, and mustard. Brush evenly over chicken skin.

Place chickens, skin side up, on a lightly greased grill 4 to 6 inches above a solid bed of medium coals. Cover barbecue and adjust dampers (or cover with a tent of heavy-duty foil). Cook until meat near thighbone is no longer pink; cut to test (40 to 50 minutes).

Meanwhile, prepare Pineapple Salsa. To serve, cut each chicken into quarters; offer salsa on the side. Makes 8 servings.

Per serving: 435 calories, 48 g protein, .24 g carbohydrates, 26 g total fat, 154 mg cholesterol, 164 mg sodium

Pineapple Salsa. Cut top from 1 small **pineapple** (about 3 lbs.). With a grapefruit knife, cut fruit from shell in chunks. Reserve shell and top. Coarsely chop pineapple and place in a colander to drain; save juice to drink. In a bowl, stir together drained pineapple; 1 medium-size mild **red onion** (minced); ¾ cup finely chopped **fresh cilantro (coriander);** 1 tablespoon **white wine vinegar;** and ½ teaspoon **liquid hot pepper seasoning.** Spoon salsa into pineapple shell; present top alongside. Makes about 3½ cups.

Per ¼ cup: 27 calories, .27 g protein, 7 g carbohydrates, .22 g total fat, 0 mg cholesterol, 5.5 mg sodium

MARINADES, SAUCES &

BUTTERS FOR CHICKEN

Adaptable chicken takes on a whole new character when it's marinated before cooking or brushed with a seasoned butter or sauce as it sizzles on the grill. Mild and mellow in flavor, this barbecue favorite takes readily to a wide range of marinades and sauces, from herb-seasoned and wine-based mixtures to soy-flavored or sweet fruit glazes.

You'll find basic grilling times and techniques for chicken on page 18.

MARINADES

The basic white wine marinade below is great for chicken or turkey; you might also try our Dijon Marinade and Teriyaki Marinade (both on page 27) for sliced turkey breast or chicken pieces.

To marinate poultry, place it in a close-fitting dish, pan, or bowl; or use a heavy-duty plastic bag. Pour in the marinade and turn the meat (or rotate the bag) to coat evenly. For maximum flavor, let marinate for at least 4 hours—or better yet, until the next day.

Basic Wine Marinade. In a blender or food processor, combine 2 large **onions** (coarsely chopped); 3 cloves **garlic;** 1 teaspoon **black pepper;** ⅛ teaspoon **ground red pepper** (cayenne); ½ cup **white wine vinegar;** 1 cup **dry white wine;** ¼ cup **salad oil;** 1½ teaspoons **thyme leaves;** ½ teaspoon grated **lemon peel;** 2 tablespoons **lemon juice;** and 1 teaspoon **honey.** Whirl until smooth. Makes about 3½ cups.

BUTTERS & BASTES

Fragrant herb butters are marvelous bastes for grilled chicken. Try easy Five-Herb Butter, or use the Basil-Garlic Butter on page 117. Brush the Sherry Butter over barbecued whole turkey; you'll find it adds a delightful spark to gravy made from the drippings.

To give the flavors time to blend, prepare any of these butters at least an hour in advance.

Five-herb Butter. Melt 6 tablespoons butter or margarine in a small pan over medium heat. Remove from heat and stir in ¾ teaspoon **pepper;** 1 clove **garlic** (minced or pressed); and ½ teaspoon *each* **dry basil, thyme leaves, rubbed sage, oregano leaves,** and **marjoram leaves.** Makes about 6 tablespoons.

Sherry Butter. Melt ¼ cup butter or margarine in a small pan over medium heat. Remove from heat; stir in ½ cup **dry sherry** and ½ teaspoon *each* **dry rosemary, marjoram leaves,** and **rubbed sage.** Makes about ¾ cup.

SAUCES & SALSAS

Brushed over the meat during the last 10 minutes or so of cooking, fruit glazes and other sweet sauces really enhance the smoky flavor of grilled chicken. Here, we offer a simple sherry-hoisin mixture and a fresh apricot sauce accented with orange and red pepper.

Tart, tangy Mediterranean Olive Salsa is a perfect accompaniment for plain barbecued chicken (try brushing the skin with olive oil before you set the meat on the grill).

Ginger-Hoisin Sauce. In a bowl, stir together ⅔ cup **hoisin sauce,** ⅓ cup **dry sherry** or water, 2 tablespoons finely chopped **fresh ginger,** 4 large cloves **garlic** (minced or pressed), and 1 tablespoon **sesame oil.** Makes about 1 cup.

Apricot Glaze. In a 3- to 4-quart pan, combine 2 cups diced **fresh apricots;** ¼ cup firmly packed **brown sugar;** 1 tablespoon grated **orange peel;** ¼ cup **orange juice;** 3 tablespoons minced **candied or crystallized ginger;** 3 tablespoons **dry white wine;** and about ¼ teaspoon **ground red pepper** (cayenne). Cook over medium-high heat, stirring often, until bubbly; then reduce heat and boil gently, uncovered, until thickened (15 to 20 minutes). Stir often to prevent sticking. Makes about 2½ cups.

Mediterranean Olive Salsa. In a bowl, stir together ¼ cup **lime juice;** ¼ cup minced **shallots** or minced green onions (including tops); 3 tablespoons **olive oil** or salad oil; 1 tablespoon minced **fresh tarragon** or 1½ teaspoons dry tarragon; ½ teaspoon **Dijon mustard;** 8 **canned anchovy fillets** (drained and minced); 1 medium-size **red, yellow, or green bell pepper** (seeded and diced); and 1 can (6 oz.) **pitted ripe olives** (drained and coarsely chopped).

If made ahead, cover and refrigerate for up to 2 days. Serve at room temperature. Makes 2½ cups.

(Pictured on facing page)

CHILI-GLAZED CHICKEN WITH PEAS

Preparation time: 10–15 minutes

Grilling time: 35–45 minutes

Lime, garlic, and chili powder make a tangy baste for chicken. Accompany the meat with peas in the pod, steamed in a heavy pan set on the barbecue (or use frozen peas, cooked on the range).

    3- to 3½-pound frying chicken, cut up
⅓ **cup butter or margarine**
2 **cloves garlic, minced or pressed**
1 **teaspoon chili powder**
¼ **teaspoon *each* ground cumin and grated lime peel**
2 **tablespoons lime juice**
2 **pounds peas in the pod**
2 **tablespoons water**

Rinse chicken and pat dry. Melt butter in a small pan over medium heat; remove from heat and stir in garlic, chili powder, cumin, lime peel, and lime juice. Generously brush over chicken.

Arrange chicken, except breast pieces, skin side up on a lightly greased grill 4 to 6 inches above a solid bed of medium coals. Cook for 15 minutes, turning and basting frequently with butter mixture. Place breast pieces on grill. Continue to cook, turning and basting often, until meat near bone is no longer pink; cut to test (20 to 30 more minutes).

Meanwhile, rinse peas; then place in a cast-iron frying pan or Dutch oven and add water. Cover with lid or foil; place on grill next to chicken during last 15 minutes of cooking, stirring peas every 5 minutes. Let guests shell their own peas to eat alongside chicken. Makes about 4 servings.

Per serving: 501 calories, 46 g protein, 13 g carbohydrates, 29 g total fat, 153 mg cholesterol, 211 mg sodium

HERB-MUSTARD CHICKEN

Preparation time: About 10 minutes

Marinating time: 4 hours or until next day

Grilling time: 35–45 minutes

A basic oil and vinegar marinade gains a zesty new dimension from spicy brown mustard. If you like mustard, you might enjoy trying other varieties in this recipe—green peppercorn or German coarse-grained mustard, for example.

    3- to 3½-pound frying chicken, cut up
½ **cup dry white wine**
⅔ **cup salad oil**
6 **tablespoons white wine vinegar**
2 **tablespoons finely chopped onion**
1 **teaspoon Italian herb seasoning or thyme leaves**
2 **cloves garlic, minced or pressed**
½ **teaspoon pepper**
¼ **cup spicy brown mustard**

Rinse chicken and pat dry. In a large bowl, stir together wine, oil, vinegar, onion, herb seasoning, garlic, pepper, and mustard. Add chicken and turn to coat. Cover and refrigerate for at least 4 hours or until next day, turning occasionally.

Lift chicken from marinade and drain briefly (reserve marinade). Place chicken, except breast pieces, skin side up on a lightly greased grill 4 to 6 inches above a solid bed of medium coals. Cook, turning and basting frequently with marinade, for 15 minutes. Place breast pieces on grill and continue to cook, turning and basting often, until meat near bone is no longer pink; cut to test (20 to 30 more minutes). Makes about 4 servings.

Per serving: 530 calories, 41 g protein, 2 g carbohydrates, 39 g total fat, 132 mg cholesterol, 204 mg sodium

A finger-food feast from the barbecue: Chili-glazed Chicken with Peas (facing page). You cook fresh peas in the pod right on the grill, then let guests shell them to eat alongside the spicy butter-basted chicken.

137

INDONESIAN CHICKEN

Preparation time: 15–20 minutes

Marinating time: 8 hours or until next day

Grilling time: 35–45 minutes

We've adapted this Indonesian recipe to suit Western tastes, using ingredients that are readily available in any supermarket.

> 1 clove garlic, quartered
> 1 small onion, quartered
> 2 tablespoons water
> 2 tablespoons salad oil
> ½ teaspoon crushed red pepper
> 6 tablespoons soy sauce
> 2 tablespoons *each* sugar and lemon juice
> ¼ teaspoon black pepper
> 3½-pound frying chicken, cut up

In a blender or food processor, whirl garlic, onion, and water until onion is finely minced. Heat oil in a wide frying pan over medium-high heat; add onion mixture and red pepper. Cook, stirring often, for 10 minutes. Remove from heat; stir in soy, sugar, lemon juice, and black pepper. Let cool.

Rinse chicken and pat dry. Place chicken in a large bowl and add soy mixture; turn chicken to coat. Cover and refrigerate for at least 8 hours or until next day.

Lift chicken from marinade and drain briefly (reserve marinade). Arrange chicken, except breast pieces, skin side up on a lightly greased grill 4 to 6 inches above a solid bed of medium coals. Cook for 15 minutes, turning and basting frequently with marinade. Place breast pieces on grill. Continue to cook, turning and basting often, until meat near bone is no longer pink; cut to test (20 to 30 more minutes). Makes about 4 servings.

Per serving: 471 calories, 48 g protein, 5 g carbohydrates, 27 g total fat, 154 mg cholesterol, 916 mg sodium

PEACH-GLAZED CHICKEN

Preparation time: 30–40 minutes

Grilling time: 1½–1¾ hours

Diced fresh peaches flavored with curry, ginger, and orange make a sweet and unusual glaze for charcoal-roasted chicken.

> 5- to 6-pound roasting chicken
> ½ teaspoon marjoram leaves
> ¼ teaspoon pepper
> 3 large ripe peaches, peeled, pitted, and diced
> ¼ cup *each* firmly packed brown sugar and orange juice
> 1 tablespoon grated orange peel
> 2 tablespoons minced candied or crystallized ginger
> 1 green onion (including top), chopped
> 3 tablespoons dry white wine
> ¾ teaspoon curry powder

Remove chicken neck and giblets; reserve for other uses, if desired. Discard lumps of fat. Rinse chicken inside and out; pat dry. Sprinkle both cavities with marjoram and pepper. Secure skin over cavities with small metal skewers; bend wings akimbo.

Barbecue chicken by indirect heat (see page 10), placing chicken, breast down, on a lightly greased grill directly above drip pan. Cover barbecue and adjust dampers as necessary to maintain an even heat. Cook for 1 hour.

Meanwhile, in a 3- to 4-quart pan, combine peaches, sugar, orange juice, orange peel, ginger, onion, wine, and curry powder. Cook over medium-high heat until bubbly; then reduce heat and boil gently, uncovered, until thickened (15 to 20 minutes). Stir often to prevent sticking.

Turn chicken over and brush generously with peach mixture. Continue to cook until a meat thermometer inserted in thickest part of thigh (not touching bone) registers 185°F or until meat near thighbone is no longer pink; cut to test (30 to 45 more minutes). Remove chicken from barbecue and transfer to a platter. Offer remaining peach mixture to spoon over individual portions. Makes 6 or 7 servings.

Per serving: 435 calories, 41 g protein, 16 g carbohydrates, 22 g total fat, 127 mg cholesterol, 126 mg sodium

 MEDITERRANEAN FRUITED CHICKEN

Preparation time: About 20 minutes

Marinating time: 2 hours

Grilling time: 1½–1¾ hours

This lemony Greek-style chicken is served with a garland of orange and avocado slices. For best flavor, be sure to use fresh lemon juice in the marinade.

    5- to 6-pound roasting chicken
    Lemon-Herb Marinade (recipe follows)
1 **lemon, cut into wedges**
1 **small onion, cut into quarters**
2 **large oranges**
1 **avocado**
1 **tablespoon lemon juice**

Remove chicken neck and giblets; reserve for other uses, if desired. Discard lumps of fat. Rinse chicken inside and out; pat dry. Prepare Lemon-Herb Marinade. Place chicken in bowl with marinade and turn to coat; then cover and refrigerate for 2 hours, turning occasionally.

    Lift chicken from marinade and drain briefly (reserve marinade). Place lemon wedges and onion quarters in body cavity. Secure skin over cavities with small metal skewers; bend wings akimbo.

    Barbecue chicken by indirect heat (see page 10), placing chicken, breast down, on a lightly greased grill directly above drip pan. Cover barbecue and adjust dampers as necessary to maintain an even heat. Cook for 1 hour; then turn chicken over and continue to cook, basting several times with marinade, until a meat thermometer inserted in thickest part of thigh (not touching bone) registers 185°F or until meat near thighbone is no longer pink; cut to test (30 to 45 more minutes).

    Remove chicken from barbecue; discard lemon and onion, then transfer chicken to a platter. Peel and thinly slice oranges. Pit, peel, and slice avocado; sprinkle with lemon juice. Garnish chicken with oranges and avocado. Makes 6 or 7 servings.

Lemon-Herb Marinade. In a large bowl, mix ⅓ cup *each* **fresh lemon juice, dry white wine,** and **olive oil;** 1 teaspoon **oregano leaves;** ½ teaspoon *each* **dry tarragon, dry rosemary,** and **pepper;** and 3 cloves **garlic** (minced or pressed).

Per serving: 498 calories, 41 g protein, 10 g carbohydrates, 32 g total fat, 127 mg cholesterol, 282 mg sodium

ONION-STUFFED CHICKEN

Preparation time: About 15 minutes

Grilling time: 1–1¼ hours

Herb-seasoned tiny onions fill this bird, flavoring the meat as it cooks.

    3½- to 4-pound frying chicken
1 **clove garlic, cut in half**
1 **can (about 1 lb.) small whole onions, drained**
2 **bay leaves**
¼ **cup butter or margarine, melted**
½ **teaspoon pepper**
¼ **teaspoon *each* thyme, oregano, and marjoram leaves**
¼ **teaspoon *each* dry basil and rubbed sage**
2 **tablespoons dry sherry**

Remove chicken neck and giblets; reserve for other uses, if desired. Discard lumps of fat. Rinse chicken inside and out; pat dry. Rub cut sides of garlic over chicken skin, then put garlic in body cavity with onions and bay leaves.

    Combine butter, pepper, thyme, oregano, marjoram, basil, sage, and sherry. Spoon 1 tablespoon of the mixture into body cavity; reserve remainder for basting. Secure skin over both cavities with small metal skewers; bend wings akimbo. Brush chicken all over with butter mixture.

    Barbecue chicken by indirect heat (see page 10), placing chicken, breast down, on a lightly greased grill directly above drip pan. Cover barbecue and adjust dampers as necessary to maintain an even heat. Cook for 30 minutes. Baste chicken with butter mixture; then turn over and continue to cook, basting occasionally, until a meat thermometer inserted in thickest part of thigh (not touching bone) registers 185°F or until meat near thighbone is no longer pink; cut to test (30 to 45 more minutes). Remove chicken from barbecue. Spoon stuffing into a serving bowl; offer with chicken. Makes 4 or 5 servings.

Per serving: 407 calories, 39 g protein, 5 g carbohydrates, 25 g total fat, 139 mg cholesterol, 510 mg sodium

Dotted with peas, diced tomatoes, and chunks of sausage,
Chorizo Rice perfectly complements savory grilled chicken
quarters. Serve Spanish-style Chicken & Rice (facing page) with
marinated tiny artichokes and cherry tomatoes, if you like.

CILANTRO & SAKE ROAST CHICKEN

Preparation time: 10–15 minutes

Marinating time: 1 hour

Grilling time: 1–1¼ hours

Here's an especially easy way to add extra flavor and aroma to a grilled whole chicken—just fill the bird with fresh herbs, celery leaves, and a generous splash of sake.

    3½- to 4-pound frying chicken
    Pepper
  1 **cup** *each* **chopped celery leaves and chopped fresh cilantro (coriander)**
  8 **fresh rosemary sprigs,** *each* **about 2 inches long, or ¾ teaspoon dry rosemary**
  ½ **cup sake**

Remove chicken neck and giblets; reserve for other uses, if desired. Discard lumps of fat. Rinse chicken inside and out; pat dry. Sprinkle both cavities with pepper.

In a bowl, combine celery leaves, cilantro, rosemary, and ¼ cup of the sake. Stuff mixture into body cavity of chicken; then secure skin over both cavities with small metal skewers. Bend wings akimbo. Cover and refrigerate for 1 hour.

Barbecue chicken by indirect heat (see page 10), placing chicken, breast down, on a lightly greased grill directly above drip pan. Cover barbecue and adjust dampers as necessary to maintain an even heat. Cook for 30 minutes; then turn chicken over. Continue to cook, brushing several times with remaining ¼ cup sake, until a meat thermometer inserted in thickest part of thigh (not touching bone) registers 185°F or until meat near thighbone is no longer pink; cut to test (30 to 45 more minutes). Remove chicken from barbecue; discard stuffing, then transfer chicken to a platter. Pass pan drippings to spoon over individual portions. Makes 4 or 5 servings.

Per serving: 341 calories, 38 g protein, 1.5 g carbohydrates, 19 g total fat, 123 mg cholesterol, 116 mg sodium

(Pictured on facing page)
SPANISH-STYLE CHICKEN & RICE

Preparation time: About 35 minutes

Grilling time: 40–50 minutes

You might call this a barbecue adaptation of Spain's famous *arroz con pollo* ("rice with chicken"). But in the classic dish, the rice is seasoned with saffron; here, it gets a spicy flavor from chorizo sausage.

    3- to 3½-pound frying chicken, quartered
  ½ **cup (¼ lb.) butter or margarine, melted**
  1 **clove garlic, minced or pressed**
  ¾ **teaspoon savory leaves**
  ½ **teaspoon paprika**
  ¼ **teaspoon** *each* **ground cinnamon and dry tarragon**
    Chorizo Rice (recipe follows)

Rinse chicken and pat dry. In a bowl, combine butter, garlic, savory, paprika, cinnamon, and tarragon. Turn chicken in butter mixture to coat, then lift out and drain briefly (reserve butter mixture). Place chicken, skin side up, on a lightly greased grill 4 to 6 inches above a solid bed of medium coals. Cook, turning and basting frequently with butter mixture, until meat near thighbone is no longer pink; cut to test (40 to 50 minutes).

Meanwhile, prepare Chorizo Rice, using 1 to 2 tablespoons of the butter mixture. Serve each chicken quarter over rice. Makes 4 servings.

Chorizo Rice. Cut 2 **chorizo sausages** (2½ to 3 oz. *each*) into ½-inch slices. Cook chorizo in a wide frying pan over medium heat until browned on all sides; pour off and discard all but 2 tablespoons fat. Add 2 medium-size **onions** (finely chopped); cook, stirring occasionally, until soft. Stir in 3 cups **cooked rice;** 1 cup **frozen peas** (thawed); and 1 **tomato** (peeled and coarsely chopped). Reduce heat to low. Cover and cook, stirring once or twice, until hot throughout (about 10 minutes); then blend in 1 to 2 tablespoons of the **butter mixture.**

Per serving: 869 calories, 55 g protein, 47 g carbohydrates, 50 g total fat, 174 mg cholesterol, 326 mg sodium

CHICKEN WITH BRANDY BASTE

Preparation time: About 20 minutes

Grilling time: 40–50 minutes

Chicken and fruit are always good together. Here, apricots and dark sweet cherries join juicy chicken quarters brushed with a buttery brandy baste. (You can use fresh or canned fruit, depending on availability.)

2 **frying chickens (3 to 3½ lbs. *each*), quartered**
   Pepper
½ **cup (¼ lb.) butter or margarine, melted**
¼ **cup *each* firmly packed brown sugar, lemon**
   juice, and brandy
6 **fresh apricots, halved and pitted**
   (or 12 canned apricot halves, drained)
1 **cup pitted fresh dark sweet cherries (or**
   canned pitted dark sweet cherries, drained)

Rinse chicken and pat dry. Sprinkle with pepper. In a bowl, combine butter, sugar, lemon juice, and brandy; turn chicken in butter mixture to coat, then lift out and drain briefly (reserve butter mixture).

Place chicken, skin side up, on a lightly greased grill 4 to 6 inches above a solid bed of medium coals. Cover barbecue and adjust dampers (or cover with a tent of heavy-duty foil). Cook, turning and basting occasionally with butter mixture, until meat near thighbone is no longer pink; cut to test (40 to 50 minutes).

Meanwhile, arrange apricots (cut side up) and cherries in 2 separate shallow metal baking pans. Brush fruit with butter mixture, then heat on grill beside chicken for last 5 to 10 minutes of cooking.

To serve, place chicken on a platter and surround with apricots; pour cherries over top. Makes 8 servings.

Per serving: 449 calories, 42 g protein, 10 g carbohydrates, 26 g total fat, 147 mg cholesterol, 184 mg sodium

ROSEMARY CHICKEN QUARTERS

Preparation time: About 10 minutes

Marinating time: 3 hours or until next day

Grilling time: 40–50 minutes

For best flavor, start this chicken marinating at least 3 hours before you barbecue.

       3- to 3½-pound frying chicken, quartered
½ **cup olive oil or salad oil**
2 **teaspoons dry rosemary**
1 **teaspoon finely chopped parsley**
2 **cloves garlic, minced or pressed**
2 **tablespoons lemon juice**
⅛ **teaspoon pepper**

Rinse chicken and pat dry. In a large bowl, combine oil, rosemary, parsley, garlic, lemon juice, and pepper. Turn chicken in marinade to coat. Cover and refrigerate for at least 3 hours or until next day, turning occasionally.

Lift chicken from marinade and drain briefly (reserve marinade). Place chicken, skin side up, on a lightly greased grill 4 to 6 inches above a solid bed of medium coals. Cook, turning and basting frequently with marinade, until meat near thighbone is no longer pink; cut to test (40 to 50 minutes). Makes 4 servings.

Per serving: 481 calories, 41 g protein, .68 g carbohydrates, 34 g total fat, 132 mg cholesterol, 124 mg sodium

⬤ GINGER CHICKEN QUARTERS

Preparation time: 10–15 minutes

Marinating time: 4 hours or until next day

Grilling time: 40–50 minutes

With the addition of toasted sesame seeds, a soy-ginger baste makes a flavorful sauce for grilled chicken quarters.

         3- to 3½-pound frying chicken, quartered
 ⅓ **cup soy sauce**
 1 **cup water**
 1 **clove garlic, minced or pressed**
 1 **tablespoon sugar**
 2 **tablespoons dry sherry or lemon juice**
 3 **tablespoons grated fresh ginger or
     1 teaspoon ground ginger**
 ¼ **cup sesame seeds**
 2 **teaspoons *each* cornstarch and water
     Hot cooked rice**

Rinse chicken and pat dry. In a large bowl, stir together soy, the 1 cup water, garlic, sugar, sherry, and ginger. Add chicken and turn to coat. Cover and refrigerate for at least 4 hours or until next day, turning occasionally.

Lift chicken from marinade and drain briefly. Reserve ⅓ cup of the marinade for basting; set remaining marinade aside for sauce. Place chicken, skin side up, on a lightly greased grill 4 to 6 inches above a solid bed of medium coals. Cook, turning and basting frequently with the ⅓ cup reserved marinade, until meat near thighbone is no longer pink; cut to test (40 to 50 minutes).

When chicken is almost done, toast sesame seeds in a wide frying pan over medium heat until golden (about 3 minutes), shaking pan often. Pour remaining marinade into pan. Blend cornstarch and the 2 teaspoons water; stir into pan. Cook, stirring, until sauce is thickened. Spoon sauce over chicken and rice. Makes 4 servings.

Per serving: 447 calories, 44 g protein, 10 g carbohydrates, 25 g total fat, 132 mg cholesterol, 1483 mg sodium

⬤ SAVORY HERB CHICKEN

Preparation time: About 15 minutes

Marinating time: 1 hour or until next day

Grilling time: 40–50 minutes

Sherry, garlic, and four kinds of herbs punctuate the marinade for these simple grilled chicken quarters.

 2 **frying chickens (3 to 3½ lbs. *each*), quartered**
 1 **cup dry sherry**
 ½ **cup salad oil**
 1 **large onion, finely chopped**
 1 **tablespoon Worcestershire**
 1 **teaspoon *each* garlic powder, thyme leaves,
     oregano leaves, marjoram leaves, dry
     rosemary, soy sauce, and lemon juice**

Rinse chicken and pat dry. In a large bowl, combine sherry, oil, onion, Worcestershire, garlic powder, thyme, oregano, marjoram, rosemary, soy, and lemon juice. Turn chicken in marinade to coat; then cover and refrigerate for at least 1 hour or until next day, turning occasionally.

Lift chicken from marinade and drain briefly (reserve marinade). Place chicken, skin side up, on a lightly greased grill 4 to 6 inches above a solid bed of medium coals. Cook, turning and basting frequently with marinade, until meat near thighbone is no longer pink; cut to test (40 to 50 minutes). Makes 8 servings.

Per serving: 432 calories, 41 g protein, 3 g carbohydrates, 27 g total fat, 132 mg cholesterol, 156 mg sodium

(from facing page)

...KEN WINGS WITH GRILLED POTATOES

...time: 10–15 minutes

Marinating time: 2 hours

Grilling time: About 30 minutes

If you're looking for a good picnic entrée, consider these grilled marinated chicken wings and garlicky potato slices. For easy turning, arrange the wings in a hinged barbecue basket before placing them on the grill.

- 4 **pounds (about 20) chicken wings**
- ½ **cup soy sauce**
- 1 **clove garlic, minced or pressed**
- 1 **teaspoon ground ginger**
- 2 **tablespoons** *each* **firmly packed brown sugar, lemon juice, and salad oil**
- 1 **tablespoon instant minced onion**
- ¼ **teaspoon pepper**
- 4 **large russet potatoes**
  Melted butter or margarine
  Garlic salt

Rinse chicken wings and pat dry. Bend wings akimbo. In a large bowl, stir together soy, garlic, ginger, sugar, lemon juice, oil, onion, and pepper. Stir in wings; cover and refrigerate for 2 hours, stirring several times.

Scrub potatoes, but do not peel. Cut lengthwise into ¼-inch slices; brush generously with butter and sprinkle with garlic salt.

Lift chicken from marinade and drain briefly (discard marinade). Place chicken and potato slices on a lightly greased grill 4 to 6 inches above a solid bed of medium coals. Cook, turning chicken and potatoes occasionally, until potatoes are soft when pierced and meat near bone is no longer pink; cut to test (about 30 minutes). Makes about 4 servings.

Per serving: 737 calories, 51 g protein, 47 g carbohydrates, 37 g total fat, 144 mg cholesterol, 1189 mg sodium

⬤ GARLIC-BASTED CHICKEN

Preparation time: About 15 minutes

Grilling time: 20–45 minutes, depending on chicken parts

Many people insist that garlic is "good for what ails you." We know it's good for flavoring chicken, especially when combined with the subtle hop overtones from beer.

- 6 **whole chicken legs, thighs attached (about 3 lbs.** *total***); or 3 whole chicken breasts (about 1 lb.** *each***), split**
- ½ **cup (¼ lb.) butter or margarine**
- 4 **cloves garlic, minced or pressed**
- ¼ **cup finely chopped onion**
- 1 **cup beer**
- 1 **tablespoon finely chopped parsley**
- ½ **teaspoon coarsely ground pepper**

Rinse chicken and pat dry. Melt butter in a small pan over medium heat; add garlic and onion and cook, stirring occasionally, until onion is soft. Add beer and bring to a boil, stirring. Remove from heat. Stir in parsley and pepper; pour into a large bowl. Turn chicken in butter mixture to coat; lift out and drain briefly (reserve butter mixture).

Place chicken, skin side up, on a lightly greased grill 4 to 6 inches above a solid bed of medium coals. Cook, turning and basting frequently with butter mixture, until meat near bone is no longer pink; cut to test (35 to 45 minutes for legs, 20 to 25 minutes for breasts). Makes 6 servings.

Per serving: 334 calories, 29 g protein, 1.4 g carbohydrates, 23 g total fat, 124 mg cholesterol, 177 mg sodium

*Soy-marinated chicken wings and buttery potato slices grill
together for a satisfying entrée (facing page). For a colorful
accompaniment, set juicy tomato halves on the barbecue for the
last 10 minutes or so.*

⬤ TANDOORI CHICKEN

Preparation time: About 20 minutes

Grilling time: 35–45 minutes

A paste of fresh ginger, garlic, and spices tucked under the skin of whole chicken legs gives the meat a pleasant bite. Temper the heat with spoonfuls of cold yogurt.

- **4 whole chicken legs, thighs attached (2 to 2½ lbs.** *total***)**
- **1 teaspoon** *each* **grated fresh ginger and ground allspice**
- **¼ to ½ teaspoon crushed red pepper**
- **2 cloves garlic, minced or pressed**
- **1 tablespoon lemon juice**
   Plain yogurt

Rinse chicken and pat dry. In a bowl, mash together ginger, allspice, red pepper, garlic, and lemon juice to make a paste. Then lift skin of each chicken leg; spread 1 teaspoon paste over flesh of thigh and top of drumstick. Brush any remaining paste evenly over skin.

Place chicken, skin side up, on a lightly greased grill 4 to 6 inches above a solid bed of medium coals. Cook, turning frequently, until meat near thighbone is no longer pink; cut to test (35 to 45 minutes). Pass cold yogurt to spoon over chicken. Makes 4 servings.

Per serving: 265 calories, 29 g protein, 1 g carbohydrates, 15 g total fat, 103 mg cholesterol, 99 mg sodium

⬤ CHICKEN WITH BAY, SQUASH & TOMATOES

Preparation time: About 20 minutes

Marinating time: 6 hours or until next day

Grilling time: 30–40 minutes

Bay leaves and a mustardy vinaigrette flavor chicken thighs, squash, and cherry tomatoes. Because the meat and vegetables have different cooking times, they're grilled on separate skewers.

- **12 chicken thighs (about 4 lbs.** *total***)**
- **3 tablespoons** *each* **Dijon mustard and white wine vinegar**
- **¾ cup olive oil or salad oil**
- **1 teaspoon coarsely ground pepper**
   About 36 fresh bay leaves (or dry bay leaves soaked in hot water for 1 hour)
- **4 medium-size crookneck squash, cut into ½-inch-thick slices**
- **3 cups cherry tomatoes, stemmed**

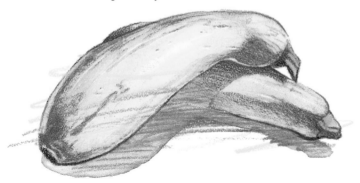

Skin chicken, if desired; then rinse and pat dry. In a large bowl, stir together mustard, vinegar, oil, pepper, and 6 of the bay leaves. Add chicken and turn to coat. Cover and refrigerate for at least 6 hours or until next day, turning occasionally.

Lift chicken from marinade and drain briefly. Add squash to marinade and stir to coat; then lift out squash and bay leaves. Discard marinade.

You will need 9 sturdy metal skewers, each about 10 inches long. On 3 of the skewers, alternate chicken with 12 of the bay leaves (including those from marinade); pierce chicken perpendicular to bone. On 3 more skewers, thread squash, piercing it through skin, and about half the remaining bay leaves. Thread tomatoes and remaining bay leaves on remaining 3 skewers.

Place chicken on a lightly greased grill 4 to 6 inches above a solid bed of medium coals. Cook, turning frequently, for 10 minutes. Place squash on grill. Continue to cook, turning squash and chicken often, until meat near thighbone is no longer pink; cut to test (20 to 30 more minutes). Set tomatoes on grill 5 minutes before chicken is done; cook, turning, until hot. Makes 6 servings.

Per serving: 556 calories, 42 g protein, 10 g carbohydrates, 39 g total fat, 146 mg cholesterol, 250 mg sodium

FIG & CHICKEN SKEWERS

Preparation time: 15–20 minutes

Marinating time: 30 minutes

Grilling time: 6–8 minutes

Ripe figs and chunks of dark-meat chicken team up for a skewer that's just right for grilling on a small portable barbecue or hibachi.

> Teriyaki Sauce (recipe follows)
> 5 chicken thighs (about 1½ lbs. *total*), skinned and boned
> 5 large ripe figs, stems trimmed
> 4 green onions
> Lemon wedges

Prepare Teriyaki Sauce; pour into a large bowl and let cool to room temperature.

Rinse chicken and pat dry. Cut each thigh into 4 equal pieces. Cut figs lengthwise into quarters. Trim root ends and any wilted tops from onions, then cut onions into 1½-inch lengths. Add figs, onions, and chicken to Teriyaki Sauce in bowl; mix gently to coat evenly. Cover and refrigerate for 30 minutes. If using bamboo skewers, soak 20 skewers in hot water to cover for 30 minutes.

Drain Teriyaki Sauce into a 1- to 1½-quart pan; bring to a boil, pour through a fine wire strainer, and set aside.

Thread one piece of chicken, one fig piece, and 3 or 4 green onion pieces on one end of each of 20 bamboo or metal skewers. Place skewers on a lightly greased grill 2 inches above a solid bed of hot coals. Cook, turning and basting with strained Teriyaki Sauce, until chicken is no longer pink in center; cut to test (6 to 8 minutes).

Serve skewers with remaining Teriyaki Sauce; offer lemon wedges to squeeze over top. Makes 3 or 4 main-dish servings or 6 to 8 appetizer servings.

Teriyaki Sauce. In a 1- to 1½-quart pan, combine ½ cup **sake** or dry sherry and ¼ cup *each* **soy sauce** and **sugar**. Bring to a boil, stirring until sugar is dissolved. Remove from heat. If made ahead, let cool; then cover and refrigerate for up to 1 week.

Per main-dish serving: 216 calories, 20 g protein, 26 g carbohydrates, 4 g total fat, 82 mg cholesterol, 622 mg sodium

GRILLED ASIAN CHICKEN

Preparation time: 10–15 minutes

Marinating time: 4 hours or until next day

Grilling time: 20–40 minutes, depending on chicken parts

A pungent blend of garlic, cilantro, and crushed peppercorns seasons this bird. You rub the mixture into the chicken, then refrigerate it for several hours to allow the flavors to penetrate the meat.

> 2 whole chicken breasts (about 1 lb. *each*), split; or 8 chicken thighs (about 2½ lbs. *total*)
> 6 cloves garlic
> ½ cup fresh cilantro (coriander) leaves
> 2 teaspoons whole black peppercorns
> 2 teaspoons soy sauce
> 1 teaspoon sugar
> 5 tablespoons salad oil
> 1 tablespoon wine vinegar

Rinse chicken, pat dry, and set aside.

In a blender or food processor, whirl garlic, cilantro, and peppercorns until finely chopped; add soy, sugar, and 4 tablespoons of the oil and whirl until a paste forms. Measure out 1½ tablespoons of the paste; cover and refrigerate. Rub remaining paste evenly all over chicken, slipping some under skin. Cover and refrigerate for at least 4 hours or until next day.

Place chicken, skin side up, on a lightly greased grill 4 to 6 inches above a solid bed of medium coals. Cook, turning often, until meat near bone is no longer pink; cut to test (20 to 25 minutes for breasts, 30 to 40 minutes for thighs). Mix reserved paste, vinegar, and remaining 1 tablespoon oil; spoon over chicken. Makes 4 servings.

Per serving: 354 calories, 37 g protein, 2.4 g carbohydrates, 21 g total fat, 103 mg cholesterol, 203 mg sodium

*Garnished with shiny lemon leaves and delicate kumquat slices,
Yakitori Chicken & Vegetables (facing page) looks elegant
enough for a party. Treat your guests to tender eggplant, meaty
shiitake mushrooms, and skewered chicken, all topped with a
sherry-soy sauce and sprinkled with toasted sesame seeds.*

⊛ CHICKEN & VEGETABLE BUNDLES

Preparation time: 30–40 minutes

Grilling time: 10–12 minutes

Tender strips of chicken or turkey are wrapped around slivers of carrot and zucchini, then skewered for easy grilling.

4 **whole chicken breasts (about 1 lb.** *each***), skinned, boned, and split; or 2 to 2½ pounds boned, skinned turkey breast, cut across the grain into ½-inch-thick slices**

3 **or 4 medium-size carrots, cut into 3-inch-long julienne strips**

1 **or 2 medium-size zucchini, cut into 3-inch-long julienne strips**

3 **tablespoons** *each* **salad oil and lemon juice**

¼ **teaspoon** *each* **salt and dry rosemary**
  Dash of pepper

Rinse poultry and pat dry. Using a flat-surfaced mallet, pound each chicken half-breast (or each turkey slice) between 2 sheets of wax paper until ¼ inch thick. Cut each half-breast in half lengthwise. For each bundle, wrap one strip of meat around 3 or 4 strips *each* of carrot and zucchini. Run 2 parallel metal skewers through each bundle (one through each end); thread 2 bundles on each pair of skewers.

In a bowl, combine oil, lemon juice, salt, rosemary, and pepper. Place skewers on a lightly greased grill 4 to 6 inches above a solid bed of medium coals. Cook, turning and brushing with oil mixture, until meat is no longer pink in center; cut to test (10 to 12 minutes). Makes 8 servings.

Per serving: 216 calories, 34 g protein, 4 g carbohydrates, 6 g total fat, 92 mg cholesterol, 125 mg sodium

⊛ *(Pictured on facing page)*
YAKITORI CHICKEN & VEGETABLES

Preparation time: 30–40 minutes

Marinating time: 1–8 hours

Grilling time: 30–35 minutes

Skewered marinated chicken breast, slim Oriental eggplants, and big shiitake mushrooms all grill together for this entrée.

2 **tablespoons sesame seeds**

3 **large whole chicken breasts (about 1½ lbs.** *each***), skinned, boned, and split**
  Sherry-Soy Marinade (recipe follows)

6 **medium-size Oriental eggplants**

15 **to 18 large fresh shiitake mushrooms or regular button mushrooms**

Toast sesame seeds in a small frying pan over medium heat until golden (about 3 minutes), shaking pan often. Set aside.

Rinse chicken and pat dry. Cut each breast half into 6 or 7 equal-size chunks, then place in a bowl. Prepare Sherry-Soy Marinade. Pour ¼ cup of the marinade over chicken in bowl and mix gently to coat (reserve remaining marinade). Cover and let stand at room temperature for 1 hour; or refrigerate for up to 8 hours. If using bamboo skewers, soak 6 skewers in hot water to cover for 30 minutes.

Lift chicken from marinade and drain briefly (discard marinade left in bowl). Thread chicken equally on 6 bamboo or metal skewers. Set aside.

Slash each eggplant lengthwise or crosswise in 4 or 5 places, making cuts ⅓ inch deep and spacing them evenly. Cut mushroom stems flush with caps.

Place eggplants on a lightly greased grill 4 to 6 inches above a solid bed of hot coals. Cook, turning often, until eggplants are slightly charred and very soft when pressed (30 to 35 minutes).

After eggplants have cooked for about 20 minutes, start cooking mushrooms and chicken. Dip mushrooms in reserved marinade, drain briefly, and set on grill. Cook for about 5 minutes; then turn over and continue to cook until softened and lightly browned (about 5 more minutes). At the same time you place mushrooms on grill, place chicken on grill and cook, turning occasionally, until meat is no longer pink in center; cut to test (10 to 12 minutes).

Arrange skewers, mushrooms, and eggplants on 1 or 2 shallow platters. Pull each eggplant apart at a slash to expose flesh. Moisten surface of chicken and vegetables with marinade and sprinkle with sesame seeds. Pass any remaining marinade at the table. Makes 6 servings.

Sherry-Soy Marinade. Stir together ⅓ cup **dry sherry**, 3 tablespoons *each* **soy sauce** and **sesame oil**, and 1½ teaspoons finely minced **fresh ginger.**

Per serving: 374 calories, 53 g protein, 15 g carbohydrates, 11 g total fat, 138 mg cholesterol, 383 mg sodium

⊛ CHICKEN & FRUIT KEBABS

Preparation time: About 45 minutes

Marinating time: 1–8 hours

Grilling time: 10–12 minutes

Juicy chunks of pineapple and papaya pair beautifully with sherry- and soy-flavored chicken. Before serving, sprinkle meat and fruit with crunchy toasted sesame seeds.

> 2 **tablespoons sesame seeds**
> 3 **large whole chicken breasts (about 1½ lbs.**
>   ***each*), skinned, boned, and split**
>   **Sherry-Soy Marinade (page 149)**
> 1 **large papaya, peeled, seeded, and cut**
>   **into 1½-inch chunks**
> 1 **small pineapple (about 3 lbs.), peeled, cored,**
>   **and cut into 1½-inch chunks**

Toast sesame seeds in a small frying pan over medium heat until golden (about 3 minutes), shaking pan often. Set aside.

Rinse chicken and pat dry. Cut each breast half into 6 or 7 equal-size chunks, then place in a bowl. Prepare Sherry-Soy Marinade. Pour ¼ cup of the marinade over chicken in bowl and mix gently to coat (reserve remaining marinade). Cover and let stand at room temperature for 1 hour; or refrigerate for up to 8 hours.

If using bamboo skewers, soak 12 skewers in hot water to cover for 30 minutes. Lift chicken from marinade and drain briefly (discard marinade left in bowl). Thread chicken equally on 6 bamboo or metal skewers. Thread fruit on 6 more skewers, alternating papaya and pineapple on each skewer.

Place chicken on a lightly greased grill 4 to 6 inches above a solid bed of hot coals. Cook, turning occasionally, until meat is no longer pink in center; cut to test (10 to 12 minutes).

Meanwhile, brush fruit with a little of the reserved marinade. Place on grill next to chicken and cook, turning occasionally, just until heated through and lightly browned (about 3 minutes).

Sprinkle chicken and fruit with some of the marinade, then with sesame seeds. Accompany with any remaining marinade. Makes 6 servings.

Per serving: 403 calories, 52 g protein, 23 g carbohydrates, 11 g total fat, 138 mg cholesterol, 381 mg sodium

⊛ CURRIED CHICKEN TORTILLA SANDWICHES

Preparation time: About 30 minutes

Marinating time: 4 hours or until next day

Grilling time: 10–12 minutes

In traditional Indian fashion, chicken is marinated in yogurt and curry spices, then grilled and served with cucumbers and a minty yogurt sauce. In place of the usual *chapaties* (Indian flat bread), we use flour tortillas for wrappers.

> 2 **whole chicken breasts (about 1 lb. *each*),**
>   **skinned, boned, and split**
> 2 **cups plain yogurt**
> 1½ **teaspoons curry powder**
> ½ **teaspoon *each* ground cumin, ground**
>   **coriander, and ground ginger**
>   **About ¼ teaspoon garlic salt**
> ¼ **to ½ teaspoon ground red pepper (cayenne)**
> 2 **tablespoons lemon juice**
> 8 **flour tortillas, *each* about 8 inches in diameter**
> 2 **tablespoons finely chopped fresh mint**
> 8 **small romaine lettuce leaves**
> 1 **small cucumber, cut in half lengthwise and**
>   **thinly sliced**

Rinse chicken, pat dry, and cut into 1-inch chunks. In a bowl, stir together 1 cup of the yogurt, curry powder, cumin, coriander, ginger, ¼ teaspoon of the garlic salt, red pepper, and lemon juice. Add chicken and stir to coat. Cover and refrigerate for at least 4 hours or until next day, stirring occasionally.

Lift chicken from marinade and drain briefly (discard marinade); then thread meat equally on 4 sturdy metal skewers. Sprinkle each tortilla with a few drops of water; then stack and wrap in heavy-duty foil.

Place chicken on a lightly greased grill 4 to 6 inches above a solid bed of hot coals. Place tortillas at edge of grill (not directly above coals). Cook, turning chicken and tortillas occasionally, until tortillas are warm and meat is no longer pink in center; cut to test (10 to 12 minutes). Keep warm.

In a bowl, stir together mint and remaining 1 cup yogurt. Season to taste with garlic salt. To eat, place a romaine leaf down center of a tortilla and top with chicken, cucumber, and yogurt sauce; roll up and eat out of hand. Makes 4 servings.

Per serving: 455 calories, 44 g protein, 54 g carbohydrates, 5 g total fat, 95 mg cholesterol, 654 mg sodium

RASPBERRY-GLAZED TURKEY TENDERLOINS

Preparation time: About 10 minutes

Grilling time: 10–12 minutes

Lean, succulent turkey tenderloins—also called fillets—are the strips of meat lying along either side of the breastbone. Here, a sweet-sharp raspberry glaze gives color and flavor to the mild white meat.

½ cup seedless red raspberry jam
6 tablespoons raspberry vinegar
¼ cup Dijon mustard
1 teaspoon grated orange peel
½ teaspoon dry or fresh thyme leaves
4 turkey breast tenderloins (about 1½ lbs. *total*)
Salt

In a 1- to 1½-quart pan, whisk together jam, vinegar, mustard, orange peel, and thyme. Bring to a boil over high heat; boil, stirring, until reduced by about ¼ and slightly thickened (2 to 3 minutes). Reserve about ½ cup of the glaze to serve with the grilled meat.

Rinse turkey pieces and pat dry; then coat each with some of the remaining raspberry glaze. Place turkey on a lightly greased grill 4 to 6 inches above a solid bed of medium coals. Cook, turning to brown evenly and basting frequently with glaze, until meat is no longer pink in thickest part; cut to test (10 to 12 minutes).

Transfer turkey to individual plates and let guests season to taste with salt. Pass reserved glaze to spoon over meat. Makes 4 servings.

Per serving: 294 calories, 40 g protein, 24 g carbohydrates, 3.5 g total fat, 106 mg cholesterol, 460 mg sodium

BUTTERFLIED TURKEY WITH LEEK DRESSING

Preparation time: 45–60 minutes

Grilling time: 1½–2 hours

A layer of stuffing tucked under the skin helps keep turkey breast meat extra moist. You can use 5 cups of just about any stuffing you like, but our leek dressing is an especially good choice.

7 large leeks (about 3½ lbs. *total*)
¼ cup butter or margarine
⅓ cup pine nuts or slivered almonds
2 large onions, thinly sliced
2 cloves garlic, minced or pressed
1½ teaspoons dry tarragon
1½ teaspoons grated lemon peel
2 tablespoons lemon juice
Salt
10- to 12-pound turkey, thawed if frozen

Trim ends and tops from leeks, leaving 3 inches of dark green leaves. Discard coarse outer leaves. Split leeks lengthwise; rinse well, then thinly slice crosswise (you need 9 cups). Set aside.

Melt butter in a wide frying pan over low heat. Add pine nuts and stir until golden (about 1 minute). Lift out with a slotted spoon. Add onions to pan; cook over medium heat, stirring often, until soft. Stir in leeks, garlic, and tarragon; cook, stirring occasionally, until leeks are very soft (about 10 minutes). Stir in lemon peel, lemon juice, and pine nuts. Season to taste with salt. Let cool.

Remove turkey neck and giblets; reserve for other uses, if desired. Discard large lumps of fat. With poultry shears or a knife, split turkey lengthwise along one side of backbone. Pull turkey open; place, skin side up, on a flat surface and press firmly, cracking breastbone slightly, until bird lies reasonably flat. Rinse and pat dry.

Separate skin from meat over entire breast. Starting at neck end, ease your hands gently under skin to loosen it; complete separation process from other end of breast, working carefully to avoid tearing skin. Using your hands, insert an even layer of dressing between meat and skin. Tuck excess neck skin under breastbone.

Barbecue turkey by indirect heat (see page 10), placing turkey, skin side up, on a lightly greased grill directly above drip pan. Cover barbecue and adjust dampers as necessary to maintain an even heat. Cook turkey until a meat thermometer inserted in thickest part of thigh (not touching bone) registers 185°F or until meat near thighbone is no longer pink; cut to test (1½ to 2 hours).

Transfer turkey to a platter; slice and serve. (To carve breast, first cut off wings; then cut under breast along ribs to free meat. Starting near wing joint, cut through dressing and breast meat to make ¾-inch-thick slices.) Makes 10 to 12 servings.

Per serving: 414 calories, 57 g protein, 11 g carbohydrates, 15 g total fat, 154 mg cholesterol, 190 mg sodium

BARBECUED TURKEY

Preparation time: 15–20 minutes

Grilling time: 4–4½ hours

Why not barbecue your holiday turkey this year? This big bird is sure to impress. It's filled with vegetable chunks and port wine for flavor, then cooked slowly on a covered grill.

- **20- to 22-pound turkey, thawed if frozen**
- 2 **teaspoons poultry seasoning**
- ¼ **teaspoon pepper**
- 1 **cup port**
- 1 **large onion, quartered**
- 2 **large carrots, cut into chunks**
- 2 **stalks celery, cut into chunks**
- 1 **clove garlic, quartered**
- 3 **or 4 fresh rosemary sprigs,** *each* **3 to 4 inches long**

Remove turkey neck and giblets; reserve for other uses, if desired. Discard large lumps of fat, then rinse turkey inside and out and pat dry.

Combine poultry seasoning and pepper. Sprinkle some of the mixture into neck and body cavities; rub remaining mixture over skin. Place turkey on its breast and spoon 1 to 2 tablespoons of the port into neck cavity; bring skin over opening and secure to back with a metal skewer. Turn turkey on its back and place onion, carrots, celery, and garlic in body cavity.

Barbecue turkey by indirect heat (see page 10), placing bird, breast up, on a lightly greased grill directly above drip pan. Pour about ⅓ cup of the remaining port into body cavity; cover barbecue and adjust dampers as necessary to maintain an even heat. Cook until a meat thermometer inserted in thickest part of thigh (not touching bone) registers 185°F or until meat near thighbone is no longer pink; cut to test. Total cooking time should be 4 to 4½ hours; allow about 12 minutes per pound.

Several times during cooking, place a rosemary sprig on the coals to add fragrance as it smolders. During last hour, brush turkey with port several times, using all remaining port. When turkey is done, discard stuffing. Makes 16 to 18 servings.

Per serving: 423 calories, 73 g protein, 1.4 g carbohydrates, 12 g total fat, 191 mg cholesterol, 186 mg sodium

---

(Pictured on facing page)

BARBECUED TURKEY BREAST WITH PEACHES & CHUTNEY

Preparation time: About 15 minutes

Grilling time: 50–55 minutes

Puréed chutney gives this succulent boned turkey breast its shiny, crusty coating. Briefly grill peach halves and green onions to serve alongside.

- ⅔ **cup Major Grey's chutney**
- 1 **teaspoon minced fresh ginger**
- 1 **turkey breast half (about 3 lbs.), boned and skinned**
- 3 **fresh firm-ripe peaches; or 6 canned peach halves, drained**
- 2 **tablespoons lemon juice (if using fresh peaches)**
- 6 **to 8 green onions**
  Salt

In a blender, whirl ⅓ cup of the chutney with ginger until smoothly puréed. Coarsely chop remaining ⅓ cup chutney and set aside. Rinse turkey breast and pat dry. Brush breast all over with some of the puréed chutney.

Barbecue turkey by indirect heat (see page 10), placing it on a lightly greased grill directly above drip pan. Cover barbecue and adjust dampers as necessary to maintain an even heat. Cook, brushing occasionally with puréed chutney, until a meat thermometer inserted in center of turkey registers 155°F (50 to 55 minutes).

Meanwhile, immerse fresh peaches in boiling water for about 30 seconds; lift from water and let cool for 1 minute. Peel, halve, and pit; then coat with lemon juice to prevent darkening. Cut root ends from onions, peel off outer layer, and trim tops, leaving about 4 inches of green leaves.

About 10 minutes before turkey is done, lay peach halves (cut side down) and onions on grill over coals. Cook, turning once and brushing several times with puréed chutney, until peaches are hot and onion tops are wilted (about 10 minutes).

Arrange turkey on a platter and surround with peaches and onions. Slice meat across the grain and serve with chopped chutney. Let guests season to taste with salt. Makes about 6 servings.

Per serving: 298 calories, 44 g protein, 27 g carbohydrates, 1 g total fat, 117 mg cholesterol, 136 mg sodium

Simple—and simply delicious. Barbecued Turkey Breast with Peaches & Chutney (facing page) features boneless, chutney-glazed turkey served with grilled whole green onions and peach halves.

Grilling fresh fruits or vegetables alongside your meat, fish, or poultry entrée is an easy way to add extra color, flavor, and nutrition to barbecue meals. On these two pages, we give basic directions for grilling an assortment of fresh produce.

GRILLING FRESH FRUITS

To grill fruits, simply cut as directed, brush with plain or seasoned butter or the basting sauce used on an accompanying entrée, and grill until hot and streaked with brown.

GRILLED FRUIT

1½ to 2 pounds fresh fruit of your choice, prepared as directed

½ cup (¼ lb.) butter or margarine, melted*; or basting sauce used on an accompanying entrée

*If desired, add 3 tablespoons firmly packed brown sugar to melted butter, then season with 1 teaspoon ground cinnamon or ground ginger

If using small pieces of fruit, thread on thin metal or bamboo skewers ahead of time, making sure fruit lies flat. (If using bamboo skewers, soak skewers in hot water to cover for 30 minutes before threading fruit.)

To grill, coat prepared fruits with plain or seasoned butter or basting sauce. Place fruit on a lightly greased grill 4 to 6 inches above a lightly dispersed bed of medium coals. Cook, turning frequently, until fruits are hot and streaked with brown (for grilling times, see specific fruits).

Serve fruits hot or at room temperature. Makes 6 to 8 servings.

GRILLING

FRUITS & VEGETABLES

FRUITS FOR GRILLING

Apples. *To prepare:* Core apples; peel, if desired. Then cut small apples into halves; cut larger apples crosswise into ¾-inch-thick rings. *Grilling time:* About 6 minutes for rings, 10 to 12 minutes for halves.

Apricots. *To prepare:* Cut into halves; discard pits. Thread on skewers, making sure fruit lies flat. *Grilling time:* 4 to 6 minutes.

Bananas. *To prepare:* Do not peel. Cut into halves lengthwise. *Grilling time:* 4 to 6 minutes.

Figs. *To prepare:* Cut into halves lengthwise; then thread on skewers, making sure fruit lies flat. *Grilling time:* 4 to 6 minutes.

Melons (firm-fleshed types such as cantaloupe or Persian). *To prepare:* Cut into 1- to 1½-inch-wide wedges; discard seeds. Peel, if desired. *Grilling time:* 3 to 4 minutes.

Nectarines. *To prepare:* Cut into halves lengthwise; discard pits. *Grilling time:* 6 to 8 minutes.

Oranges or tangerines. *To prepare:* Do not peel. Cut small oranges into halves crosswise; cut large ones crosswise into ¾-inch-thick slices. *Grilling time:* 4 to 5 minutes for slices; 10 to 12 minutes for halves.

Papayas. *To prepare:* Peel, if desired; then cut crosswise into ¾-inch-thick rings or cut lengthwise into quarters. Remove and discard seeds. *Grilling time:* 5 to 8 minutes.

Peaches. *To prepare:* Peel and cut into halves lengthwise; discard pits. *Grilling time:* 6 to 8 minutes.

Pears. *To prepare:* Peel, if desired. Cut small pears into halves lengthwise; remove cores. Cut large pears into ¾-inch-wide wedges and remove cores; thread on skewers, making sure fruit lies flat. *Grilling time:* About 6 minutes for wedges, 10 to 12 minutes for halves.

Pineapple. *To prepare:* Peel and core pineapple; then cut crosswise into ¾-inch-thick rings or cut lengthwise into 1-inch-wide wedges. *Grilling time:* 6 to 8 minutes.

GRILLING FRESH VEGETABLES

Before grilling, prepare vegetables as directed for each type; some require cooking or blanching ahead of time, others do not. Then brush with plain or herb-seasoned butter or oil, or the basting sauce used on an accompanying entrée. Cook on the barbecue until hot, tender, and streaked with brown.

GRILLED VEGETABLES

About 2 pounds fresh vegetables of your choice, prepared as directed

⅓ to ½ cup olive oil*, salad oil*, melted butter or margarine*, or basting sauce used on an accompanying entrée

*If desired, add 2 tablespoons chopped fresh thyme, rosemary, oregano, or tarragon (or 2 teaspoons dry herbs) to oil or melted butter or margarine

If using small vegetables or pieces, thread on thin metal or bamboo skewers ahead of time, making sure vegetables lie flat. (If using bamboo skewers, soak skewers in hot water to cover for 30 minutes before threading vegetables.)

To grill, coat prepared vegetables with plain or seasoned oil or butter or basting sauce. Place vegetables on a lightly greased grill 4 to 6 inches above a lightly dispersed bed of medium coals. Cook, turning frequently, until vegetables are streaked with brown and tender when pierced (check grilling times under specific vegetables).

Serve vegetables hot or at room temperature. Makes 6 to 8 servings.

VEGETABLES FOR GRILLING

Artichokes. *To prepare:* Trim off stem and coarse outer leaves; cut off top third. Trim thorny tips. Rinse artichokes well, then plunge into acidulated water (3 tablespoons vinegar per quart of water). When all artichokes have been prepared, drain; then cook in boiling water to cover until stem end is tender when pierced (30 to 45 minutes). Drain; cut into halves lengthwise. *Grilling time:* 5 to 8 minutes.

Bell peppers or fresh chiles. *To prepare:* Rinse and pat dry. *Grilling time:* 8 to 10 minutes.

Cabbage (red or green) or radicchio. *To prepare:* Cut cabbage into quarters lengthwise. Cut radicchio into halves. *Grilling time:* 6 to 10 minutes.

Carrots. *To prepare:* Cook whole baby carrots or small regular carrots in boiling water to cover until just tender (5 to 10 minutes). Drain. Thread baby carrots on skewers. *Grilling time:* 8 to 10 minutes.

Corn in husks. *To prepare:* Pull off dry outer husks until you reach light green inner husks; tear several outer husks into ¼-inch strips to use as ties later. Gently pull back inner husks without tearing from cobs. Remove and discard silk. Spread corn with oil, butter, or baste. Lay inner husks back in place around corn; tie with strips of husks at top to enclose. Immerse in cold water to cover for 15 to 30 minutes. Drain well. *Grilling time:* 15 to 20 minutes.

Corn out of husks. *To prepare:* Peel off and discard all husks and silk. *Grilling time:* About 8 minutes.

Eggplants. *To prepare:* Cut off stem end of Oriental or small regular eggplants. Cut Oriental eggplants into halves lengthwise; cut regular eggplants lengthwise into 1½-inch-

wide wedges. *Grilling time:* 12 to 15 minutes.

Fennel. *To prepare:* Cut off and discard woody stems. Cut vertically into 4 equal slices. *Grilling time:* About 20 minutes.

Leeks. *To prepare:* Trim root ends; trim tops, leaving 2 inches of green leaves. Split lengthwise to within ½ inch of root ends. Rinse well. *Grilling time:* 4 to 6 minutes.

Mushrooms (regular or shiitake). *To prepare:* Cut off tough stem ends. Thread smaller mushrooms on skewers. *Grilling time:* About 10 minutes.

Onions, dry (yellow, white, red). *To prepare:* Do not peel. Cut small onions into halves. Cut larger ones into quarters and thread on skewers, making sure onions lie flat. *Grilling time:* 15 to 20 minutes.

Onions, green. *To prepare:* Trim root ends and top 2 inches of green tops. *Grilling time:* 6 to 8 minutes.

Potatoes (thin-skinned or russet), sweet potatoes, or yams. *To prepare:* Cut small potatoes into halves. Cut large ones lengthwise into 1-inch-wide wedges. Cook in boiling water to cover until tender when pierced (6 to 8 minutes). *Grilling time:* 8 to 10 minutes.

Squash, summer (crookneck, pattypan, or zucchini). *To prepare:* Leave small squash (1 inch or less in diameter) whole. Cut larger squash into halves lengthwise. *Grilling time:* 10 to 15 minutes.

Tomatoes. *To prepare:* Cut tomatoes into halves. *Grilling time:* 8 to 12 minutes.

Bold stripes from the barbecue accent cantaloupe wedges and Turkey Steaks with Cashew Butter (facing page). For an autumn dinner, accompany grilled meat and melon with wild rice and fresh figs.

(Pictured on facing page)

TURKEY STEAKS WITH CASHEW BUTTER

Preparation time: About 10 minutes

Marinating time: 8 hours or until next day

Grilling time: About 8 minutes

This speedy entrée is ideal for company. It requires little preparation or cooking time, and the results are sure to win you raves.

	About 3 pounds boned turkey breast, skinned
1	**cup dry sherry**
2	**teaspoons chicken stock base**
½	**teaspoon fresh rosemary leaves or dry rosemary**
	Cashew Butter (recipe follows)
¼	**cup butter or margarine, melted**
	Fresh rosemary or parsley sprigs
	Lemon wedges

Rinse turkey and pat dry. Cut across the grain into ⅜-inch-thick slices. In a large baking dish, combine sherry, stock base, and rosemary leaves. Stir to dissolve stock base. Add turkey and turn to coat. Cover and refrigerate for at least 8 hours or until next day, turning occasionally.

Prepare Cashew Butter; keep warm. Lift turkey from marinade and drain briefly (discard marinade). Place turkey on a lightly greased grill 4 to 6 inches above a solid bed of medium coals. Cook turning and basting occasionally with plain melted butter, until meat is no longer pink in center; cut to test (about 8 minutes). Transfer turkey to a platter and garnish with rosemary sprigs and lemon wedges. Pass Cashew Butter to spoon over individual portions. Makes about 8 servings.

Per serving: 223 calories, 37 g protein, 2 g carbohydrates, 7 g total fat, 116 mg cholesterol, 262 mg sodium

Cashew Butter. In a small pan, melt ½ cup (¼ lb.) **butter** or margarine. Add 1 tablespoon **lemon juice** and ¾ cup **salted cashews.** Set at side of grill to keep warm. Makes about 1¼ cups.

Per tablespoon: 70 calories, .8 g protein, 1.7 g carbohydrates, 7 g total fat, 12 mg cholesterol, 80 mg sodium

GRILLED TURKEY CUTLETS PICCATA

Preparation time: 10–15 minutes

Marinating time: 30 minutes–2 hours

Grilling time: 3–4 minutes

Thinly sliced and quickly grilled, turkey breast gives you a lowfat but flavor-packed variation on classic veal piccata.

1½	**tablespoons capers with liquid**
¼	**cup lemon juice**
1	**tablespoon olive oil**
⅛	**teaspoon pepper**
1	**pound boned, skinned turkey breast**
	Lemon wedges
	Salt

Drain caper liquid into a shallow dish; cover drained capers and refrigerate. Stir lemon juice, oil, and pepper into caper liquid. Rinse turkey and pat dry. Cut meat across the grain into ¼-inch-thick slices, then turn each slice in lemon juice mixture to coat. Cover and refrigerate for at least 30 minutes or up to 2 hours, turning slices over once or twice.

Lift turkey slices from marinade and drain briefly (reserve marinade). Place slices on a lightly greased grill 4 to 6 inches above a solid bed of hot coals. Cook, turning once and brushing often with marinade, until meat is no longer pink in center; cut to test (3 to 4 minutes).

Transfer meat to a platter and sprinkle with drained capers; garnish with lemon wedges. Let guests season to taste with salt. Makes about 3 servings.

Per serving: 195 calories, 36 g protein, .7 g carbohydrates, 5 g total fat, 94 mg cholesterol, 159 mg sodium

BARBECUED TURKEY SALTIMBOCCA

Preparation time: 10–15 minutes

Grilling time: About 6 minutes

Fresh sage leaves, prosciutto, and Swiss cheese are layered atop turkey breast slices for a rich-tasting entrée. Like Grilled Turkey Cutlets Piccata (page 157), this is a lower-fat version of a traditional Italian veal dish.

1 turkey breast half (about 3 lbs.),
  boned and skinned
1 large clove garlic, cut in half
2 teaspoons olive oil
16 to 20 large fresh sage leaves
¼ pound thinly sliced prosciutto
4 or 5 slices (about 1 oz. *each*) Swiss cheese

Rinse turkey and pat dry. Cut meat across the grain into ½-inch-thick slices. Rub each slice all over with cut garlic, then rub with oil. Press one sage leaf onto one side of each turkey slice. Cut prosciutto and cheese into equal-size pieces; you need one prosciutto slice and one cheese slice for each turkey slice. Set aside.

Place turkey, sage side up, on a lightly greased grill 4 to 6 inches above a solid bed of hot coals. Cook for 3 minutes, then turn slices over. Quickly top each piece with a slice of prosciutto, a slice of cheese, and another sage leaf. Cover barbecue and adjust dampers (or cover with a tent of heavy-duty foil). Cook until meat is no longer pink in center; cut to test (about 3 more minutes). Using a wide metal spatula, transfer turkey to individual plates. Makes 4 or 5 servings.

Per serving: 374 calories, 62 g protein, 2 g carbohydrates, 12 g total fat, 175 mg cholesterol, 446 mg sodium

SKEWERED TURKEY

Preparation time: 15–20 minutes

Marinating time: 1 hour or until next day

Grilling time: About 15 minutes

Turkey or lamb? These skewers may have you guessing. The chunks of turkey thigh taste much like lamb when treated to an unconventional mint-lime marinade, then grilled.

1 turkey thigh (about 2 lbs.)
¼ cup *each* salad oil and dry white wine
¼ cup mint jelly, melted
¼ teaspoon grated lime peel
1 tablespoon lime juice
⅛ teaspoon pepper
  Hot cooked rice

Pull off and discard turkey skin. Rinse turkey and pat dry; then place skin side down on a flat surface and find the thick bone with your fingers. Run a

sharp knife along bone to cut meat free; lift out bone with your other hand as you cut. Discard bone. Cut meat into 1-inch chunks.

In a bowl, stir together oil, wine, jelly, lime peel, lime juice, and pepper; stir in meat. Cover and refrigerate for at least 1 hour or until next day, stirring several times.

Lift meat from marinade and drain briefly (reserve marinade). Thread meat equally on 4 metal skewers. Place skewers on a lightly greased grill 4 to 6 inches above a solid bed of medium coals. Cook, turning as needed and basting several times with marinade, until turkey is well browned on all sides and no longer pink in center; cut to test (about 15 minutes).

To serve, mound rice on a platter; arrange skewers on top. Makes 4 servings.

Per serving: 305 calories, 35 g protein, 7 g carbohydrates, 14 g total fat, 131 mg cholesterol, 142 mg sodium

STUFFED TURKEY THIGHS

Preparation time: About 30 minutes

Grilling time: 50–60 minutes

If you're craving turkey and dressing but don't want to end up with a mountain of leftovers, this is the recipe for you. Boned and stuffed, two turkey thighs yield just six servings—and take only an hour to cook.

- 2 **cups coarsely crushed packaged stuffing mix**
- ⅓ **cup finely chopped celery**
- 3 **tablespoons** *each* **chopped parsley and thinly sliced green onions (including tops)**
- ¼ **cup butter or margarine, melted**
- 1 **teaspoon chicken stock base**
- ½ **teaspoon poultry seasoning**
- ½ **cup hot water**
- 2 **turkey thighs (about 2 lbs.** *each***)**
- 1 **can (8 oz.) jellied cranberry sauce**

In a large bowl, combine stuffing mix, celery, parsley, onions, butter, stock base, poultry seasoning, and hot water. Set aside.

Rinse turkey and pat dry. Place each thigh skin side down on a flat surface and find the thick bone with your fingers. Run a sharp knife along bone to cut meat free; lift out bone with your other hand as you cut. Discard bones. Place 3 to 4 tablespoons stuffing in center of each thigh where bone was removed. Bring meat up over stuffing and secure skin with metal skewers along 2 sides. If possible, tuck more stuffing into open end, then secure skin across it with another skewer to completely enclose meat and stuffing in a neat bundle. Wrap remaining stuffing in a double thickness of heavy-duty foil.

Barbecue turkey by indirect heat (see page 10), placing turkey and foil packet on a lightly greased grill directly above drip pan. Cover barbecue and adjust dampers as necessary to maintain an even heat. Cook until a meat thermometer inserted into center of thigh registers 185°F or until meat in thickest part is no longer pink; cut to test (50 to 60 minutes).

To serve, melt cranberry sauce in a small pan over low heat. Transfer stuffing from foil packet to a serving bowl. Remove skewers from turkey, then cut each thigh crosswise into thick slices. Pass cranberry sauce at the table to spoon over individual portions. Makes about 6 servings.

Per serving: 360 calories, 27 g protein, 32 g carbohydrates, 13 g total fat, 109 mg cholesterol, 685 mg sodium

CURRIED TURKEY DRUMSTICKS

Preparation time: About 15 minutes

Grilling time: 55–65 minutes

Grilled turkey drumsticks make an economical meal. You slip a curry-seasoned butter under the skin to flavor the meat during cooking, then pass a peppery peanut sauce at the table.

- ¼ **cup butter or margarine, at room temperature**
- 4 **teaspoons curry powder**
- ¼ **teaspoon** *each* **ground ginger and ground cloves**
  Dash of pepper
- 4 **turkey drumsticks (about 1¼ lbs.** *each***)**
- ¼ **cup butter or margarine, melted**
  Peanut-Pepper Sauce (recipe follows)

In a small bowl, blend room-temperature butter, curry powder, ginger, cloves, and pepper. Set aside. Rinse turkey and pat dry. Carefully peel back skin on each drumstick and spread butter mixture evenly over meat. Pull skin back into place and secure with small metal skewers.

Arrange drumsticks on a lightly greased grill 4 to 6 inches above a solid bed of medium coals. Cover barbecue and adjust dampers (or cover with a tent of heavy-duty foil). Cook, basting often with melted butter and turning as needed to cook evenly, until meat near bone is no longer pink; cut to test (55 to 65 minutes).

Meanwhile, prepare Peanut-Pepper Sauce. Pass sauce at the table to spoon over individual servings. Makes 4 servings.

Per serving: 630 calories, 69 g protein, 1.4 g carbohydrates, 37 g total fat, 317 mg cholesterol, 508 mg sodium

Peanut-Pepper Sauce. In a small serving bowl, stir together ½ cup *each* **apple juice** and **crunchy peanut butter.** Stir in 1 teaspoon **crushed red pepper.** Makes about 1 cup.

Per tablespoon: 51 calories, 2 g protein, 2 g carbohydrates, 4 g total fat, 0 mg cholesterol, 33 mg sodium

(Pictured on facing page)

GRILLED BIRDS WITH JALAPEÑO JELLY GLAZE

Preparation time: 45–60 minutes

Grilling time: 7–40 minutes, depending on type of bird

Spicy glaze adds a lively dimension to grilled game hens or quail. You'll find the jalapeño jelly in specialty food stores and some well-stocked supermarkets.

>   6 **to 8 Rock Cornish game hens (1¼ to 1½ lbs.** ***each*) or 18 to 24 quail (3 to 4 oz.** ***each*), thawed if frozen**
>   ¼ **cup butter or margarine**
>   ⅔ **cup jalapeño jelly**
>   2 **tablespoons lime juice**
>   **Salt and pepper**

Remove poultry necks and giblets; reserve for other uses, if desired. If using game hens, cut in half. If using quail, cut through backbone of each bird with poultry shears or a knife. Place quail, skin side up, on a flat surface and press firmly,

cracking bones slightly, until birds lie flat. Rinse poultry and pat dry.

In a pan, combine butter and jelly. Stir over medium heat until melted. Stir in lime juice; set aside. Place birds, skin side up, on a lightly greased grill 4 to 6 inches above a solid bed of medium coals (for game hens) or hot coals (for quail).

Cook game hens until meat near thighbone is no longer pink; cut to test (30 to 40 minutes). Turn several times during cooking; during last 15 minutes, baste often with jelly mixture.

Cook quail until skin is browned and breast meat is cooked through but still slightly pink near bone; cut to test (7 to 8 minutes). Turn several times during cooking; during last 5 minutes, baste often with jelly mixture.

Sprinkle birds lightly with salt and pepper before serving. Makes 6 to 8 servings.

Per serving: 785 calories, 75 g protein, 19 g carbohydrates, 43 g total fat, 259 mg cholesterol, 292 mg sodium

SPINACH-STUFFED GAME HENS

Preparation time: 45–55 minutes

Grilling time: 45–60 minutes

Here's a nice company entrée. Each little hen holds a spinach-rice mixture accented with rosemary and water chestnuts. (Heat leftover stuffing to serve alongside.)

>   2 **Rock Cornish game hens (1¼ to 1½ lbs.** ***each*),** **thawed if frozen**
>   **Spinach-Rice Stuffing (recipe follows)**
>   **Green Onion Baste (recipe follows)**

Remove game hen necks and giblets; reserve for other uses, if desired. Rinse birds inside and out; pat dry. Prepare Spinach-Rice Stuffing; put ¾ to 1 cup stuffing in body cavity of each hen. Secure body openings with metal skewers and tie legs together. Secure skin across neck openings with skewers and bend wings akimbo. Prepare Green Onion Baste.

Barbecue game hens by indirect heat (see page 10), placing birds, breast up, on a lightly greased grill directly above drip pan. Cover barbecue and adjust dampers as necessary to maintain an even heat. Cook, brushing often with Green Onion Baste, until meat near thighbone is no longer pink; cut to test (45 to 60 minutes).

To serve, split each bird in half with poultry shears, if desired. Makes 2 or 4 servings.

Spinach-Rice Stuffing. Heat 2 tablespoons **salad oil** in a wide frying pan over medium-high heat. Add 4 cups thinly sliced **fresh spinach** leaves (about ¾ lb., stems removed); 1 can (about 8 oz.) whole **water chestnuts,** drained and slivered; and ½ cup *each* minced **green onions** (including tops) and diced **celery.** Cook, stirring, until spinach is wilted (about 3 minutes); remove from heat. Add 2 cups **cooked rice** and ¼ teaspoon **dry rosemary;** season to taste with **salt** and **pepper.** Let cool.

Green Onion Baste. Beat ½ cup (¼ lb.) **butter** or margarine (at room temperature) until fluffy; blend in 1½ tablespoons *each* finely chopped **parsley** and finely minced **green onions** (including tops), ½ teaspoon *each* **dry mustard** and **fines herbes,** ¼ teaspoon **garlic powder,** ⅛ teaspoon **liquid hot pepper seasoning,** and a dash of freshly ground **pepper.**

Per serving: 621 calories, 39 g protein, 35 g carbohydrates, 36 g total fat, 141 mg cholesterol, 288 mg sodium

For an impressive main dish that's surprisingly quick to prepare, serve up plump Grilled Birds with Jalapeño Jelly Glaze (facing page). Fresh pineapple wedges and crunchy coleslaw complement the succulent game hen halves.

APRICOT-GLAZED GAME HENS

Preparation time: About 30 minutes

Grilling time: 30–40 minutes

Apricot jam, orange-flavored liqueur, and a savory herb butter season these birds.

  Herb Butter (recipe follows)
4 Rock Cornish game hens (1¼ to 1½ lbs. *each*), thawed if frozen
¼ cup apricot jam
1 tablespoon orange-flavored liqueur
  Watercress sprigs

Prepare Herb Butter; set aside. Remove game hen necks and giblets; reserve for other uses, if desired. With poultry shears or a knife, split hens lengthwise along one side of backbone. Pull hens open; place, skin side up, on a flat surface and press firmly, cracking bones slightly, until hens lie reasonably flat. Rinse and pat dry.

Brush hens all over with Herb Butter; then place, skin side up, on a lightly greased grill 4 to 6 inches above a solid bed of medium coals. Cook for 15 minutes, turning and brushing occasionally with any remaining Herb Butter.

Meanwhile, stir jam in a small pan over medium-low heat until melted; stir in liqueur. Brush evenly over hens and continue to cook, turning occasionally, until meat near thighbone is no longer pink; cut to test (15 to 25 more minutes). Garnish with watercress. Makes 4 to 8 servings.

Herb Butter. In a pan, melt ⅓ cup **butter** or margarine with ¼ teaspoon *each* **dry rosemary** and **dry tarragon** and ⅛ teaspoon **white pepper.** Remove from heat and stir in 1 tablespoon **lemon juice.**

Per serving: 363 calories, 34 g protein, 8 g carbohydrates, 21 g total fat, 120 mg cholesterol, 144 mg sodium

BANGKOK-STYLE BARBECUED BIRDS

Preparation time: About 1 hour

Grilling time: 8–40 minutes, depending on type of bird

Threading small butterflied birds on parallel skewers keeps them flat for more even cooking. There's another advantage, too: skewered birds can be turned all at once.

  Thai Sauce (recipe follows)
8 Rock Cornish game hens (1¼ lbs. *each*), 8 squab (1 lb. *each*), or 24 quail (3 to 4 oz. *each*), thawed if frozen
½ cup minced fresh cilantro (coriander)
⅓ cup coarsely ground pepper
24 cloves garlic, minced or pressed

Prepare Thai Sauce and refrigerate. Remove poultry necks and giblets; reserve for other uses, if desired. With poultry shears or a knife, split birds of your choice lengthwise through breastbone. Pull birds open; place, skin side up, on a flat surface and press firmly, cracking bones slightly, until birds lie reasonably flat. Rinse and pat dry.

Thread birds on sturdy 18-inch-long metal skewers as follows. Force one skewer into drumstick and through thigh, then under backbone, through other thigh, and out other drumstick. Run a second skewer parallel to the first, forcing it through one side of breast and middle section of one wing, then over backbone, through middle section of other wing, and out other side of breast. Each pair of 18-inch skewers holds 2 or 3 game hens or squab or up to 6 quail.

Mash together cilantro, pepper, and garlic; rub evenly over poultry. Place poultry on a lightly greased grill 4 to 6 inches above a solid bed of medium coals. Cook, turning as needed, until meat near thighbone of game hens is no longer pink; cut to test (30 to 40 minutes). Cook squab until breast meat is cooked through but still pink near bone; cut to test (about 20 minutes). Cook quail until breast meat is cooked through but still slightly pink near bone; cut to test (8 to 10 minutes). Serve with Thai Sauce. Makes 8 servings.

Per serving: 609 calories, 69 g protein, 2.9 g carbohydrates, 34 g total fat, 220 mg cholesterol, 207 mg sodium

Thai Sauce. In a blender or food processor, combine 1 can (8 oz.) **tomato sauce,** 3 tablespoons firmly packed **brown sugar,** 6 cloves **garlic,** ⅛ to ½ teaspoon **ground red pepper** (cayenne), and ¼ cup **cider vinegar.** Whirl until blended. Add 1¼ cups **golden raisins** and ⅓ cup **water;** whirl until raisins are coarsely chopped. Pour sauce into a 2- to 3-quart pan; bring to a boil over high heat. Boil, stirring, until reduced to 1½ cups. Let cool, then cover and refrigerate until cold. Makes 1½ cups.

Per tablespoon: 34 calories, .4 g protein, 9 g carbohydrates, .04 g total fat, 0 mg cholesterol, 59 mg sodium

(Pictured on page 132)

GAME HENS OR SQUAB WITH APPLE JUICE

Preparation time: About 30 minutes

Marinating time: 4 hours or until next day

Grilling time: 15–40 minutes, depending on type of bird

Crushed fennel seeds add an interesting accent to a sweet apple juice marinade for small birds. Accompany with grilled apple, pear, and onion halves, if you wish (see pages 154 and 155).

- **4 Rock Cornish game hens (1¼ to 1½ lbs. *each*) or 4 squab (1 lb. *each*), thawed if frozen**
- **1 cup apple juice**
- **2 tablespoons *each* lemon juice and salad oil**
- **1 tablespoon crushed fennel seeds or caraway seeds**

Remove poultry necks and giblets and reserve for other uses, if desired. With poultry shears or a knife, split each bird lengthwise along one side of backbone. Place birds, skin side up, on a flat surface and press firmly, cracking bones slightly, until birds lie reasonably flat. Rinse birds, pat dry, and place in a large heavy-duty plastic bag.

In a small bowl, combine apple juice, lemon juice, oil, and fennel seeds. Pour into bag over birds. Seal bag securely, rotate to distribute marinade, and place in a shallow baking pan. Refrigerate for at least 4 hours or until next day, turning bag over several times.

Lift birds from marinade and drain briefly (reserve marinade). Arrange birds, skin side up, on a lightly greased grill 4 to 6 inches above a solid bed of medium coals (for game hens) or hot coals (for squab).

Cook game hens until meat near thighbone is no longer pink; cut to test (30 to 40 minutes). Cook squab until skin is browned and breast meat is cooked through but still pink near bone; cut to test (15 to 20 minutes). During cooking, baste birds with marinade and turn often. Makes 4 servings.

Per serving: 645 calories, 68 g protein, 4 g carbohydrates, 37 g total fat, 220 mg cholesterol, 207 mg sodium

GAME HENS WITH CASSIS-MUSTARD SAUCE

Preparation time: About 30 minutes

Grilling time: 30–40 minutes

The mild-flavored meat of game hens takes well to additional seasonings. Here, the hens are finished off with a pungent-sweet sauce made with Dijon mustard and black currant liqueur.

- **4 Rock Cornish game hens (1¼ to 1½ lbs. *each*), thawed if frozen**
- **⅓ cup butter or margarine, melted**
  Cassis-Mustard Sauce (recipe follows)
  Parsley sprigs

Remove game hen necks and giblets; reserve for other uses, if desired. With poultry shears or a knife, split hens lengthwise along one side of backbone. Pull hens open; place, skin side up, on a flat surface and press firmly, cracking bones slightly, until hens lie reasonably flat. Rinse hens; pat dry.

Brush hens all over with butter; then place, skin side up, on a lightly greased grill 4 to 6 inches above a solid bed of medium coals. Cook for 25 minutes, turning and brushing occasionally with any remaining butter.

Meanwhile, prepare Cassis-Mustard Sauce. Brush evenly over hens, using about 1 tablespoon per bird. Continue to cook, turning occasionally, until meat near thighbone is no longer pink; cut to test (5 to 15 more minutes). Remove hens to a platter; garnish with parsley and pass remaining sauce to spoon over individual portions. Makes 4 to 8 servings.

Cassis-Mustard Sauce. Melt 1½ tablespoons **butter** or margarine in a 1- to 1½-quart pan over medium heat. Add ¼ cup minced **shallots** (or ½ small onion, minced) and 2 cloves **garlic** (minced or pressed). Cook, stirring often, until shallots are soft (about 2 minutes). Stir in ⅓ cup **black currant liqueur** (crème de cassis) or ½ cup red currant jelly. Then add ¼ cup **Dijon mustard** and stir until smoothly blended. Makes about ⅔ cup.

Per serving: 355 calories, 34 g protein, 2.5 g carbohydrates, 22 g total fat, 123 mg cholesterol, 265 mg sodium

Rich, full-flavored domestic duck is easy to barbecue by indirect heat. Glistening Duck with Citrus-Chile Marinade (facing page), flanked with halved kiwi fruit and grilled pineapple and yam wedges, makes a memorable entrée for an intimate party of three.

BUTTERFLIED PHEASANT WITH WHITE TERIYAKI SAUCE

Preparation time: 10–15 minutes

Marinating time: 4 hours or until next day

Grilling time: About 30 minutes

For an elegant, intimate occasion, try a farm-raised pheasant. Check your supermarket's freezer section for frozen birds, usually sold whole; or order a fresh one from your meat market.

> 1 **pheasant (about 2½ lbs.), thawed if frozen**
> ½ **cup sake or dry white wine**
> ¼ **cup rice wine vinegar or distilled white vinegar**
> 1 **tablespoon sugar**
> 2 **tablespoons minced fresh ginger**
> ½ **teaspoon sesame oil**
> **Salt and pepper**
> **Watercress sprigs**

Remove pheasant neck and giblets; reserve for other uses, if desired. With poultry shears or a knife, split pheasant lengthwise along one side of backbone. Pull bird open; place, skin side up, on a flat surface and press firmly, cracking breastbone slightly, until bird lies reasonably flat. Rinse bird and pat dry. With a small, sharp knife, pierce breast in 6 to 8 places. Place bird, breast down, in a 9- by 13-inch dish.

In a small bowl, stir together sake, vinegar, sugar, and ginger; pour over pheasant. Cover and refrigerate for at least 4 hours or until next day, turning pheasant over several times.

Barbecue pheasant by indirect heat (see page 10). Lift pheasant from marinade and drain briefly (reserve marinade). Place bird, breast down, on a lightly greased grill directly above drip pan. Cover barbecue and adjust dampers as necessary to maintain an even heat. Cook, turning bird every 10 minutes and generously basting with marinade, until breast meat is white with a touch of pink at breastbone (about 30 minutes). To test, cut to breastbone parallel to wing joint—meat should look moist, not soft and wet.

Transfer pheasant to a platter; brush with sesame oil. Cut into serving-size pieces and sprinkle lightly with salt and pepper. Garnish with watercress. Makes 3 or 4 servings.

Per serving: 462 calories, 55 g protein, 3.8 g carbohydrates, 23 g total fat, 0 mg cholesterol, 100 mg sodium

(Pictured on facing page)

DUCK WITH CITRUS-CHILE MARINADE

Preparation time: 10–15 minutes

Marinating time: 6 hours or until next day

Grilling time: About 2 hours

Use one duck or two for this recipe, depending on the number of servings you need. (Expect plenty of sauce if you cook just one duck.)

> 1 **or 2 ducks (4½ to 5 lbs.** *each***), thawed if frozen**
> ⅓ **cup sugar**
> 1½ **cups orange juice**
> ¾ **cup lime juice**
> ½ **to 1 teaspoon crushed dried hot red chiles**
> 1 **tablespoon** *each* **grated orange peel and lime peel**
> 1 **tablespoon** *each* **cornstarch and water**

Remove duck neck and giblets; reserve for other uses, if desired. Discard lumps of fat. Rinse duck inside and out and pat dry. Place duck in a large heavy-duty plastic bag.

In a small bowl, combine sugar, orange juice, lime juice, chiles, orange peel, and lime peel. Stir until sugar is dissolved; then pour into bag over duck. Seal bag securely, rotate to distribute marinade, and place in a shallow baking pan. Refrigerate for at least 6 hours or until next day, turning bag over several times.

Lift duck from marinade and drain briefly (reserve marinade). Fasten neck skin to back with a small metal skewer. Barbecue duck by indirect heat (see page 10), placing duck, breast up, on a lightly greased grill directly above drip pan. Cover barbecue and adjust dampers as necessary to maintain an even heat. Cook for 1¼ hours; then baste with marinade. Continue to cook, basting frequently, until meat near bone at hip socket is no longer pink; cut to test (about 45 more minutes).

Transfer duck to a platter and keep warm. In a 2-quart pan, combine cornstarch and water; stir in remaining marinade and bring to a boil over high heat, stirring. Pour into a bowl and pass at the table to spoon over duck. Makes 3 to 6 servings.

Per serving: 935 calories, 50 g protein, 16 g carbohydrates, 73 g total fat, 217 mg cholesterol, 157 mg sodium

SHERRY-ORANGE BARBECUED DUCK

Preparation time: 20–25 minutes

Marinating time: 6 hours or until next day

Grilling time: 7–9 minutes

More tender and more predictable in flavor than wild ducks, farm-raised mallards offer the added advantage of year-round availability. Be aware, though, that they're generally rather expensive and must usually be ordered from your meat market well in advance.

    12 wild or farm-raised boned mallard duck
        breast halves (about 3 oz. *each*, skinned);
        or 4 or 5 wild or farm-raised mallard ducks
        (about 2 lbs. *each*), cut up
    ¾ cup soy sauce
    1 can (6 oz.) frozen orange juice concentrate,
        thawed
    ½ cup dry red wine
    2 tablespoons Worcestershire
        Wine Sauce (recipe follows)

Rinse duck pieces and pat dry. With a fork, pierce each piece all over.

In a large heavy-duty plastic bag, mix soy, orange juice concentrate, wine, and Worcestershire. Add duck pieces. Seal bag securely and rotate to distribute marinade. Place in a shallow baking pan and refrigerate for at least 6 hours or until next day, turning bag over occasionally.

Pour off 1½ cups of the marinade and use it to prepare Wine Sauce. Set Wine Sauce aside.

Lift duck from remaining marinade and drain briefly (reserve marinade). Arrange duck pieces on a lightly greased grill 4 to 6 inches above a solid bed of hot coals. Cook, basting with remaining marinade and turning to brown evenly, until meat is done to your liking. For medium-rare duck, cook until meat is pinkish red in center; cut to test (about 9 minutes for legs, 7 minutes for breasts).

To serve, pass Wine Sauce to spoon over individual portions. Makes 4 to 6 servings.

Wine Sauce. Heat 2 tablespoons **salad oil** in a 3- to 4-quart pan over medium-high heat; add 1 cup finely chopped **onion** and cook until soft (about 10 minutes). Stir in the 1½ cups **reserved marinade.** Mix ½ cup **cream sherry** and 1½ tablespoons **cornstarch;** add to pan. Bring to a boil over high heat, stirring. (At this point, you may set aside for up to 1 hour; reheat to continue.) Stir in 2 tablespoons **sesame oil.**

*Per serving: 247 calories, 21 g protein, 21 g carbohydrates,
9 g total fat, 0 mg cholesterol, 1803 mg sodium*

WHOLE WILD DUCK

Preparation time: About 5 minutes

Grilling time: 20–30 minutes

Wild ducks are smaller than the domestic birds; they're lower in fat, too, so you need to baste them with butter to keep the meat moist. Stuff these ducks with onion or apple for flavor.

    2 ducks (2 to 3½ lbs. *each*), thawed if frozen
        Onion or apple slices (optional)
        Melted butter or margarine

Rinse ducks inside and out and pat dry. Place a few slices of onion or apple in body cavity of each duck for flavoring, if desired. Secure skin over body cavities with small metal skewers.

Barbecue ducks by indirect heat (see page 10), placing ducks, breast up, on a lightly greased grill directly above drip pan. Cover barbecue and adjust dampers as necessary to maintain an even heat. Cook for about 10 minutes, then baste with butter. Continue to cook, basting every 5 minutes, until ducks are done to your liking; cut to test (10 to 20 more minutes for rare). Makes about 4 servings.

*Per serving: 581 calories, 33 g protein, 0 g carbohydrates,
49 g total fat, 145 mg cholesterol, 102 mg sodium*

BARBECUED DUCK WITH HOISIN

Preparation time: About 30 minutes

Marinating time: 6 hours or until next day

Grilling time: About 40 minutes

Skinned duck pieces, spicy with hoisin, cook on the grill; the skin bakes crisp in the oven.

  2 **ducks (4½ to 5 lbs.** *each***), thawed if frozen**
  1 **cup hoisin sauce**
  ½ **cup raspberry vinegar or red wine vinegar**
  ½ **cup orange juice**
    Baked Duck Skin (optional; recipe follows)

Remove duck necks and giblets; reserve for other uses, if desired. Discard lumps of fat. Rinse ducks inside and out and pat dry. With a sharp knife, cut legs from body at hip joints (near center back); also cut wings from breast. Pull skin off breast and trim breast meat from ribs, sliding knife parallel to bones. Reserve carcass for other uses, or discard. If desired, cover and refrigerate skin to use for Baked Duck Skin.

In a large bowl, stir together hoisin, vinegar, and orange juice. Add duck pieces and turn to coat. Cover and refrigerate for at least 6 hours or until next day, turning duck pieces several times.

Lift duck pieces from marinade and drain briefly (reserve marinade). Set breast pieces aside.

Barbecue duck by indirect heat (see page 10), placing duck legs and wings on a lightly greased grill directly above drip pan. Cover barbecue and adjust dampers as necessary to maintain an even heat. Cook for 30 minutes, basting once with marinade after 15 minutes. (If you're preparing the Baked Duck Skin, start baking it when you put duck leg and wing pieces on barbecue.)

Uncover barbecue. Place breast pieces directly over coals (not over drip pan). Cook, turning after 5 minutes, until meat in thickest portion is no longer red (it should still look pink); cut to test. Cooking takes about 10 minutes *total*. When breasts are done, meat near thighbone in leg pieces should be firm but still slightly pink.

Bring remaining marinade to a boil and pass at the table to spoon over individual portions, if desired. Serve duck pieces with Baked Duck Skin, if desired. Makes about 6 servings.

Per serving: 397 calories, 41 g protein, 12 g carbohydrates, 19 g total fat, 152 mg cholesterol, 1131 mg sodium

Baked Duck Skin. Cut **duck skin** into pieces about 4 inches square. Arrange in a single layer, fat side down, on a wire rack in a rimmed baking pan. Bake in a 350° oven until crisp (about 45 minutes). Makes 6 servings.

BARBECUED RABBIT

Preparation time: About 5 minutes

Marinating time: 1 hour or until next day

Grilling time: About 35 minutes

Mild-flavored, fine-textured rabbit tastes much like chicken; it takes well to grilling, too.

    3- to 3½-pound frying rabbit, cut up
    Tarragon-Dijon Marinade or Paprika
    Marinade (recipes follow)

Rinse rabbit and pat dry. Arrange in a single layer in a shallow dish.

Prepare your choice of marinade; pour over rabbit. Cover and refrigerate for at least 1 hour or until next day, turning occasionally.

Lift rabbit from marinade and drain briefly (reserve marinade). Barbecue rabbit by indirect heat (see page 10), placing rabbit on a lightly greased grill directly above drip pan. Cover barbe-

cue and adjust dampers as necessary to maintain an even heat. Cook, basting often with marinade, until meat is no longer pink near bone; cut to test (about 35 minutes). Makes 4 or 5 servings.

Tarragon-Dijon Marinade. In a bowl, whisk together ½ cup **salad oil**, ¼ cup *each* **Dijon mustard** and **white wine vinegar**, and 2 teaspoons **dry tarragon** until smoothly blended. Makes about 1 cup.

Paprika Marinade. In a bowl, whisk together ½ cup **salad oil**, ¼ cup **red wine vinegar**, 2 tablespoons **paprika**, 1 tablespoon **Worcestershire**, and 1 clove **garlic** (minced or pressed). Makes about 1 cup.

Per serving with Tarragon-Dijon Marinade: 498 calories, 53 g protein, 1 g carbohydrates, 30 g total fat, 165 mg cholesterol, 262 mg sodium

Per serving with Paprika Marinade: 495 calories, 54 g protein, 1 g carbohydrates, 29 g total fat, 165 mg cholesterol, 91 mg sodium

Hawaiian-style curry served from the barbecue is the featured dish at our Malihini Luau Party (page 170). Grilled chicken and shrimp skewers are served with a curried coconut cream sauce, rice, and condiments.

SMALL PARTIES TO EXTRAVAGANZAS

Parties centered around the barbecue have a relaxed ambience that makes entertaining easy on the hosts, whether the occasion is casual or quite elegant. To help you plan your parties, we've assembled 21 menus geared to gatherings of different sizes; you'll find ideas for as few as four or as many as 180 guests.

For extravaganzas—club parties, block parties, fundraisers— we offer two impressive barbecues. The first features a spit-roasted whole pig; the second focuses on a large beef roast cooked in an underground pit.

For more typical occasions, with guest lists of 12 to 16, you might decide on a turkey fiesta, a Greek-style *doner kebab* barbecue, a whole meal of Spanish *tapas,* or a fancy sit-down dinner starring a whole beef tenderloin. If you're serving a smaller group of eight to twelve, choose a Hawaiian-style curry, authentic-tasting Italian pizza baked on the grill, or two meals that get guests involved in the cooking—a hot dog roast and a barbecued burrito party. And for just four to six guests, try Jamaican-style spareribs, a shellfish picnic at the beach, or a hearty Venetian mixed grill.

All our menus include recipes or suggestions for accompaniments to the main course, plus hints for shopping and serving. To help you carry off your party smoothly and successfully, we provide a timetable with each menu.

MALIHINI LUAU PARTY

Pictured on page 168

Malihini is Hawaiian for "newcomer"—an appropriate label for the mixture of ethnic ingredients that have become important in Hawaiian cuisine. This barbecue meal for eight, blending the flavors of Southeast Asian and Indian curries with tropical fruits, is a good example of the Islands' malihini cooking styles.

Pupus (Appetizers) of Your Choice

Hawaiian-style Curry:
Skewered Grilled Chicken Legs & Shrimp
with Curried Coconut Cream Sauce

Hot Cooked Rice   Pineapple Wheels

Condiments: Pickled Onions, Coconut, Mango Chutney, Banana Slices, Chopped Macadamia Nuts, Lime Wedges, Fresh Cilantro Leaves, Dried Hot Chiles

Tropical Fruit Spritzers

Sliced Papayas with Lime Sherbet

The day before the party, you can prepare the curry sauce and start marinating the chicken and shrimp; the pickled onions can also be prepared a day ahead of time. On the day of the party, arrange all the condiments in their serving dishes and start the barbecue fire about 1½ hours before serving. While the chicken and shrimp are on the grill, reheat the curry sauce and cook the rice.

To make Tropical Fruit Spritzers, let guests mix equal parts of dry white wine, sparkling mineral water, and a tropical fruit juice (such as guava, papaya, or passion fruit).

 HAWAIIAN-STYLE CURRY

Curried Coconut Cream Sauce (recipe follows)
16 **chicken drumsticks (4 to 6 oz. *each*)**
40 **medium-size raw shrimp (about 1¼ lbs. *total*), shelled and deveined**
    Pickled Onions (facing page)
15 **green onions**
 8 **to 10 cups hot cooked rice**
 1 **large ripe pineapple (about 5 lbs.), peeled and cut crosswise into 8 slices**
    Condiments (suggestions on facing page)
    Small dried hot red chiles, whole or crushed

Prepare Curried Coconut Cream Sauce. Pour 1 cup of the sauce into a large heavy-duty plastic bag. Rinse chicken and pat dry, then add to sauce in bag; mix to coat. Seal bag securely. In another heavy-duty plastic bag, combine shrimp and ½ cup of the sauce; mix to coat, then seal bag. Place bags in a large, shallow baking pan; refrigerate for at least 4 hours or until next day, turning bags over occasionally. Also cover and refrigerate remaining sauce. Meanwhile, prepare Pickled Onions.

If using bamboo skewers, soak about 26 skewers in hot water to cover for 30 minutes. Trim root ends and any wilted tops from green onions; then cut onions into 2-inch lengths. On a pair of parallel bamboo or metal skewers, thread 3 or 4 drumsticks alternately with onion pieces (see photo on page 168). Repeat with remaining chicken, using 3 or 4 more pairs of skewers. Thread 5 shrimp on a pair of parallel skewers, alternating with onion pieces; repeat with remaining shrimp, using 7 more pairs of skewers.

Place chicken skewers on a lightly greased grill 4 to 6 inches above a solid bed of medium coals. Cook, turning frequently, for 20 minutes. Set shrimp skewers on grill next to chicken. Cook, turning shrimp and chicken occasionally, until chicken is no longer pink near bone (cut to test— about 10 more minutes) and shrimp turn pink (about 5 minutes).

Meanwhile, place remaining Curried Coconut Cream Sauce in a 3- to 4-quart pan and heat over medium heat, stirring frequently, until hot (about 15 minutes). Pour sauce into a 1½-quart serving bowl.

Spoon rice over half of a large platter; arrange pineapple slices over other half. Present grilled chicken and shrimp skewers on top.

To serve, place about 1 cup rice and one pineapple slice on each individual plate; slide chicken and shrimp from skewers onto plates. Top foods with curry sauce, then spoon condiments and Pickled Onions alongside. For extra heat, cautiously add chiles. Makes 8 servings.

Per serving: 638 calories, 46 g protein, 68 g carbohydrates, 19 g total fat, 188 mg cholesterol, 198 mg sodium

Curried Coconut Cream Sauce. Melt 6 tablespoons **butter** or margarine in a wide frying pan over medium-high heat. Add 3 large **onions** (chopped), 3 cloves **garlic** (minced or pressed), and 2 tablespoons minced **fresh ginger.** Cook, stirring occasionally, until onions are soft (about 15 minutes). Stir in ¼ cup **all-purpose flour,** 3 tablespoons **curry powder,** 1 tablespoon **sugar,** and ½ teaspoon **crushed red pepper.** Cook, stirring occasionally, until hot and bubbly. Remove from heat and smoothly blend in 4 cans (12 to 14 oz. *each*) **unsweetened coconut milk,** thawed if frozen. (As an alternative to coconut milk, you may use

6 cups half-and-half or light cream mixed with 1 tablespoon *each* sugar and coconut extract.)

Bring sauce to a boil over medium heat, stirring frequently. Continue to cook, uncovered, stirring frequently, until sauce is reduced to about 6 cups (15 to 20 minutes). Season to taste with **salt**. Makes about 6 cups.

Per tablespoon: 38 calories, .4 g protein, 1.3 g carbohydrates, 3.8 g total fat, 2 mg cholesterol, 9 mg sodium

Pickled Onions. Thinly slice 2 large mild **red onions** and separate into rings. Place in a bowl and mix in 1½ tablespoons **salt**. Knead onions with your hands until limp. Place onions in a colander and rinse thoroughly with **cold water;** drain, place in a bowl, and add ¼ cup *each* **sugar** and **white wine vinegar**. Mix gently but thoroughly. If made ahead, let stand at room temperature until next day. Makes about 2½ cups.

Per ¼ cup: 36 calories, .6 g protein, 9 g carbohydrates, .12 g total fat, 0 mg cholesterol, 221 mg sodium

Condiments. Choose 4 or 5 of the following: 1 cup **dried unsweetened flaked coconut;** 1 cup coarsely chopped **mango chutney;** 3 medium-size **bananas,** sliced and coated with 1 tablespoon **lemon juice;** 1 cup **macadamia nuts** or peanuts, coarsely chopped; 2 **limes,** cut into wedges; and ¾ cup lightly packed **fresh cilantro (coriander) leaves.**

BURRITO BARBECUE

Aromatic foods grilling on street braziers in Mexico inspired this informal garden party. To begin the meal, roast corn over hot coals until the kernels are sweet and slightly parched. Then, as the barbecue's heat decreases, let guests fill, fold, and grill flour tortillas to make big, crisp burritos.

Barbecued Corn, Mexican Style

Barbecued Burritos Filled with Corned Beef or Pastrami, Cheese, Tomatoes, Onions, Fresh Cilantro Sprigs

Seasonal Fresh Fruit Salad

Sangría   Lemonade

Ahead of time, you can husk the corn; you should also assemble all the burrito ingredients in separate dishes or in separate piles on a large tray. The recipe makes 12 burritos—6 to 12 servings, depending on appetites.

Start the barbecue fire 30 to 40 minutes before you plan to start roasting the corn.

BARBECUED CORN, MEXICAN STYLE

For each serving, you will need 1 or 2 ears of **corn;** ½ juicy **lime,** cut into wedges; and **salt.**

Strip husks and silk from corn. Lay corn on a lightly greased grill 4 to 6 inches above a solid bed of medium coals. Cook, turning occasionally, until kernels are lightly browned on several sides (10 to 12 minutes). Push cooked corn to a cooler area of the barbecue to keep warm.

To serve, squeeze lime wedges over corn and sprinkle with salt; eat out of hand. Offer napkins or plates to catch any drips.

Per ear of corn: 79 calories, 3 g protein, 18 g carbohydrates, 1 g total fat, 0 mg cholesterol, 146 mg sodium

BARBECUED BURRITOS

12 **large flour tortillas,** *each* **about 12 inches in diameter**

6 **cups (1½ lbs.) shredded Cheddar or jack cheese**

2 **large cans (7 oz.** *each***) whole green chiles, drained and seeded**

1½ **to 2 pounds thinly sliced corned beef or pastrami**

About 6 large tomatoes, thinly sliced

About 3 large mild red or white onions, thinly sliced

1 **or 2 bunches fresh cilantro (coriander), separated into sprigs**

If coals are low, assemble burritos on grill. If coals are hotter, fill and fold burritos next to barbecue, then place them on grill to heat.

To assemble each burrito: Working quickly, distribute cheese in a band down center of a tortilla to within 2 inches of top and bottom edges. Top with a chile and some of the corned beef, tomatoes, onions, and cilantro. Fold ends over filling; then fold one side over filling and roll up.

Place burrito, folded side down, on grill. Cook until tortilla is toasted and crisp; then turn over and toast on other side. If coals are too hot for you to turn burrito with your fingers, it will toast in 2 to 3 minutes per side; turn with a wide metal spatula and watch to avoid scorching. If coals are low, burrito may take up to 6 to 8 minutes per side.

Serve burritos immediately, or push to a cooler area of the barbecue to keep warm until ready to eat. Makes 12 large burritos (6 to 12 servings).

Per burrito: 553 calories, 30 g protein, 39 g carbohydrates, 30 g total fat, 115 mg cholesterol, 1470 mg sodium

INDIAN-STYLE SALMON BAKE

Pictured on facing page

The dramatic focus of this beach picnic is a butterflied salmon, woven onto a wood frame and cooked over an open fire. It's a cooking method borrowed from the Northwest coastal Indians, who traditionally use three-legged frames of alder to hold the salmon; we've modified the design of the frame to a two-piece central stake. The butterflied fish is "woven" against the main stake with smaller strips of wood. Pounded into sand or soft soil, the stake holds the salmon fillet upright and flat at about 2 feet above the fire, so it cooks evenly.

Hot Sipping Soup of Your Choice

Indian-style Baked Salmon
&
Roasted Potatoes with Lemon-Garlic Butter

Coleslaw

S'mores

A day ahead, prepare the wood for the frame. Early on the day of the picnic, rinse the salmon and put it in the brine. Carry the salmon to the beach in a plastic bag; be sure to bring along fresh water for rinsing the fish at the picnic site.

At the beach, frame the salmon and build the fire, then erect the framed salmon in place to cook. Wrap small potatoes in foil and push them down into the hot coals to roast. Baste the fish with lemon-garlic butter as it cooks; reserve any remaining butter to spoon over the potatoes.

INDIAN-STYLE BAKED SALMON

    1 or 2 whole salmon (6 to 8 lbs. *each*)
       Light brine (¼ cup salt to each 4 quarts water)
       Frame (directions follow)
    ¼ cup butter or margarine, melted
    1 clove garlic, minced or pressed
    2 tablespoons lemon juice

At the fish market, have your fishman remove salmon head, tail, and back fin, then butterfly salmon from stomach side (do not separate fillets along back) and bone it, leaving skin intact. At home, trim any white membrane from belly area of fish. Rinse fish, pat dry, and place in a deep pan or a large heavy-duty plastic bag set in a shallow baking pan. Cover completely with brine; let stand for 45 minutes to 1½ hours. (Brining firms fish and gives it a moister, more succulent texture.)

Prepare frame. Lay one 6-foot section of frame flat. Wrap a piece of foil slightly longer than fish

smoothly around center of stake. Position 3 of the 1½-foot frame pieces at right angles to stake, centering pieces and spacing evenly apart.

Lift fish from brine; rinse and pat dry. Align center of fish with long stake; lay fish on top of 1½-foot frame pieces (wide end of fish should be pointed toward sharpened end of stake). Adjust position of 1½-foot pieces so entire edge of fish overlaps them by 2 to 3 inches at top and bottom.

On top of salmon, place remaining two 1½-foot frame pieces, centered between and parallel to frame pieces beneath fish.

Foil-wrap the second 6-foot stake as you did the first. Lay second stake directly over first, sharpened ends together, with fish and short frame pieces sandwiched between. Tightly wrap wire around the 2 long stakes above and below fish.

If cooking a second fish, repeat framing steps.

As you are framing salmon, start fire in a location sheltered from wind. The ideal fire is a driftwood fire built against the base of a large rock or rocky cliff. The firebed should be at least twice as long as width of fish when fish are placed side by side. Burn fire until you have a solid bed of glowing coals—this takes at least 30 minutes. Add more wood to keep a gentle blaze going while fish is cooking.

Face fish toward heat. With a hammer, pound sharpened ends of double stakes into sand (or soft soil) at least 1 foot from firebed until bottom edge of fish is about 2 feet above fire. If fire is against a rock, angle stake at about a 60° angle over fire. If fire is in the open, angle stake at a 45° angle over fire. (You can control angle of stakes by wedging a rock between base of stakes and sand.) Push fire around beneath fish to control heat.

Cook fish for 25 minutes; mix butter, garlic, and lemon juice and baste fish several times as it cooks. Then carefully pull out stakes, rotate fish so back is toward the fire, and cook until it flakes readily when prodded in thickest part (about 25 more minutes); baste several times.

Push fire away or move fish back from heat. To serve, let guests pull chunks of fish from frame.

Each salmon makes about 8 servings.

Per serving: 194 calories, 23 g protein, .18 g carbohydrates, 10 g total fat, 73 mg cholesterol, 906 mg sodium

Frame. *For each frame,* you'll need nonresinous milled lumber: two 6-foot-long pieces, ¾- by ¾-inch stock; five 1½-foot-long pieces, ¼- by ¾-inch stock; and 2 feet of 22-gauge or heavier wire. Sharpen one end of each of the 6-foot stakes.

Soak wood in water overnight so it won't burn; wrap 1½-foot pieces smoothly with foil.

*Indian-style Baked Salmon (facing page) is the center of
attention at this out-of-the-ordinary beach barbecue. You weave
the butterflied salmon onto a wooden frame, then bake
it above an open fire.*

SPIT-ROASTED PIG—THE
ULTIMATE BARBECUE

Spit-roasting a whole pig is not for the faint of heart: pulling off the project successfully involves a serious commitment of time, effort, and funds. The hard work pays off in the results, though—a succulent pig that makes a memorable show and a grand feast for a large crowd.

Briefly, here's what you must do. *First*, find a source and order a pig well ahead of time. *Second*, rent a spit (check the Yellow Pages under "Barbecue Equipment & Supplies"). *Third*, select and prepare the cooking area; you'll need to use the spit for this step, so prepare the firebed after you've picked up the spit but before you pick up the pig. *Fourth*, secure the pig on the spit; and *fifth*, keep the pig cool until you're ready to start cooking.

The pig takes about 12 hours to roast, so be prepared to get up very early on the day of serving to have the meat ready to eat by late afternoon or evening. Once you start working with the pig, you'll need at least one reasonably strong partner—and, ideally, someone to relieve both of you from time to time.

Enlist your guests' help in completing the menu with assorted salads, cold vegetables, breads, desserts, and beverages.

The pig. Order a pig weighing 100 pounds *or less*. A meat market or supermarket that cuts up carcasses can usually make the arrangements, but you may have to wait for up to 30 days to get the size pig you want. Check prices when you order, and shop around for the best value.

If the pig arrives a day or so ahead, have it held for you in the market's refrigerator. After spitting the pig, you can keep it cold for up to 14 hours. Place pig on a plastic sheet in a cool place; drape it with sealed plastic bags filled with ice. Cover with another sheet of plastic; protect from animals and insects. Replace ice as it melts.

Spit-roasting equipment. You need a spit that's at least 7 feet long, spit forks to keep the pig from slipping, spit supports to hold the pig over the heat, and a means to turn the spit (manual or motorized).

You can rent a spit at some shops that sell barbecue equipment. Reserve it well ahead; before leaving the shop, make sure you have all the parts and check them for defects.

Preparing the firebed. For the cooking site, choose a spot protected from wind and rain.

You'll need this equipment: a shovel, the spit-roasting equipment, 20 pounds of sand, 14 concrete blocks (6- by 6- by 12-inch size), about 120 pounds of long-burning charcoal briquets, fire starter and matches, a garden rake, long-handled tongs, potholder mitts, and a large box of baking soda.

Clear a level 3- by 5-foot area down to the soil. Down the center, spread sand in a 1½- by 3-foot rectangle.

Set spit supports at 3-foot ends of rectangle and put spit in position.

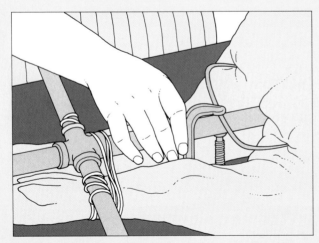

Insert spit through mouth and out tail of pig; secure legs. Then push spit fork into rump.

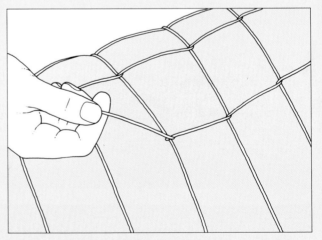

Netting made of string holds skin in place as pig cooks. Weave strings at right angles to form 3-inch squares.

Adjust supports so that spit is 20 to 24 inches above ground and centered over rectangle. Line perimeter of 3- by 5-foot area with concrete blocks (with open sides up) to make a solid wall.

Spitting & tying the pig: a team operation. Allow at least 2 hours for spitting and tying. First, insert spit through mouth and out tail of pig; one person pushes spit, the other guides it along backbone. Spit should not pierce any bone or meat. Make sure pig is centered on length of spit.

Next, wire spine to spit. You'll need three 2-foot lengths of heavy wire (such as baling wire), an ice pick, and pliers.

At mid-back, make a hole on each side of spine with an ice pick, poking from rib side out through skin. Working from skin side, force the ends of one wire through holes into pig cavity. With pliers, twist wire ends together over spit, securely uniting spit and spine (spine curves and may not actually touch spit). Position remaining 2 wires about 1 foot away from center wire on either side.

Use double strands of heavy cotton string to tie front and rear legs to spit. Because legs are stiff, this task may require a little brute strength.

Force spit forks firmly and securely into thickest parts of hind and shoulder ends; clamp or wire spit forks tightly to secure to spit.

To hold skin in place as it cooks, make a string net over rib loin sections, as follows. Suspend spit between 2 counters or set it on spit supports so you can pass string under and around pig. First tie string tightly at 3-inch intervals around body between front and rear legs. Then wrap strings at right angles to make 3-inch squares.

Once pig is spitted and tied, position it on spit supports and rotate it to make sure that equipment works and that pig is balanced. (Adjust spit forks or tighten netting if necessary.) A well-balanced pig that doesn't shift its weight on the spit is essential if equipment is motor-operated.

Remove pig and keep it cool while you start the fire.

Roasting the pig. Pile 10 pounds of briquets at each end of firebed and ignite. When coals are ash-covered and glowing hot (about 1 hour), set spitted pig on supports. Rake coals into an even layer underneath pig. Begin rotating motor-operated spit, or manually rotate pig a quarter-turn every 5 to 10 minutes. Continue rotating throughout cooking.

After about 1 hour, when fat begins to drip, rake briquets from directly beneath pig to expose sand. (Sand catches grease and reduces flare-ups.) Arrange coals so most are underneath thickest parts of pig, with a 6- to 8-inch-wide band of coals along sides of pig.

To keep skin from charring, sprinkle any grease fires with baking soda to smother flames. About every 30 minutes, rake briquets to knock off ash. Add 10 pounds of briquets about every hour to maintain heat; make a single row along sides and distribute balance at each end.

After about 10 hours, fat will cease dripping excessively; at this point, rake hot coals back beneath pig, concentrating heat under thighs and shoulders. Internal temperature in thickest part of animal at bone (inside thigh or neck section of shoulder) should be 140°F on a meat thermometer; use a rapid-reading thermometer to check temperature in several places. (A spit-cooked pig exposed to the air often reaches only 140° to 150°F, but if cooking continues at this temperature for at least 1 hour, the meat is both safe to eat and very palatable.)

Cooking typically takes 10 to 12 hours, though breezy or cool weather will slow it down.

If the pig is ready before the rest of the meal, rake coals from beneath pig so it will cease cooking but stay hot; keep hot on spit for up to 1 hour.

To serve, transfer spitted pig to a table topped with a pig-size tray of heavy-duty foil; pull out spit and cut off strings. Garnish pig with parsley. Pull off skin; tear or carve meat from bones. Season with salt and pepper.

A 100-pound pig makes 100 servings.

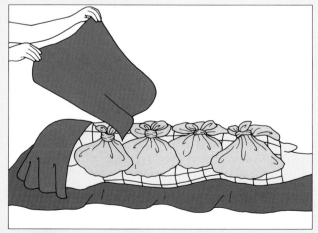

Ice-filled plastic bags, wet towels, and a plastic sheet keep spitted pig cold overnight.

To maintain heat, add 10 pounds of charcoal to fire every hour; rake coals regularly to knock off ash.

A sandy beach provides a fitting background for this finger-food picnic of fresh shellfish (facing page). Diners dunk grilled shrimp, mussels, clams, and oysters in lemon-garlic butter before eating.

BEACH BARBECUE

Pictured on facing page

Oysters, clams, mussels, and shrimp are the natural stars in this easy-to-manage beach barbecue for four to six picnickers.

The shellfish cook on a portable barbecue while a flavorful garlic butter melts alongside. Serving is easy—guests simply pluck the shellfish from their shells and dunk them in butter. Offer chunks of French bread and crisp raw vegetables as additional dippers.

Vegetables for Dipping: Asparagus Spears, Radishes, Small Red or Yellow Tomatoes

Barbecued Shellfish with Garlic Butter

Crusty French Bread

Cappelletti Pesto Salad

White Wine such as Chardonnay

Pears & Grapes   Cookies

If you plan to buy your shellfish at or en route to the beach, take along a water pan and a scrub brush for cleaning them. If you purchase the shellfish in advance, scrub them at home, then carry them in an ice-filled cooler or insulated bag.

BARBECUED SHELLFISH

Garlic Butter (recipe follows)
20 **to 24** *each* **clams, mussels, and medium-size oysters, scrubbed in fresh water**
About 1 pound extra-large raw shrimp (about 20 per lb.), shelled and deveined

Prepare Garlic Butter; pour into a small heatproof container that can sit on the barbecue.

To cook, place container of Garlic Butter on a lightly greased grill 2 to 4 inches above a solid bed of hot coals. Also arrange as many clams, mussels, oysters, and shrimp on grill as will fit. Cook, turning once, until clams and mussels pop wide open (about 3 minutes), oysters open slightly (about 4 minutes), and shrimp turn pink (3 to 4 minutes).

To eat clams, mussels, and oysters, protect your fingers with a napkin and drain shellfish juices into Garlic Butter. Then pluck out meat with a fork, dip in butter, and eat. To eat shrimp, just dip in Garlic Butter. Makes 4 to 6 servings.

Per serving: 157 calories, 25 g protein, 5 g carbohydrates, 3 g total fat, 144 mg cholesterol, 248 mg sodium

Garlic Butter. In a small pan, melt 1 cup (½ lb.) **butter** or margarine. Stir in 1 tablespoon **lemon juice** and 2 cloves **garlic** (minced or pressed). Makes 1 cup.

Per tablespoon: 102 calories, .14 g protein, .18 g carbohydrates, 11 g total fat, 31 mg cholesterol, 117 mg sodium

CAPPELLETTI PESTO SALAD

Pesto (recipe follows)
8 **ounces cappelletti or other medium-size fancy-shaped dry pasta**
⅓ **cup olive oil**
2 **tablespoons white wine vinegar**
1 **clove garlic, minced or pressed**
Freshly ground pepper (optional)

Prepare Pesto; set aside.

In a 5- to 6-quart pan, bring 3 quarts water to a boil over high heat. Add pasta; let water return to a boil and cook, uncovered, just until tender to bite (about 10 minutes). Or cook according to package directions. Drain well, rinse with cold water, and drain well again.

In a large bowl, combine oil, vinegar, garlic, and ⅓ cup of the Pesto; mix until well blended. (Reserve remaining Pesto for other uses.) Add pasta and mix gently. Cover and refrigerate for at least 1 hour or until next day. Just before serving, sprinkle with pepper, if desired. Makes 4 to 6 servings.

Pesto. In a blender or food processor, combine 1 cup lightly packed **fresh basil leaves,** ½ cup (about 2½ oz.) grated **Parmesan cheese,** and ¼ cup **olive oil;** add 1 clove **garlic** (minced), if desired. Whirl until basil is finely chopped. Use at once; or place in a small jar, top with a thin layer of **olive oil** to keep pesto from darkening and refrigerate for up to a week. Freeze for longer storage. Makes about ⅔ cup.

Per serving: 477 calories, 11 g protein, 45 g carbohydrates, 28 g total fat, 7 mg cholesterol, 169 mg sodium

A GREEK-STYLE DONER KEBAB PARTY

This barbecue party for 12 centers around a *doner kebab*—spit-roasted meat that's popular in Greece. There, street-side vendors carve thin slivers of meat from the roast, then tuck them into sandwiches to sell to passersby.

Rotating on its vertical spit, a doner kebab looks like a single large chunk of meat. In fact, though, it's many thin slices, stacked and skewered. Barbecuing meat this way carries some definite advantages. Marinades penetrate sliced meat more thoroughly than they do an uncut roast—with extra-tender, flavorful results. And when the meat is carved, it falls naturally into small pieces, just right for filling pocket bread.

To make a doner kebab, purchase a boneless beef, lamb, or pork roast and have it cut into steaks at the meat market. Marinate the steaks, then reassemble them into a roast for cooking on an outdoor rotisserie. Once the meat is done, cut it into thin strips, using the spit as your anchor. Guests pile the meat strips into halves of pocket bread, then add toppings of mint leaves, tomatoes, cucumbers, onions, and yogurt.

Feta Cheese Spread (page 190) with Fresh Vegetables for Dipping

Greek-style Doner Kebab

Pocket Bread   Mint Leaves

Yogurt   Diced Tomatoes, Cucumbers & Red Onions

Red Wine such as Chianti

Fruit   Butter Cookies or Pastry

The day before the party, purchase the meat and have it cut into ½-inch-thick steaks; marinate the steaks overnight.

On the day of serving, prepare appetizer, dessert, and toppings for the doner kebab. Assemble the sliced meat into a roast and impale it on the spit as directed. About 2½ hours before serving, start the barbecue fire.

GREEK-STYLE DONER KEBAB

- 2½- to 3-pound boneless roast (such as beef crossrib, pork leg or loin, or leg of lamb), cut into ½-inch-thick steaks
- ¼ cup *each* olive oil and dry white wine
- 3 tablespoons lemon juice
- ¼ teaspoon *each* oregano leaves, pepper, and cracked bay leaves
- 1 teaspoon salt
- 2 cloves garlic, minced or pressed
- 2 tablespoons minced parsley
- 12 pocket breads, *each* about 7 inches in diameter, cut into halves
- 2 cups *each* diced tomatoes, diced peeled cucumbers, and diced mild red onions
- 1 cup fresh mint leaves (optional)
- About 2 cups plain yogurt

Arrange sliced meat in a deep, close-fitting bowl or dish. In a small bowl, stir together oil, wine, lemon juice, oregano, pepper, bay leaves, salt, garlic, and parsley. Pour mixture over meat and turn to coat; then cover and refrigerate for at least 8 hours or until next day, turning meat several times.

Lift meat from marinade and drain briefly (discard marinade). To assemble doner kebab, stack meat slices to resemble a roast again, then tie them securely with string to make a compact stack. Insert a rotisserie spit through center of meat and secure spit forks.

Prepare fire as directed for spit-roasting on page 19. Set spit on barbecue and start rotisserie motor. Place a drip pan beneath and to the front of roast. Immediately add about 7 coals; add 7 more coals every 30 minutes or as needed to maintain a constant fire temperature.

Cook meat until a meat thermometer inserted in thickest portion registers 135° to 140°F for beef, 140° to 145°F for lamb, or 150° to 155°F for pork; total cooking time is 1½ to 2 hours. Lift spit onto a platter and let meat stand for 10 minutes before carving.

To carve, remove one spit fork; use other fork to push meat to end of spit. Remove strings and cut meat down its length so slivers fall onto platter. Let guests pile meat into pocket bread halves; top with tomatoes, cucumbers, onions, mint leaves (if desired), and yogurt. Makes about 12 servings.

Per serving: 535 calories, 25 g protein, 44 g carbohydrates, 28 g total fat, 72 mg cholesterol, 535 mg sodium

BREAKFAST FROM THE GRILL

Why not take advantage of a lovely warm-weather morning by enjoying a leisurely breakfast on the patio? Our menu for six begins with skewers of fresh fruit and smoked sausage that cook quickly right over the coals. The rest of the meal—a chive-flecked omelet and extra-large corn muffins—"bakes" by indirect heat in a covered barbecue.

Mimosas

Fruit & Sausage Skewers

Baked Chive Omelet

Giant Corn Muffins

About 50 minutes before serving time, prepare the barbecue for cooking by indirect heat (see page 10). When the coals are almost ready, prepare the muffin batter; then make the omelet mixture.

When the coals are hot, bank half of them on either side of the barbecue, then cook the sausage and fruit directly over the coals on both sides of the grill. Remove and keep warm. Set the omelet and muffins in the center of the grill (not over coals). Cover the barbecue and bake the omelet and muffins as directed. Mix equal parts of champagne and fresh orange juice to make the mimosas.

FRUIT & SAUSAGE SKEWERS

Honey-Lime Sauce (recipe follows)
2 pounds fully cooked sausages such as kielbasa (Polish sausage), cut into 1-inch pieces
1 small pineapple (about 3 lbs.), peeled, cored, and cut into 1-inch pieces
1 large cantaloupe, peeled, seeded, and cut into 1-inch pieces

Soak 12 bamboo skewers in hot water to cover for 30 minutes. Meanwhile, make Honey-Lime Sauce.

Thread sausage pieces on skewers alternately with pineapple and cantaloupe. Brush skewers all over with Honey-Lime Sauce and place on a lightly greased grill about 4 inches above the banked coals (see directions above). Cook, turning often, until sausages and fruit are well browned and hot (about 5 minutes). Transfer skewers to a platter; brush with Honey-Lime Sauce, then cover with foil and keep warm until serving time. Makes 6 servings.

Honey-Lime Sauce. In a small bowl, stir together ½ cup **lime juice** and 3 tablespoons **honey.**

Per serving: 622 calories, 23 g protein, 35 g carbohydrates, 44 g total fat, 106 mg cholesterol, 1341 mg sodium

BAKED CHIVE OMELET

8 eggs, separated
2 tablespoons all-purpose flour
3 tablespoons milk
2 tablespoons chopped chives
½ teaspoon salt
¼ teaspoon Worcestershire
Dash of pepper
1½ cups (6 oz.) shredded sharp Cheddar cheese

In a large bowl, beat egg yolks until creamy; gradually beat in flour, milk, chives, salt, Worcestershire, and pepper. In another large bowl, beat egg whites until stiff but not dry. Fold yolk mixture and cheese into beaten whites. Spoon mixture into a well-buttered shallow 2-quart metal pan or heatproof baking dish.

Place omelet in center of grill in a barbecue prepared for cooking by indirect heat (see page 10), making sure that no part of pan is directly over coals. Cover barbecue and adjust dampers as necessary to maintain an even heat. Cook until top of omelet is golden brown and firm to the touch (12 to 15 minutes). Serve hot. Makes 6 servings.

Per serving: 254 calories, 16 g protein, 4 g carbohydrates, 17 g total fat, 396 mg cholesterol, 456 mg sodium

GIANT CORN MUFFINS

1 cup *each* all-purpose flour and yellow cornmeal
2 teaspoons baking powder
½ teaspoon *each* salt and baking soda
⅓ cup sugar
1 cup buttermilk
1 egg

In a bowl, stir together flour, cornmeal, baking powder, salt, baking soda, and sugar. In a cup or bowl, beat buttermilk and egg until well blended. Pour buttermilk mixture into dry ingredients and stir just until moistened.

Spoon batter evenly into 6 well-buttered 1-cup custard cups or foil pans. Place in center of grill in a barbecue prepared for cooking by indirect heat (see page 10), making sure that no part of muffin cups is directly over coals. Cover barbecue and adjust dampers as necessary to maintain an even heat. Cook until muffins are lightly browned and firm to the touch (10 to 12 minutes). Makes 6 large muffins.

Per muffin: 249 calories, 6 g protein, 47 g carbohydrates, 4 g total fat, 52 mg cholesterol, 467 mg sodium

AN ELEGANT SIT-DOWN DINNER FOR TWELVE

Pictured on facing page

Barbecue meals don't have to be casual, as the spinach-stuffed beef tenderloin featured in this menu demonstrates. To make this show-stopping entrée for 12, you simply cut a pocket in a whole fillet of beef, slip in a fennel-seasoned spinach mixture, and grill by indirect heat on a covered barbecue.

Accompany the roast with vegetables grilled over the coals and a Madeira sauce made from the meat drippings.

First-course Soup of Your Choice

Spinach-stuffed Beef Tenderloin with Madeira Sauce

Grilled New Potatoes, Mushrooms, Baby Carrots & Leeks (page 155)

Dinner Rolls

Red Wine such as Cabernet Sauvignon

Raspberries with Orange Liqueur & Custard Sauce

Ahead of time, order the beef tenderloin (sometimes called a whole fillet of beef) from your meat market. Early on serving day, stuff the roast and prepare the vegetables (you'll need 8 to 12 *each* new potatoes and leeks, 1½ pounds mushrooms, and 2 pounds baby carrots). Start the barbecue fire 1½ to 2 hours before serving.

After cooking, keep the roast warm while you prepare the Madeira sauce and grill the vegetables.

SPINACH-STUFFED BEEF TENDERLOIN

Spinach Stuffing (recipe follows)
5- to 6-pound whole beef tenderloin (fillet of beef), trimmed of excess fat
1 tablespoon minced or pressed garlic (4 to 6 large cloves)
1½ teaspoons *each* fennel seeds and cracked pepper
1½ teaspoons salt (optional)
1 cup regular-strength beef broth
1 cup Madeira or dry sherry

Prepare Spinach Stuffing; set aside.

With a sharp knife, make a lengthwise slash in center of beef fillet, cutting to within 1 inch of opposite side and both ends to form a pocket. Spoon stuffing evenly into pocket, then pat in firmly. Sew roast closed, using a large embroidery needle and strong thread (or dental floss) and making stitches ½ inch apart.

Blend garlic, fennel seeds, pepper, and, if desired, salt; with your fingers, pat mixture all over roast.

Barbecue roast by indirect heat (see page 10), placing roast on a lightly greased grill directly above drip pan. Cover barbecue and adjust dampers as necessary to maintain an even heat. Cook roast until a meat thermometer inserted in thickest part registers 135° to 140°F for rare (about 1 hour). Transfer roast to a platter and keep warm.

Pour meat drippings into a 2- to 3-quart pan; add broth and Madeira. Bring to a boil over high heat, then boil until reduced to 1½ cups; keep warm.

To serve, cut beef into 1-inch-thick slices; offer sauce to spoon over individual portions. Makes about 12 servings.

Spinach Stuffing. Discard tough leaves and stems from 1 pound **spinach.** Rinse leaves, drain briefly, and place in a wide frying pan. Cover and cook over medium heat just until spinach is wilted (2 to 3 minutes), stirring once or twice. Remove from heat; then uncover, let cool, and coarsely chop. Squeeze out excess water with your hands.

Melt 2 tablespoons **butter** or margarine in frying pan over medium-high heat. Add ½ pound **mushrooms,** chopped; cook, stirring occasionally, until mushrooms are soft and all liquid has evaporated. Remove from heat.

In a large bowl, mix mushrooms with spinach, 1½ cups (6 oz.) shredded **Swiss cheese,** 1 **egg,** beaten, and 1 teaspoon *each* **fennel seeds** and **sage leaves.** Season to taste with **salt** and **pepper.** If made ahead, let cool; then cover and refrigerate until next day.

Per serving: 329 calories, 37 g protein, 5 g carbohydrates, 17 g total fat, 135 mg cholesterol, 237 mg sodium

A stunning entrée for guests: Spinach-stuffed Beef Tenderloin
(facing page), filled with a fennel-seasoned spinach mixture.
Complete the meal with assorted grilled vegetables and
a Madeira sauce to drizzle over all.

PAELLA IN THE GARDEN

Cooking paella in a wok nestled in a barbecue may be a bit unorthodox, but it's certainly a showy way to feed 6 to 8 guests at a patio party. The wok's shape makes it a practical choice for cooking over charcoal: the curved bowl rests more comfortably in a barbecue than does a flat-bottomed paella pan, and lets you stir the food and control the heat more easily.

While the paella cooks, let guests help themselves to *tapas* (Spanish-style appetizers): salted almonds, oil-cured olives, honeydew melon wrapped in prosciutto, and feta cheese with unsalted crackers. Finish the meal with fruit, chocolates, and your favorite cream sherry.

Tapas

Patio Paella

Mixed Green Salad   French Bread

Sangría

Strawberries on the Stem   Chocolate Bonbons

Cream Sherry   Coffee

About 1½ hours before you plan to serve, start the barbecue fire. To keep the paella ingredients fresh outdoors, arrange them on ice in trays.

 PATIO PAELLA

Bell Pepper Sauce (recipe follows)

- ¾   **pound linguisa sausage, cut into ½-inch-thick slanting slices**
- 1½   **pounds chicken thighs, cut in half along bone**
- 2½   **cups short-grain rice (such as pearl)**
- ½   **teaspoon ground turmeric**
- ¼   **teaspoon ground saffron**
- 6   **cups regular-strength chicken broth**
- 1½   **pounds firm-textured white fish (cut into 1-inch chunks), giant squid steaks (cut into ¼-inch strips), or medium-size raw shrimp (30 to 32 per lb.), shelled and deveined; or use a mixture of fish, squid, and shrimp**
  - **Shellfish (choices follow)**
- ⅔   **cup frozen tiny peas**
- 2   **lemons, *each* cut into 6 wedges**

Prepare Bell Pepper Sauce; set aside.

Mound and ignite 50 charcoal briquets on fire grate of a barbecue (at least 22 inches wide) with lid; open dampers. When coals are covered with gray ash (after about 30 minutes), push them out to form a circle just large enough to accommodate a metal wok stand in the center. To maintain heat, scatter 12 more briquets over coals; also scatter 12 more briquets over coals at 30-minute intervals throughout remainder of cooking time until directed otherwise.

Set a 2-handled 14- to 16-inch wok on stand. Add linguisa to wok; with tongs or a long-handled slotted spoon, stir frequently until well browned (about 1 minute), pushing sausage slices up sides of wok where wok is hottest. Transfer sausage to a plate, leaving fat in wok.

Add chicken to wok; turn to coat in fat, then push up onto wok sides. Turn frequently until golden brown (10 to 15 minutes). Lift from wok; transfer to plate with sausage.

Add Bell Pepper Sauce to wok; stir frequently until pepper is softened. Add rice, turmeric, and saffron. Stir frequently until rice begins to turn opaque (about 10 minutes). Add broth; cook, stirring often, for 10 minutes.

Lay chicken and sausage (with any accumulated juices), fish, and shellfish on rice. Scatter peas over top. (From this point on, add no more briquets.) Cover barbecue and close dampers; let paella cook until rice is tender to bite and clams or mussels pop open (about 20 minutes). Remove lid. If coals are almost extinguished, push as far from wok as possible; serve paella from wok. If coals are still hot, lift wok and stand from barbecue and set on a counter to serve. Offer lemon wedges to squeeze onto individual portions. Makes 6 to 8 servings.

Bell Pepper Sauce. In a bowl, mix ¼ cup chopped **onion**; 1 small **green bell pepper** (seeded and cut into ¼-inch slices); 1 large ripe **tomato** (seeded and diced); and 1 small clove **garlic** (minced or pressed).

Shellfish. Purchase 2½ pounds *total* of one kind or combine any of the following.

Spiny lobster. Buy cooked tails or whole lobster. Rinse shells. Twist tail off whole lobster, reserving head section to use for decoration. With scissors, snip out underside shell of tail. Pull meat free, slice into ½-inch pieces, and return to shell.

Dungeness crab. Buy cooked crab in the shell, cleaned and cracked.

Small live hard-shell clams or mussels. Scrub shells under running water; pull off mussel beards.

Per serving: 714 calories, 45 g protein, 55 g carbohydrates, 34 g total fat, 108 mg cholesterol, 874 mg sodium

JAPANESE HIBACHI PARTY

Yakitori is chicken carefully cut and grilled over hot coals—and in this party menu for six, you skewer and grill every part of the chicken, even the giblets and skin. The hosts assemble the skewers beforehand; at party time, guests cook their choice of foods, first dipping them in a clinging glaze, then grilling them over hot coals.

Clear Soup for Sipping

Yakitori

Assorted Japanese Pickles Made from Cucumber, Onion, Burdock Root, Daikon, or Mixed Vegetables

Hot Cooked Rice

White Wine such as Gewürztraminer or Riesling

Strawberries & Orange Slices

Many of the ingredients for this menu—a Japanese mix for the soup, assorted Japanese pickles, and sake and mirin for the yakitori glaze—can be purchased at a Japanese market or a well-stocked supermarket that carries Asian foods.

Assembling skewered foods takes time, so make sure to get the skewers ready well ahead of your party. Start the barbecue fire about half an hour in advance.

⊙ YAKITORI

Chicken Balls (recipe follows)
Yakitori Glaze (recipe follows)
2   frying chickens with giblets (3 to 4 lbs. *each*), cut up
    Extra giblets (optional)
5   to 7 green onions (white part only), cut into 1-inch lengths
½   red or green bell pepper, seeded and cut into ¼- by 1-inch strips
6   to 12 large shiitake or regular button mushrooms
1   can (about 6 oz.) ginkgo nuts, drained
    Soy sauce, salt, and pepper

Soak about 10 dozen 8- or 9-inch bamboo skewers in hot water to cover for 30 minutes.

Prepare Chicken Balls and Yakitori Glaze; set aside.

Rinse chicken and all giblets and pat dry. Pull off chicken skin and cut it into 1- by 3-inch strips. Thread each piece of skin lengthwise on a skewer.

Bone breasts, thighs, and drumsticks. Cut meat into ¾- to 1-inch cubes (cut thin pieces slightly larger and fold to this size). Thread breast meat on skewers alternately with onion, using 3 pieces of meat and 3 onion pieces per skewer. Thread dark (thigh or drumstick) meat on skewers alternately with bell pepper, using 3 pieces of meat and 3 pepper strips per skewer.

Cut wings apart at joints. Skewer each section separately, running skewer alongside bone. Cut livers and gizzards apart where a natural separation occurs. Thread livers, gizzards, and hearts on skewers, using 2 or 3 pieces per skewer. Thread mushrooms and ginkgo nuts on separate skewers, using 1 mushroom and 4 or 5 nuts per skewer.

Arrange all skewers on a large tray. (At this point, you may cover and refrigerate until next day.)

To cook, pour Yakitori Glaze into a narrow glass or jar. Dip skewered foods into glaze; lift out and drain briefly, then place on a lightly greased hibachi (or other small barbecue) grill 2 to 4 inches above a solid bed of hot coals. Cook foods, turning frequently, until done. Skin should be crisp and brown; breast meat, dark meat, and Chicken Balls should no longer be pink in center (cut to test). Giblets should be firm but still moist in center (cut to test); mushrooms and ginkgos should be hot and well glazed. Cooking times range from 5 to 12 minutes.

After grilling, remove foods from skewers and season to taste with soy, salt, and pepper. Makes about 6 servings.

Chicken Balls. Bone and skin 1 **chicken breast** (about 1 lb.). Coarsely chop meat, then place in a food processor or blender and whirl until finely chopped (you should have 1½ cups). Stir in 3 tablespoons **soy sauce,** 2 tablespoons **sake** or dry sherry, 1 tablespoon minced **fresh ginger,** and ¼ teaspoon **salt.** Shape mixture into 1-inch balls.

Place ¾ cup **fine dry bread crumbs** in a shallow bowl. Roll each Chicken Ball in crumbs to coat. Thread Chicken Balls on skewers, 2 per skewer.

Yakitori Glaze. In a 2- to 3-quart pan, combine 1¼ cups **sake** or dry sherry, ⅔ cup **mirin** or cream sherry, ¾ cup **sugar,** and ⅓ cup **soy sauce.** Bring to a boil over high heat; then boil, uncovered, until reduced to 1½ cups. If made ahead, cover and refrigerate until next day.

Per serving: 787 calories, 79 g protein, 42 g carbohydrates, 30 g total fat, 275 mg cholesterol, 1475 mg sodium

Fireworks and barbecued chicken are a natural part of many Fourth of July celebrations. To feed a crowd, serve Chicken for a Hungry Dozen (facing page)—grilled chicken quarters coated with a tomato-based barbecue sauce.

FIREWORKS BARBECUE FOR A DOZEN

Pictured on facing page

Perfect for a Fourth of July celebration is this All-American menu of barbecued chicken, roasted corn, baked beans, and homemade ice cream. The featured recipe—chicken quarters grilled with an old-fashioned sweet-sour tomato sauce—is sure to satisfy guests of any age.

Cheese & Crackers

Chicken for a Hungry Dozen

Grilled Corn in Husks (page 155)

Baked Beans

Mixed Green Salad

Homemade Vanilla Ice Cream with Fresh Strawberries and/or Blueberries

Wine Coolers   Soft Drinks

You can make the barbecue sauce several days in advance if you wish; refrigerate it in a covered container until ready to use. Early on the day of the party, mix up the beans and prepare the ice cream mixture as directed in your favorite recipe; also cut the chickens into quarters and get the corn ready for roasting in the husks.

About 2 hours before serving time, put the beans in the oven to bake. About 1½ hours ahead, start the barbecue fire. While the chicken is cooking, grill the corn, toss the salad, and have a few strong volunteers churn the ice cream.

CHICKEN FOR A HUNGRY DOZEN

All-purpose Barbecue Sauce (recipe follows)
3 frying chickens (3 to 3½ lbs. *each*), quartered

Prepare All-purpose Barbecue Sauce; set aside.

Rinse chicken, pat dry, and place on a lightly greased grill 4 to 6 inches above a solid bed of medium coals. Cook, turning occasionally, for 20 minutes; then brush generously with barbecue sauce. Continue to cook, turning and basting several times, until meat near thighbone is no longer pink; cut to test (20 to 30 more minutes). Heat any remaining sauce and pass at the table to spoon over individual servings. Makes 12 servings.

Per serving: 397 calories, 41 g protein, 7 g carbohydrates, 22 g total fat, 132 mg cholesterol, 310 mg sodium

All-purpose Barbecue Sauce. Heat 2 tablespoons **salad oil** in a 3-quart pan over medium heat. Add 1 medium-size **onion** (chopped); cook, stirring often, until soft (about 10 minutes). Stir in 3 cans (8 oz. *each*) **tomato sauce,** ½ cup *each* **red wine vinegar** and firmly packed **brown sugar,** 2 tablespoons **Worcestershire,** and 1 teaspoon **cracked pepper.** Bring to a boil; then reduce heat and simmer, uncovered, until thickened (about 45 minutes). Stir occasionally to prevent sticking. If made ahead, let cool, then cover and refrigerate for up to 2 weeks. Makes about 3 cups.

Per tablespoon: 19 calories, .22 g protein, 4 g carbohydrates, .6 g total fat, 0 mg cholesterol, 93 mg sodium

BAKED BEANS

12	slices bacon, crisply cooked and crumbled
4	cans (28 oz. *each*) pork and beans
1	cup firmly packed brown sugar
1⅓	cups catsup
2	teaspoons dry mustard
2	medium onions, finely chopped

In a large bowl, stir together bacon, beans, sugar, catsup, mustard, and onions. Spoon into a 3- to 4-quart bean pot or casserole. (At this point, you may cover and let stand at room temperature for up to 6 hours.) Bake, uncovered, in a 350° oven until thickened and bubbly (1½ to 2 hours), stirring several times to ensure even heating. Makes 12 to 16 servings.

Per serving: 317 calories, 11 g protein, 59 g carbohydrates, 5 g total fat, 7 mg cholesterol, 964 mg sodium

A FIRST-TIME BARBECUE FOR YOUNG COOKS

Budding chefs are sure to enjoy preparing this simple, tasty meal for six. With adult supervision, girls and boys from 8 to 12 years old can easily follow our detailed directions for marinating, skewering, and grilling chicken drumettes and potatoes.

Skewered Chicken Mini-drumsticks & Potatoes

Cherry Tomatoes   Carrot Sticks   Celery Stalks

Lemonade

Barbecued Banana Splits (facing page)

This meal takes about 1½ hours to prepare. The first step is to make the marinade and soak the chicken pieces in it. Next, clean and refrigerate the vegetables; allow 3 or 4 cherry tomatoes, 1 or 2 carrots, and 1 or 2 celery stalks for each person. Also have an adult help you cut the potatoes in half and blanch them.

About 50 to 60 minutes before serving, set up the barbecue and ignite the coals. Combine self-starting briquets (impregnated with fire starter) with regular briquets, so you can light the fire with just a match (have an adult there to supervise).

Skewer the chicken and potatoes while the coals are burning; after the chicken and potatoes are done, put the bananas on the grill.

SKEWERED CHICKEN MINI-DRUMSTICKS & POTATOES

        Paprika Marinade (recipe follows)
36 chicken wing drumettes (the meatiest part of the wing)—about 4 pounds *total*
10 self-starting charcoal briquets
40 regular charcoal briquets
 6 small red or white thin-skinned potatoes, scrubbed, cut into halves, and blanched as directed on page 155
        Salt and pepper

If using bamboo skewers, soak 20 skewers in hot water to cover for 30 minutes.

Prepare Paprika Marinade and set aside. Rinse chicken; pat dry. Place chicken in a 9- by 13-inch pan and pour in marinade; mix to coat. Cover and let stand at room temperature while you start the fire.

To prepare fire, put fire grate in place and open all dampers on barbecue. Stack self-starting charcoal briquets neatly in center of grate. Surround with regular briquets, stacking them on top of first mound. Use a long fireplace match to reach into center of pile to light charcoal. Let charcoal burn, checking occasionally, until coals are covered with gray ash; this takes about 30 minutes.

Meanwhile, skewer chicken and potatoes. Lift wings, one at a time, from marinade and drain briefly (let excess marinade drain back into pan). Holding onto bony end of wing, push a bamboo or metal skewer perpendicular (at a right angle) to bone through meaty part of wing. Push a second skewer, parallel to and ½ inch away from the first, through wing in same direction. Repeat to skewer all the wings; put 6 or 7 wings on each pair of skewers and keep each piece ½ inch from the next.

Place potato halves, cut side down, on a cutting board. With your hand on top of a half to keep it in place, hold a skewer parallel to board and push it through middle of potato. Then push it through 2 or 3 more halves the same way. Push a second skewer through potatoes parallel to first skewer and 1½ inches away from it; keep one hand flat on top of potatoes so you won't poke yourself with skewer. Ask an adult for help, if needed.

Skewer remaining potato halves the same way. Brush some of the marinade all over potatoes.

Using long-handled tongs, push coals out in a single layer, with no spaces between. Put cooking grill in place 4 to 6 inches above fire grate.

Arrange chicken on grill and cook until browned on bottom (10 to 15 minutes), basting once or twice with marinade (do not let it drip onto coals). Using padded mitts or tongs, turn skewers over. Arrange potatoes on grill; continue to cook until potatoes and chicken are browned all over and chicken is no longer pink near bone; cut to test (about 10 more minutes). Turn skewers as needed for even browning; baste occasionally. Keep an eye on foods as they cook; if drips cause flames, extinguish flare-ups with a spray of water (use a spray mister).

Lift skewers from grill and place foods on a tray. Pull out skewers and serve foods to eat with your fingers. Let guests season foods to taste with salt and pepper. Makes 6 servings.

Paprika Marinade. In a bowl, mix ½ cup **salad oil,** ¼ cup **red wine vinegar,** 2 tablespoons each **soy sauce** and **paprika,** and 1 teaspoon **thyme leaves.**

Per serving: 530 calories, 43 g protein, 32 g carbohydrates, 25 g total fat, 130 mg cholesterol, 311 mg sodium

If you're preparing a grilled entrée, why not make a "barbecued" dessert as well? Grilled whole bananas, split lengthwise and filled with ice cream and chocolate sauce, are the perfect sweet conclusion to our First-time Barbecue for Young Cooks (facing page). At a casual patio party for four to six, you might offer Dessert Fondue with fresh fruit and cake or cookies for dipping. And if you'd like a dessert to bake in a covered barbecue while you're enjoying the main course, try rich Chocolate Sundae Pudding.

DESSERT FONDUE

When enough low coals remain on the fire grate to keep the sauce warm, dessert fondue is a perfect way to end an informal meal.

For each serving, allow about ¾ cup **fresh fruit** (strawberries with stems, peach slices, apple cubes, banana chunks, papaya slices, or grapes) and 4 to 6 **pound cake** cubes, ladyfingers, or butter cookies.

Prepare **Orange Honey Sauce** or **Swiss Chocolate Sauce** (recipes follow); offer fruit and cake as dippers. Makes 4 to 6 servings.

Orange Honey Sauce. In a 3- to 4-cup heatproof bowl or pan, combine ½ cup (¼ lb.) **butter** or margarine (melted), 1 cup **whipping cream,** and ¼ cup *each* **sugar, honey,** and **orange marmalade.** Place bowl on grill 4 to 6 inches above low coals. Bring to a full, vigorously foaming boil, stirring. Stir for 30 seconds; then move to a cooler part of grill to keep warm. Stir in ¼ cup **orange-flavored liqueur.** Makes 2½ cups.

Per tablespoon: 56 calories, .15 g protein, 5 g carbohydrates, 4 g total fat, 13 mg cholesterol, 26 mg sodium

DESSERTS FROM THE GRILL

Swiss Chocolate Sauce. In a 2- to 3-cup heatproof bowl or pan, combine 12 ounces **milk chocolate** (chopped) or milk chocolate chips and ¾ cup **whipping cream.** Set bowl on grill 4 to 6 inches above low coals; stir until chocolate begins to melt. Move bowl to a cooler part of grill and continue to stir until chocolate is completely melted and smooth. Stir in 3 tablespoons **orange- or coffee-flavored liqueur.** Move sauce back and forth from cooler to warmer area of grill to maintain dipping consistency; be careful not to scorch chocolate. Makes about 2 cups.

Per tablespoon: 73 calories, .93 g protein, 7 g carbohydrates, 5 g total fat, 8 mg cholesterol, 12 mg sodium

CHOCOLATE SUNDAE PUDDING

As this rich dessert bakes, a dark fudge sauce forms below a delicate cake layer. Serve it hot, with whipped cream.

In a bowl, stir together 1 cup **all-purpose flour,** 2 teaspoons **baking powder,** ½ teaspoon **salt,** 2 tablespoons **unsweetened cocoa,** and ⅔ cup **sugar;** stir to blend. Then mix in ½ cup *each* **milk** and chopped **nuts,** 1 teaspoon **vanilla,** and 2 tablespoons **butter** or margarine (melted). Pour into a well-greased 9-inch square baking pan.

To prepare topping, stir together ¼ cup *each* **granulated sugar** and firmly packed **brown sugar,** 3 tablespoons **unsweetened cocoa,** and 1 teaspoon **vanilla.**

Sprinkle topping evenly over batter in pan. Slowly pour 1 cup **boiling water** over all; do not stir.

Place pan in center of grill in a barbecue prepared for cooking by indirect heat (see page 10). Cover barbecue and adjust dampers as necessary to maintain an even heat. Cook until pudding is slightly crusty on top and firm to the touch (45 to 60 minutes).

To serve, spoon into individual dishes; top with **whipped cream,** if desired. Makes 6 to 8 servings.

Per serving: 267 calories, 4 g protein, 46 g carbohydrates, 9 g total fat, 10 mg cholesterol, 284 mg sodium

BARBECUED BANANA SPLITS

While the chicken and potatoes in the First-time Barbecue for Young Cooks (facing page) finish grilling, let the kids put bananas for these sundaes on the barbecue.

Lay 6 small (6- to 8-inch-long) unpeeled ripe **bananas** in center of grill 4 to 6 inches above a solid bed of low to medium coals. Cook, turning once, until skin darkens and fruit feels very soft when pressed (about 10 minutes). You don't have to watch closely, but check every few minutes.

Lift bananas from grill and put each on a plate. With a knife, make a slit lengthwise through banana skin; pull skin away from fruit to make a "boat." Put a scoop of **vanilla ice cream** on top of each banana, then pour 2 to 3 tablespoons **purchased or homemade chocolate sauce** over ice cream. Makes 6 servings.

Per serving: 300 calories, 4 g protein, 59 g carbohydrates, 8 g total fat, 30 mg cholesterol, 95 mg sodium

ITALIAN PIZZA PATIO BUFFET

Pictured on facing page

Pizza on the barbecue? The idea may sound far-fetched, but in fact, pizzas cooked on the grill are deliciously similar to those baked in wood-burning Italian ovens—crisp-crusted and slightly aromatic from the smoldering embers.

The process is simple. You ignite coals for barbecuing by indirect heat (see page 10) and arrange them around the edge of the barbecue, then sprinkle them with soaked wood chips and let the pizza bake in the swirling smoke.

For this party for ten, you'll need to make two pizzas. We suggest you try a different topping on each—sprinkle one with artichokes and roasted red peppers, the other with sausage, olives, onions, and red bell peppers. Start the meal with assorted antipasti; to complete the menu, add a marinated vegetable salad and a homemade or purchased fresh fruit dessert.

Antipasto Platter: Olives, Salami, Cheese Cubes, Purchased Eggplant Caviar, Fresh Vegetables

Artichoke & Red Bell Pepper Pizza

Sausage & Red Pepper Pizza

Marinated Vegetable Salad

Fresh Fruit Dessert

Beer   Wine Coolers

You can do much of the work for the party early in the day. Prepare the antipasto platter, then cover and chill it; also make your favorite vegetable salad. Defrost the bread dough for the pizza crust according to package directions.

Start the fire about 45 minutes before serving; while the coals burn down, assemble the pizzas.

ARTICHOKE & ROASTED RED PEPPER PIZZA

1 jar (about 1 lb.) marinara sauce
2 cups hickory or mesquite wood chips
   Olive oil
1 tablespoon cornmeal
1 loaf (1 lb.) frozen white bread dough, thawed
2 cups (8 oz.) shredded mozzarella cheese
1 cup (4 oz.) shredded jack cheese
1 jar (6 oz.) marinated artichoke hearts, drained
⅓ cup crumbled crisp-cooked bacon
1 jar (7 oz.) roasted red peppers, drained
¼ to ⅓ cup calamata or Niçoise olives (optional)
   Fresh basil leaves

Pour marinara sauce into a 5- to 6-quart pan. Bring to a boil over medium-high heat; boil, stirring often to prevent sticking, until reduced to ¾ cup.

Soak wood chips in about 2 cups warm water for at least 30 minutes or up to 4 hours.

On the fire grate of a barbecue with a lid, ignite charcoal briquets—50 briquets for a 22- to 24-inch round barbecue, 57 for an 18- by 32-inch rectangular barbecue. When coals are covered with gray ash (after about 30 minutes), push them out in a circle or rectangle just larger than pizza pan. (If you plan to cook more than one pizza, at this time add 10 briquets to round barbecue, 20 to rectangular one; space evenly.) Set grill 4 to 6 inches above coals. Cover barbecue, open dampers, and heat until temperature in barbecue is 400° to 450°F (about 15 minutes). To test, set an oven thermometer in center of grill, not over coals; or refer to thermostat on barbecue, which should read hot.

Meanwhile, oil a 14-inch-diameter pizza pan or a 10- by 15-inch rimmed baking pan. Sprinkle with cornmeal. Roll out dough on a lightly floured board. For pizza pan, roll dough into a 15- to 16-inch-diameter circle; for rectangular pan, roll into an 11- by 16-inch rectangle. Lift dough into pan; it tends to shrink, so pat out firmly to pan edges.

Spread reduced marinara sauce over dough to within 1 inch of edges. Mix cheeses; scatter over sauce. Top with artichokes, bacon, peppers, and olives (if desired). Let stand until barbecue is ready.

Drain wood chips and sprinkle over coals. Place pizza on grill within (not over) rim of coals; cover barbecue. Cook with dampers open until crust is well browned on bottom (lift with a wide spatula to check) and cheese is melted (about 15 minutes); check crust after 10 minutes. Remove from barbecue, top with basil leaves, and cut into wedges to serve. Makes 5 or 6 servings.

Per serving: 512 calories, 22 g protein, 52 g carbohydrates, 25 g total fat, 54 mg cholesterol, 1323 mg sodium

SAUSAGE & RED PEPPER PIZZA

Line pan with dough, spread with sauce, and sprinkle with cheeses as directed for **Artichoke & Roasted Red Pepper Pizza.** Omit artichokes, bacon, and roasted red peppers; olives are optional. For toppings, break 1 pound **mild Italian sausages** (casings removed) into bite-size pieces; cook in a wide frying pan over medium-high heat, stirring occasionally, until browned (15 minutes). Also use ½ small **onion** (thinly sliced crosswise) and ½ small **red bell pepper** (thinly sliced).

Per serving: 629 calories, 31 g protein, 50 g carbohydrates, 35 g total fat, 93 mg cholesterol, 1595 mg sodium

*Aromatic and irresistible, our crisp-crusted Artichoke &
Roasted Red Pepper Pizza (facing page) bakes in just 15 minutes
in a covered barbecue. Try the sausage and bell pepper version,
too—or dream up your own toppings.*

YUGOSLAVIAN BARBECUE BUFFET

Yugoslavian cuisine is influenced by the five different ethnic groups that make up the country—Serbs, Croatians (including Dalmatians), Slovenes, Macedonians, and Montenegrins. Cooking styles vary from region to region, but grilled meat kebabs and vegetable stews seem to be national favorites.

The pork and veal kebabs featured in this menu for 16 to 20 are called *raznjici*. To make the mild kebabs spicier, top them with spoonfuls of two vegetable relishes; *ajvar*, a mellow eggplant and bell pepper mixture, and a zippier tomato-chile relish.

To complete the menu, serve a creamy feta cheese appetizer and an assortment of other traditional Yugoslavian dishes, homemade or purchased.

Feta Cheese Spread with Crusty White Bread & Prosciutto

Grilled Pork & Veal Kebabs

Serbian Tomato Relish (double recipe; page 114)

Eggplant Relish

Stuffed Cabbage Leaves

Potato Salad

Bean Salad

Fruity White Wine or Apple Cider

Apple Strudel

Plan to marinate the meat for kebabs and prepare the cheese spread and relishes at least a day in advance; also prepare or purchase the bread, salads, and other dishes ahead of time.

On the day of the party, start the barbecue fire about 1 hour before serving.

FETA CHEESE SPREAD

    8 ounces feta cheese
    2 large packages (8 oz. *each*) cream cheese, at room temperature
    ½ cup whipping cream
      Crusty white bread and prosciutto

Crumble feta cheese into large bowl of an electric mixer. Add cream cheese and beat until blended. With mixer on low speed, blend in cream. If made ahead, cover and refrigerate for up to 5 days. Serve at room temperature, with slices of bread and prosciutto. Makes about 2½ cups.

Per tablespoon: 63 calories, 2 g protein, .6 g carbohydrates, 6 g total fat, 21 mg cholesterol, 98 mg sodium

GRILLED PORK & VEAL KEBABS

    3 pounds *each* boneless leg of pork and boneless leg of veal, cut into 1½-inch cubes
      Salt and pepper
    ½ cup olive oil
    2 cups thinly sliced onions
    30 fresh bay leaves (or dry bay leaves soaked in hot water for 1 hour)

Sprinkle meat lightly with salt and pepper; then mix meat with oil. In a large bowl, layer oil-meat mixture and onions. Cover and refrigerate for at least 6 hours or until next day.

Thread meat and bay leaves on 10 to 16 sturdy metal skewers—a pork cube, a veal cube, then a bay leaf—until all ingredients are used.

To cook, place skewers on a lightly greased grill 4 to 6 inches above a solid bed of medium coals. Cook, turning occasionally, until pork is no longer pink in center; cut to test (20 to 25 minutes).

Slide meat from skewers. Let guests top meat with Serbian Tomato Relish (page 114) and Eggplant Relish (below). Makes 16 to 20 servings.

Per serving: 267 calories, 26 g protein, .3 g carbohydrates, 17 g total fat, 93 mg cholesterol, 52 mg sodium

EGGPLANT RELISH

    2 eggplants (about 1 lb. *each*)
    ⅔ cup olive oil
    5 *each* large red and green bell peppers
    2 cloves garlic, minced or pressed
    2 tablespoons white wine vinegar
    ½ cup finely chopped parsley
      Salt and pepper

Cut eggplants in half lengthwise. Brush cut sides with some of the oil. Arrange eggplant halves, cut side up, in a 10- by 15-inch rimmed baking pan. Set whole bell peppers on their sides in another 10- by 15-inch rimmed baking pan. Bake in a 450° oven (place peppers on lowest rack and turn occasionally) until vegetables are soft (about 45 minutes).

Enclose peppers in plastic bags and let cool. Peel and halve; discard skin, stems, and seeds.

Finely chop peppers and unpeeled eggplant; place in a bowl and stir in garlic and vinegar. With a heavy spoon, beat in remaining oil. Stir in parsley; season to taste with salt and pepper. If made ahead, cover and refrigerate for up to 3 days. Serve at room temperature. Makes about 4½ cups.

Per tablespoon: 24 calories, .21 g protein, 1.4 g carbohydrates, 2 g total fat, 0 mg cholesterol, .9 mg sodium

A KOREAN-STYLE BARBECUE

Six diners gather around a hibachi to grill and enjoy the marinated beef strips called *bul gogi* ("fire meat") at this cook-your-own Korean-style barbecue. To complement the sesame- and soy-seasoned meat, offer hot steamed rice and tangy seasoned cucumbers, providing individual bowlfuls for each guest. Beer, wine, and sparkling water are all good for sipping with the meal; for dessert, try juicy fresh pineapple spears or ripe persimmons.

Korean Barbecued Beef Strips

Steamed Rice

Seasoned Cucumbers

Beer   Wine   Sparkling Water

Fresh Pineapple or Fresh Ripe Persimmons

Prepare the cucumbers at least 4 hours in advance (or make them the evening before). Several hours ahead of time, cut the beef into thin strips and marinate it.

About 35 minutes before serving, start the fire in a hibachi or other small barbecue. While the coals burn down, prepare the rice; also lift the beef strips from the marinade and arrange them on a platter, ready for guests to cook.

KOREAN BARBECUED BEEF STRIPS

- 1 **tablespoon sesame seeds**
- 6 **tablespoons soy sauce**
- 2 **tablespoons *each* sugar and sesame oil**
- 1 **green onion (including top), thinly sliced**
- 2 **cloves garlic, minced or pressed**
- 1 **teaspoon grated fresh ginger**
     Dash of pepper
- 1½ **pounds lean boneless beef (sirloin or top round), cut across the grain into ⅛-inch-thick slices**

Toast sesame seeds in a small frying pan over medium heat until golden (about 3 minutes), shaking pan often. Using a mortar and pestle, crush seeds; then pour them into a medium-size bowl and stir in soy, sugar, sesame oil, onion, garlic, ginger, and pepper. Add meat and turn to coat

thoroughly with marinade. Cover and refrigerate for 1½ hours, turning meat several times.

Lift meat from marinade and drain briefly (discard marinade). Arrange meat on a platter. To cook, place meat on a lightly greased grill about 4 inches above a solid bed of hot coals. Cook, turning once, until meat is browned on both sides but still pink in center; cut to test (2 to 3 minutes). Serve immediately. Makes about 6 servings.

Per serving: 221 calories, 27 g protein, 4 g carbohydrates, 10 g total fat, 76 mg cholesterol, 571 mg sodium

SEASONED CUCUMBERS

- 2 **large cucumbers**
- 2 **teaspoons salt**
- 1 **green onion (including top), thinly sliced**
- 1 **clove garlic, minced or pressed**
- ½ **teaspoon *each* sugar and minced fresh ginger**
- ¼ **to ½ teaspoon Korean red pepper or ground red pepper (cayenne)**

With the tines of a fork, score cucumbers lengthwise. Cut each cucumber in half lengthwise; scoop out and discard seeds. Cut each half in half lengthwise; then cut each piece crosswise into 1-inch lengths. Place cucumbers in a bowl with salt; mix well and let stand at room temperature for 15 minutes. Rinse well, drain, and return to bowl along with onion, garlic, sugar, ginger, and red pepper. Cover and refrigerate for at least 4 hours or until next day. Makes about 3 cups (about 6 servings).

Per serving: 16 calories, .6 g protein, 3.6 g carbohydrates, .14 g total fat, 0 mg cholesterol, 185 mg sodium

Thanksgiving Fiesta (facing page) features barbecued butterflied turkey seasoned with oregano and lime. Partners for the moist meat include sausage-stuffed chiles, hominy, cranberry salsa, and shredded sweet potatoes.

THANKSGIVING FIESTA

Pictured on facing page

"Crazy turkey" is the centerpiece for this Thanksgiving dinner. Following a popular Mexican technique for barbecuing chicken, we've split the turkey through the backbone, then laid it out flat for grilling. Prepared this way, it cooks quickly and browns all over. Accompaniments for the bird—chorizo-stuffed chiles and a spirited cranberry and orange salsa—are also inspired by Mexican cooking.

Pineapple & Jicama with Chili Salt

Turkey Loco

Stuffed Chiles (page 194)   Grilled Onions (page 155)

Cranberry Salsa (page 194)

Sweet Potatoes with Tequila & Lime (page 194)

Warm Corn Tortillas

Buttered Hominy

White Wine such as Sauvignon Blanc   Limeade

Flan or Pumpkin Pie

You can do a lot of the work a day ahead—butterfly the turkey, get the chiles ready to bake, prepare the appetizer, and make the salsa. On the day of your party, start the barbecue fire 2½ to 3 hours before serving. While the bird cooks, bake the chiles and prepare the sweet potatoes.

PINEAPPLE & JICAMA WITH CHILI SALT

Cut 1 medium-size ripe **pineapple** (3½ to 4 lbs.) crosswise into ½-inch slices. Remove core from each slice, but do not peel. Cut each slice into quarters. Scrub, peel, and rinse 1½ pounds **jicama;** cut into ¼- by ¼- by 3-inch sticks. Coat pineapple and jicama with about ½ cup **lime juice,** then arrange on a tray. (At this point, you may cover with plastic wrap and refrigerate for up to 1 day.)

In a small dish, mix 2 tablespoons **chili powder** and 1 teaspoon **salt.** Place chili salt on tray with pineapple and jicama. To eat, dip foods in salt mixture. If desired, offer **lime wedges** to squeeze over foods. Makes 6 servings.

Per serving: 122 calories, 2 g protein, 29 g carbohydrates, 1 g total fat, 0 mg cholesterol, 403 mg sodium

TURKEY LOCO

10- to 12-pound turkey, thawed if frozen
About 4 limes, cut into halves
About 4 teaspoons oregano leaves
Salt and pepper

Remove turkey neck and giblets; reserve for other uses, if desired. Discard large lumps of fat. With poultry shears or a knife, split turkey lengthwise along one side of backbone. Pull turkey open; place, skin side up, on a flat surface and press firmly, cracking breastbone slightly, until bird lies reasonably flat. Rinse and pat dry. (At this point, you may cover and refrigerate until next day.)

Before cooking, squeeze 1 or 2 lime halves and rub over turkey; sprinkle with oregano, then lightly sprinkle with salt and pepper.

Barbecue turkey by indirect heat (see page 10), placing turkey, skin side up, on a lightly greased grill directly above drip pan. Cover barbecue and adjust dampers as necessary to maintain an even heat. Cook turkey until a meat thermometer inserted in thickest part of thigh (not touching bone) registers 185°F or until meat near thighbone is no longer pink; cut to test (1½ to 2 hours). Every 30 minutes, squeeze 1 or 2 lime halves and rub over turkey.

Transfer turkey to a platter. To carve, cut off wings and slice breast. Cut off legs and slice meat from thighs. Makes 12 to 16 servings.

Per serving: 236 calories, 41 g protein, .23 g carbohydrates, 7 g total fat, 108 mg cholesterol, 104 mg sodium

(Continued on next page)

STUFFED CHILES

Chorizo Stuffing (recipe follows)
16 fresh green or red Anaheim (California) chiles (2 to 2¼ lbs. *total*)

Prepare stuffing and set aside. Leave stems on chiles. Split chiles lengthwise, then pull out seeds and ribs. Fill chiles with stuffing; place side by side, stuffed side up, in a 10- by 15-inch rimmed baking pan. (At this point, you may cover and refrigerate until next day.)

Bake, uncovered, in a 400° oven until chiles are soft and lightly browned (about 25 minutes). Makes about 16 servings.

Chorizo Stuffing. Crumble ¾ pound **chorizo sausage** or bulk pork sausage into a wide frying pan. Add 1 large clove **garlic** (minced or pressed), ¾ teaspoon **ground cumin,** and ½ teaspoon **oregano leaves.** Cook over medium-high heat, stirring frequently, until meat is browned (about 10 minutes). Discard all but 2 tablespoons fat.

While sausage cooks, discard tough leaves and stems from 2 pounds **spinach.** Rinse leaves, then drain and coarsely chop. Finely chop ½ pound **mushrooms.** Add spinach and mushrooms to sausage and cook, stirring frequently, until liquid has evaporated (about 10 minutes). Remove from heat and stir in 2 cups **soft bread crumbs,** ¾ cup shredded **jack cheese,** and 1 **egg** (beaten). Mix well; season to taste with **salt.**

Per serving: 128 calories, 7 g protein, 10 g carbohydrates, 7 g total fat, 35 mg cholesterol, 162 mg sodium

SWEET POTATOES WITH TEQUILA & LIME

1½ cups (¾ lb.) butter or margarine
4 pounds sweet potatoes or yams
¼ cup sugar
¼ cup tequila
2 tablespoons lime juice
Salt and pepper
Lime wedges or halves

Place a rimmed baking pan (about 12 by 17 inches) on 2 burners over medium heat; add butter and stir until melted. Set aside.

Peel potatoes; then shred, using a food processor or coarse holes of a hand grater. Immediately mix potatoes into butter in pan, then sprinkle with sugar. Cook over medium heat on the 2 burners, uncovered, until potatoes begin to look caramelized and slightly translucent (about 15 minutes). Turn occasionally with a wide spatula, being careful not to mash or break up shreds.

Stir in tequila and lime juice. Cook, stirring, for about 3 more minutes. Season to taste with salt and pepper. If made ahead, cover and refrigerate until next day; 15 minutes before serving, reheat, covered, on 2 burners over medium-low heat, stirring occasionally. To serve, pour into a bowl and garnish with lime wedges. Makes 12 to 16 servings.

Per serving: 251 calories, 2 g protein, 23 g carbohydrates, 18 g total fat, 47 mg cholesterol, 187 mg sodium

CRANBERRY SALSA

2 cups fresh cranberries
4 teaspoons grated orange peel
2 large oranges, peeled (white membranes removed), chopped, and drained
¼ cup *each* minced onion and salad oil
1 tablespoon *each* minced fresh cilantro (coriander) and minced fresh ginger
1 small fresh hot green (jalapeño or serrano) chile, stemmed, seeded, and minced
Salt

Chop cranberries in a food processor or blender, half at a time. Combine cranberries, orange peel, drained oranges, onion, oil, cilantro, ginger, and chile. Stir to blend; season to taste with salt. If made ahead, cover and refrigerate until next day. Makes about 3 cups.

Per tablespoon: 17 calories, .06 g protein, 2 g carbohydrates, 1 g total fat, 0 mg cholesterol, .08 mg sodium

VENETIAN MIXED GRILL

Pictured on page 6

Though it's typically thought of as British fare, the mixed grill is interpreted in a variety of ways around the world. This Italian version includes six different meats—all small cuts—that grill quickly over hot coals. Accompaniments include grilled tomato halves and slices of rosemary-seasoned polenta.

Appetizers of Your Choice

Grilled Meats: Italian Sausages, Chicken Thighs, Beef Skirt Steak, Lamb Chops, Calf's Liver, Veal Chops

Rosemary Polenta

Grilled Tomato Halves

Hot Cooked Artichokes with Melted Butter

Red Wine

Gelato

This menu serves four diners very generously, six a bit less amply. Start the barbecue fire about 45 minutes ahead of time. When you're ready to serve, cut larger pieces of meat into smaller portions so diners can enjoy a bit of everything.

Unless your barbecue is very large, you won't be able to grill all the foods at once. We suggest grilling half the foods at a time and keeping them warm until everything is ready to eat.

⬤ VENETIAN MIXED GRILL

Rosemary Polenta (recipe follows)
¼ cup mixed chopped fresh herbs such as rosemary, tarragon, thyme, oregano, and marjoram
1 clove garlic, minced or pressed
¼ cup olive oil or salad oil
2 or 3 Italian sausages (½ to ¾ lb. *total*)
2 chicken thighs (about ¾ lb. *total*), skinned and boned
1 slice calf's liver (about 1 lb.), cut 1 to 1½ inches thick
1 beef skirt steak (about ¾ lb.), trimmed of excess fat
4 lamb rib chops (about 1 lb. *total*), cut 1 inch thick
4 veal rib chops with kidneys (about 1¼ lbs. *total*), cut ¾ inch thick
4 to 6 medium-size tomatoes

Prepare Rosemary Polenta and set aside.

In a 1-cup glass measure, stir together herbs, garlic, and oil. Cover and set aside for at least 1 hour or until next day.

Prick sausages in several places. Place in a wide frying pan and add enough water to cover. Bring to a boil; reduce heat and simmer, uncovered, for 5 minutes, turning several times. Drain; set aside.

Place each chicken thigh between 2 pieces of wax paper or plastic wrap; pound with a flat-surfaced mallet until ¼ inch thick. Cut out and discard any tubes and membranes from liver. Cut steak in half crosswise. Brush chicken, liver, steak, lamb chops, and veal chops on both sides with some of the herb-oil mixture; set aside.

Cut tomatoes in half crosswise. Turn polenta out of pan and cut crosswise into ¾- to 1-inch-thick slices. Brush tomatoes and polenta slices all over with some of the herb-oil mixture.

Place sausages on a lightly greased grill 4 to 6 inches above a solid bed of hot coals, setting them on a cooler area near edge of grill. In center of grill, arrange lamb chops, veal chops, and liver. Cook meats, turning once, until sausages are well browned and hot throughout (about 10 minutes) and liver, lamb, and veal are well browned but still pink in center; cut to test (10 to 12 minutes). Remove from grill and keep warm until all foods are cooked.

Place steak and chicken in center of grill; place tomatoes (cut side down) and polenta slices at edge of grill. Cook, turning foods once, until beef is browned on outside but still pink in center and chicken is no longer pink in center; cut to test (5 to 7 minutes). Cook tomatoes and polenta until hot throughout (5 to 10 minutes).

Arrange meats, tomatoes, and polenta on a large platter. Serve hot, cutting meats to make 4 to 6 portions. Makes 4 to 6 servings.

Per serving: 761 calories, 60 g protein, 8 g carbohydrates, 53 g total fat, 395 mg cholesterol, 428 mg sodium

Rosemary Polenta. In a 4- to 5-quart pan, bring 3 cups **water** to a boil over high heat. Meanwhile, in a bowl, stir together 1½ cups *each* **polenta** (Italian-style cornmeal) and **water.**

Using a long-handled spoon, gradually stir polenta mixture into boiling water. Reduce heat and simmer, stirring constantly, until polenta has the consistency of thick porridge (10 to 15 minutes). Remove from heat and mix in 3 tablespoons **butter** or margarine and 2 tablespoons chopped **fresh rosemary leaves** or 2 teaspoons dry rosemary. Season to taste with **salt.** Spread evenly in a 4½- by 8½-inch loaf pan. Let cool. If made ahead, cover cooled polenta with plastic wrap and refrigerate for up to 3 days. Makes 4 to 6 servings.

Per serving: 178 calories, 3 g protein, 27 g carbohydrates, 6 g total fat, 16 mg cholesterol, 59 mg sodium

JAMAICAN BARBECUE

Pictured on facing page

In Jamaica, aromatic columns of spicy smoke from roadside *ramadas* offer passersby a clue that "jerk pork" is cooking. To make this popular street snack, Jamaicans rub pork spareribs with a mixture of crushed spices, pepper, and fresh garlic, then slowly smoke the meat over green wood from the allspice tree.

To approximate the flavor of "jerk pork" in our Caribbean barbecue menu for six, we rub spareribs with the traditional spicy-hot mixture, then cook them in a covered barbecue with smoldering wood chips.

While the pork cooks, offer guests pineapple wedges and crisp sticks of jicama to dip in seasoned salt. Round out the meal with appropriately tropical accompaniments: whole unpeeled bananas baked alongside the ribs, papaya wedges, and avocados filled with a hot-sweet dressing.

Pineapple & Jicama with Chili Salt (page 193)

Jamaican-style Spareribs with Baked Bananas & Papaya Wedges

Avocados with Lime Dressing

Spiced Iced Tea

Coconut Cream Pie

Early on the day of serving, prepare the spice rub for the ribs. While the ribs marinate, prepare the appetizer and the dressing for the avocados. About 2½ hours before you plan to serve, start the barbecue.

JAMAICAN-STYLE SPARERIBS WITH BAKED BANANAS & PAPAYA WEDGES

- 1 slab pork spareribs (3 to 4 lbs.), trimmed of excess fat
- ¾ cup coarsely chopped onion
- 4 cloves garlic, quartered
- 2 to 4 fresh or canned jalapeño chiles, stemmed, seeded, and chopped
- 2 tablespoons ground allspice
- 1 tablespoon *each* minced fresh ginger and salad oil
- 1 teaspoon *each* ground nutmeg and salt
  About 12 fresh bay leaves (or dry bay leaves soaked in hot water for 1 hour)
- 6 small green-ripe bananas
- 1 large papaya
  Lime wedges

Make ¼-inch-deep slashes between ribs on both sides of sparerib slab.

In a food processor or blender, combine onion, garlic, chiles, allspice, ginger, oil, nutmeg, and salt. Whirl until puréed. Rub spice purée over surface and into slashes on both sides of sparerib slab. Cover and let stand for 1 to 2 hours (or refrigerate until next day).

Barbecue ribs by indirect heat (see page 10). Distribute bay leaves over meaty side of ribs; then place ribs, meat side up, on a lightly greased grill directly above drip pan. Arrange unpeeled bananas around meat, setting them on grill directly above coals. Cover barbecue and adjust dampers as necessary to maintain an even heat. Cook, turning bananas occasionally, until bananas are black all over and feel soft when pressed, and until ribs are well browned on outside and meat near bone is no longer pink; cut to test (1 to 1¼ hours). Near end of cooking time, cut papaya into wedges.

To serve, peel back banana skins to expose flesh; place bananas on a tray. Cut sparerib slab into 2- to 3-rib portions. Arrange on a large platter with papayas and Avocados with Lime Dressing (below). Offer lime wedges to squeeze over meat, bananas, and papayas. Makes 6 servings.

Per serving: 492 calories, 27 g protein, 31 g carbohydrates, 29 g total fat, 107 mg cholesterol, 362 mg sodium

AVOCADOS WITH LIME DRESSING

In a small bowl, stir together 3 tablespoons *each* **lime juice** and **salad oil,** 1 teaspoon **sugar,** and ⅛ teaspoon *each* **crushed red pepper** and **oregano leaves.** Season to taste with **salt.** (At this point, you may cover and refrigerate for up to 1 day.)

Cut 3 large ripe **avocados** in half lengthwise; pit, but do not peel. Pour equal amounts of lime dressing into each avocado cavity, making sure all cut surfaces are coated. Makes 6 servings.

Per serving: 266 calories, 2.5 g protein, 10 g carbohydrates, 26 g total fat, 0 mg cholesterol, 14 mg sodium

*Allspice- and chile-seasoned spareribs take center stage at
a Jamaican Barbecue (facing page). Papayas, mangoes, coconut,
and avocado halves filled with a sweet-hot lime dressing
complement the rich, satisfying meat.*

PIT-BARBECUED BEEF FOR A CROWD

If you're preparing beef for a big crowd, pit barbecuing is one cooking method you'll want to consider. In essence, a pit barbecue is a primitive oven, lined with rocks and preheated by a hardwood fire that produces a thick bed of red-hot coals. The meat is seasoned, wrapped in foil and damp burlap, and lowered onto the coals, then covered with a metal lid and a layer of earth to seal out all air. Kept airtight, the meat slowly steams in its own juices, becoming moist and succulent.

To find out more about pit-barbecue methods, we consulted experts who stage four or five such barbecues a year. Below, you'll find their advice for putting on a party for 36 to 180 guests—step-by-step directions for digging the pit, building and tending the fire, and preparing the meat. To cook a single 25-pound roast, you can build a small pit; for two to five roasts, you'll need a large pit. Each 25-pound roast serves about three dozen diners.

To complete the menu, have your guests contribute appetizers, salads, baked beans, crusty breads or rolls, and an array of cakes and pies.

Appetizers of Your Choice

Pit-barbecued Beef with Homemade or Purchased Barbecue Sauce

Baked Beans

Selection of Salads   Crusty Breads or Rolls

Cakes & Pies

Beverages of Your Choice

Well ahead of time, choose the site for your barbecue, making sure it's a large, open area that's free of gopher or squirrel tunnels (these let air into the pit and cause the meat to burn). You can also dig the pit well in advance; line it with rocks, then cover it with sheet metal to keep the interior dry.

About 24 hours before you plan to serve, build the fire in the pit. While it burns down, season and wrap the roasts in foil, burlap, and baling wire. Eighteen hours before serving, lower the roasts into the prepared pit and cover the pit with dirt.

Equipment. You'll need the following materials and tools to prepare your pit barbecue.

Stones. Have ready a sufficient quantity of large (6-inch-diameter), hard, dry stones to make a 1½-foot-thick layer in a small pit or a 2-foot layer in a large pit.

Fuel. You need newspaper, kindling, and at least ¼ cord dry split oak or other hardwood (same amount for small or large pit).

Metal cover. To cover the pit, use a piece of sheet metal, 3/16 inch thick and 3½ feet square.

Tools. Have at hand shovels for digging, a rake for leveling coals, and a long hook to lower meat into pit.

Wrapping. You'll need 1½-foot-wide heavy-duty foil; 2 pieces of burlap (each about 3½ by 5 feet) for each roast; baling wire; and heavy-duty gloves.

Digging the pit. To make any size pit, you dig a larger, shallower pit centered with a smaller, deeper pit in which the meat will cook. The floor

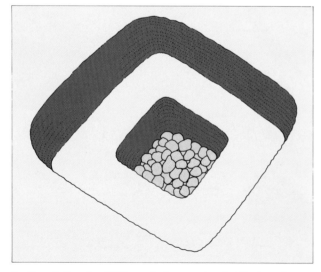

Ignite oak fire about 24 hours before serving. Let fire burn for four hours, then rake coals level.

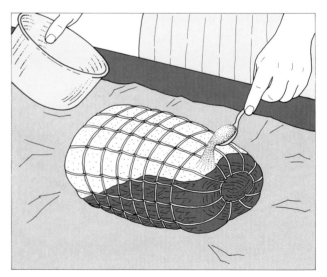

Place beef roast on heavy-duty foil, drizzle with liquid smoke, and rub with seasoned salt mixture.

of the shallow pit serves as a "ledge" to support the sheet-metal cover for the smaller pit.

For one roast, dig a hole 4 feet square by 14 inches deep; then dig a 20-inch-square inner pit, 3 feet deep. For 2 to 5 roasts, you'll need a 6½-foot-square pit, 20 inches deep; in center of this pit, mark off a 3-foot square and dig down 4 more feet. Fill inner pits with stones: a 1½-foot layer in small pit, a 2-foot layer in large pit.

Make balls of newspaper to cover stones. Arrange kindling on top in shape of a teepee. Over this, in similar teepee fashion, place dry split oak. Start fire and let it burn for about 4 hours to develop a bed of coals—1 foot deep in small pit, 1½ feet deep in large pit. Rake coals to form an even layer, discarding any uncharred pieces of wood.

Preparing & cooking the meat. To serve each group of 36, you'll need a 25- to 27-pound **boned and tied beef chuck roast.** For each roast, stir together ½ cup **salt,** ¼ cup *each* **pepper** and **sugar,** 8 cloves **garlic** (minced or pressed), and 1 tablespoon **oregano leaves.** Then place 2 pieces of heavy-duty foil, *each* 1½ by 5 feet, on top of each other. Along one 5-foot side, fold over a narrow hem 3 times to secure foil pieces. Open to make one large piece of foil. Place roast on foil, sprinkle with 1 to 2 tablespoons **liquid smoke,** and rub all over with salt mixture. Turn roast fat side up and arrange 3 or 4 medium-size mild **white onions** (cut into ½-inch-thick slices) on top of it. Bring up long sides of foil and fold them together down to surface of roast to seal securely. Then bring foil ends up over top to completely enclose roast.

Dampen two 3½- by 5-foot pieces of burlap. Spread burlap out, one piece on top of the other; place foil-wrapped roast in center. Wrap burlap around roast as you did foil. Using baling wire as you would string on a package, secure bundle tightly, wrapping wire around it several times both lengthwise and crosswise.

When coals are ready, use a hose to lightly wet burlap-wrapped meat. Using a long-handled hook (tuck hook under wire), carefully lower roast onto coals. Immediately cover pit with sheet metal, resting it on ledge. Quickly shovel dirt back over metal, stamping it well to compact. Shovel dirt until no steam escapes and dirt over metal cover is 1½ to 2 feet deep. Inspect pit several times during first hour to see that no steam is escaping; if you see any steam holes, cover them with more dirt. If pit and fire are properly prepared, meat will be ready in 12 hours (one roast or 5 roasts).

To remove roasts, lift dirt off pit down to ledge, exposing metal cover. With a rake, lift off cover and set aside. Using your hook, lift out bundles of meat. Transport meat from pit to serving area in a wheelbarrow, if desired. Replace metal cover to prevent accidents and preserve pit for future barbecues.

Wearing heavy-duty gloves, remove wire and burlap from one roast at a time. Open up burlap and place foil-wrapped roast on a rimmed platter or board to catch juices; then unwrap. Remove any string and cut meat across the grain into thick slices. Each roast makes about 36 servings.

Per serving: 744 calories, 51 g protein, 2 g carbohydrates, 57 g total fat, 194 mg cholesterol, 1627 mg sodium

Seal beef in foil, wrap in damp burlap, and tie securely in both directions with baling wire.

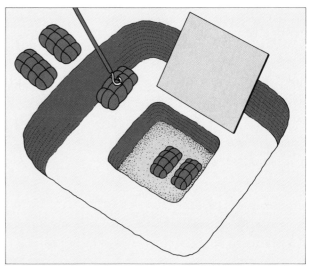

Rake oak coals level; then lower dampened bundles into pit with long-handled hook.

Coming right up—hot dogs with "the works"! Guests at our Latin American Hot Dog Roast (facing page) build their own sandwiches from juicy grilled sausages, warm flour tortillas, and half a dozen toppings.

LATIN AMERICAN HOT DOG ROAST

Pictured on facing page

The all-American hot dog takes on a Latin look in this casual patio party for eight to ten diners. For these south-of-the-border dogs, you pass up the familiar frankfurter buns for large, soft flour tortillas. And instead of the usual catsup, mustard, and relish, offer assorted Latin-style condiments.

Grilled Cheese (page 42)

Assorted Sausages

Embellishments: Hot Black Beans, Pickled Cabbage, Fresh Tomato Relish, Cheddar Cheese, Guacamole, Salsa or Taco Sauce

Watermelon Slices

Beer   Soft Drinks

Ice Cream Cones

This menu requires little attention from you after the guests arrive. You can make the black beans, pickled cabbage, tomato relish, and guacamole ahead of time. Start the fire about 45 minutes before serving; shortly before the party begins, arrange sausages, warm tortillas, and embellishments at one end of a table near the barbecue.

⊚ LATIN AMERICAN HOT DOGS

> **Hot Black Beans (recipe follows)**
> **Pickled Cabbage (recipe follows)**
> **Fresh Tomato Relish (recipe follows)**
> **Guacamole (recipe follows)**
> 18 to 24 large (*each* about 12 inches in diameter) or medium-size (*each* about 8 inches in diameter) flour tortillas
> 2 to 4 pounds (¼ to ½ lb. per person) fully cooked sausages such as old-fashioned frankfurters, knackwurst, garlic sausages, slender veal sausages, smoke-flavored pork links, and kielbasa (Polish sausage)
> About 4 cups (1 lb.) shredded Cheddar cheese
> Prepared salsa or taco sauce

Prepare Hot Black Beans, Pickled Cabbage, Fresh Tomato Relish, and Guacamole.

To heat tortillas, sprinkle each one with a few drops of water. Stack tortillas, wrap in heavy-duty foil, and bake in a 350° oven until warm (about 15 minutes). Serve wrapped in foil to keep warm.

Let guests cook their own sausages. To cook sausages, place them on a lightly greased grill 4 to 6 inches above a solid bed of medium coals. Cook, turning often, until well browned and hot through-out (5 to 10 minutes, depending on diameter of sausage). Wrap each sausage in a warm tortilla and add spoonfuls of Hot Black Beans, Pickled Cabbage, Fresh Tomato Relish, Guacamole, cheese, and salsa. Makes 8 to 10 servings.

Per serving: 803 calories, 31 g protein, 57 g carbohydrates, 49 g total fat, 104 mg cholesterol, 2023 mg sodium

Hot Black Beans. Sort 1 pound **dried black beans** and remove any debris. Rinse beans and drain. Place beans in a 4- to 5-quart pan and add 9 cups **water;** 1 large **onion,** cut into chunks; and ½ cup lightly packed **fresh cilantro (coriander) leaves.** Bring to a boil over high heat; then reduce heat, cover, and simmer until beans mash easily with a fork (2½ to 3 hours). Whirl, half at a time, in a food processor or blender until puréed. Season to taste with **salt** and **ground red pepper** (cayenne); transfer to a heatproof serving dish. If made ahead, cover and refrigerate until next day. To reheat, cover and bake in a 350° oven until hot throughout (35 to 45 minutes). Serve hot. Makes 3 cups.

Per tablespoon: 33 calories, 2 g protein, 6 g carbohydrates, .13 g total fat, 0 mg cholesterol, .57 mg sodium

Pickled Cabbage. Using a food processor or a sharp knife, coarsely shred about 1 pound **cabbage;** you should have 4 cups. Place cabbage in a bowl and add ½ cup *each* chopped **onion** and shredded **carrot,** ⅓ cup **white wine vinegar,** and ½ teaspoon **oregano leaves.** Mix well; season to taste with **salt.** Cover and refrigerate for at least 4 hours or until next day. Stir before serving. Makes 5 cups.

Per ¼ cup: 9 calories, .33 g protein, 2 g carbohydrates, .05 g total fat, 0 mg cholesterol, 5 mg sodium

Fresh Tomato Relish. In a bowl, combine 2 large **tomatoes** (peeled, seeded, and chopped); ½ cup *each* diced **green bell pepper** and chopped **onion;** 2 tablespoons chopped **fresh mint** or 2 teaspoons dry mint; 1 tablespoon chopped **fresh cilantro (coriander);** and ⅛ teaspoon **crushed red pepper.** Mix well; season to taste with **salt.** Cover and refrigerate for at least 2 hours or until next day. Makes 2½ cups.

Per ¼ cup: 9 calories, .37 g protein, 2 g carbohydrates, .09 g total fat, 0 mg cholesterol, 2.5 mg sodium

Guacamole. Halve and pit 3 large ripe **avocados.** Scoop flesh into a bowl and mash coarsely with a fork. Add ⅓ cup **lemon juice;** stir until blended. Season to taste with **salt** and **liquid hot pepper seasoning.** Cover and refrigerate for up to 4 hours. Stir before serving. Makes 2½ to 3 cups.

Per tablespoon: 25 calories, .3 g protein, 1 g carbohydrates, 2.4 g total fat, 0 mg cholesterol, 2 mg sodium

SPANISH TAPAS PARTY

Spanish *tapas* are varied "little snacks," ranging from olives and salted nuts to sturdier dishes such as grilled sausages and pasta. In Spain, tapas are served at taverns to fill the gap between lunch and a very late dinner; sometimes, they replace dinner entirely.

Centered around the barbecue, our make-ahead tapas party for 12 to 16 lets your guests sample a wide variety of foods. The menu includes grilled Polish or andouille sausages, shrimp, and vegetables; purchased tapas such as cheese, fruit, bread, and smoked fish; and a selection of beverages, among them wines, sparkling water, and traditional Spanish sherries.

To set up the party, arrange courses of tapas on separate tables as indicated below. Have small plates and forks available at the first two tables; set out glasses for drinks at the third.

Table #1: Ready-to-Grill Foods

**Polish or Andouille Sausages   Shrimp
Multicolor Bell Pepper Strips**

**Leek Halves   Mushrooms
Plantains or Green-ripe Bananas**

Table #2: Ready-to-Eat Foods

Crusty Bread or Rolls   Fresh Fruit

Wedges of Asiago, Jack, Jarlsberg, or Goat Cheese

Spanish-style Olives   Spanish Peanuts

Thin-sliced Cooked Ham or Prosciutto; or Smoked Fish such as Salmon, Trout, or Whitefish

Deviled Eggs

Table #3: Beverages

Spanish Sherries such as Fino, Manzanilla, Amontillado, or Oloroso; or California Dry or Medium-dry Sherries

Chardonnay or Dry Sauvignon Blanc and Cabernet Sauvignon Wines

Sparkling Water   Ice

Almost all the work for this party can be completed in advance. A day or two ahead of time, purchase the ready-to-eat tapas (suggested amounts follow). On the day of the party, skewer foods to be grilled; cover and refrigerate. Half an hour or so before guests arrive, set out foods and drinks and start the barbecue fire; during the party, only the grill needs tending.

TABLE #1: READY-TO-GRILL FOODS

If you're using bamboo skewers, soak them in hot water to cover for at least 30 minutes before using.

To avoid flare-ups as you cook, arrange the coals in the barbecue as follows. First, ignite 70 charcoal briquets on fire grate in a barbecue with a lid. When coals are covered with gray ash (after about 30 minutes), push them up against one side of fire grate in an even layer; they should cover only ¼ of grate. Place grill 4 to 6 inches above coals.

To barbecue, lay foods on grill over empty part of grate (not above coals). Cover barbecue, open dampers, and cook each food as directed. If you'll be cooking for more than 45 minutes, add 5 briquets to fire every 30 minutes to maintain a constant fire temperature.

Brush shrimp and vegetables with this baste as they cook:

Garlic Baste. Mix 2 tablespoons **olive oil** with 1 clove **garlic** (minced or pressed) for *each* type of vegetable and for every 6 servings of shrimp.

Sausage. Thread 1 pound **kielbasa (Polish sausage) links** or 3-inch sections of andouille sausage crosswise on a 12- to 16-inch thin metal or bamboo skewer; space sausage pieces slightly apart. Run another skewer through sausage, parallel to but slightly apart from the first, to hold meat flat. Barbecue as directed above until sausages are hot in center and lightly browned (about 4 minutes per side). Push sausages off skewers; slice 1 inch thick.

Per ounce: 92 calories, 4 g protein, .46 g carbohydrates, 8 g total fat, 20 mg cholesterol, 249 mg sodium

Shrimp. Allow 3 or 4 **medium-size raw shrimp** (30 to 32 per lb.) for each person. Shell and devein shrimp. Thread shrimp crosswise through midsection on 12- to 16-inch thin metal or bamboo skewers; space shrimp slightly apart. Run a second skewer through shrimp, parallel to but slightly apart from the first, to hold them flat. Barbecue as directed above until shrimp turn pink (about 4 minutes per side), brushing several times with **Garlic Baste** (above).

Per shrimp: 32 calories, 2 g protein, .18 g carbohydrates, 2 g total fat, 17 mg cholesterol, 16 mg sodium

Leeks. Trim tops from 6 slender **leeks** (1 to 1½ lbs. *total*), leaving 3 inches of green leaves. Peel off tough outer layers. Trim root ends, but leave enough of the bottom so layers are attached. Split leeks in half lengthwise; rinse well. Barbecue as directed above until tops are limp and leeks are streaked light brown (about 5 minutes per side), brushing several times with **Garlic Baste** (facing page).

Per half-leek: 30 calories, .25 g protein, 2 g carbohydrates, 2 g total fat, 0 mg cholesterol, 3 mg sodium

Multicolor Bell Pepper Strips. Stem and seed 1 *each* large **green, red, and yellow bell pepper.** Cut peppers lengthwise into 1½-inch-wide strips. Thread a third of the strips (alternating colors) crosswise on a 12- to 16-inch thin metal or bamboo skewer; space slightly apart. Run another skewer through pepper strips, parallel to but slightly apart from the first, to hold strips flat. Repeat to skewer remaining peppers.

Barbecue as directed on facing page until peppers are streaked light brown (5 to 6 minutes per side), brushing several times with **Garlic Baste** (facing page).

Per strip: 12 calories, .08 g protein, .5 g carbohydrates, 1 g total fat, 0 mg cholesterol, .3 mg sodium

Mushrooms. Rinse and drain 1 pound **mushrooms** (with about 1½-inch caps); trim stems. Thread mushrooms through stems and caps onto three 12- to 16-inch thin metal or bamboo skewers. Barbecue as directed on facing page until mushrooms are streaked light brown (about 4 minutes per side), brushing several times with **Garlic Baste** (facing page).

Per mushroom: 18 calories, .47 g protein, 1 g carbohydrates, 1 g fat, 0 mg cholesterol, .9 mg sodium

Plantains. Peel 3 large, very ripe **plantains** (with black skins) or green-ripe bananas; cut each in half lengthwise. Barbecue as directed on facing page until plantains are browned and soft when pressed (about 5 minutes per side), brushing several times with **Garlic Baste** (facing page). To serve, cut each plantain half in half.

Per quarter-plantain: 112 calories, 1 g protein, 24 g carbohydrates, 2.5 g total fat, 0 mg cholesterol, 3 mg sodium

TABLE #2: READY-TO-EAT FOODS

Make the deviled eggs yourself; the other items at this table can all be purchased.

Bread. Offer 3 different types of **crusty bread** or rolls. You'll need 3 pounds in all.

Fruit. Choose the season's best: **grapes, peaches, melon wedges, berries, apricots.** You'll need about 6 pounds in all. Rinse and drain fruit; arrange on platters for guests to eat out of hand.

Cheese. Buy by the chunk to cut and eat. Choose 2 or 3 kinds, such as **Asiago, jack, Jarlsberg, or goat cheese.** You'll need about 3 pounds in all.

Olives. Choose one or more kinds: **Spanish-style green or black ripe, salt-cured, seasoned, or other favorite olives.** You'll need about 4 cups.

Nuts. Choose one or more kinds of roasted shelled nuts: **Spanish or other peanuts, pistachios, almonds, walnuts, sunflower seeds.** Allow 4 cups in all.

Ham or Smoked Fish. You need about 1½ pounds of either one. Serve whole smoked fish on a plate so guests can break it apart to eat.

Deviled Eggs. Shell 18 **hard-cooked eggs** and cut them in halves lengthwise. Separate yolks from whites. In a small bowl, mash yolks with 3 to 4 tablespoons **mayonnaise;** season to taste with **dry mustard, salt,** and **pepper.** Spoon yolk mixture evenly into reserved whites. Cover and refrigerate for up to 1 day. Before serving, sprinkle eggs with **paprika** or garnish each with a slice of pimento-stuffed olive. Makes 36 deviled egg halves.

Per half-egg: 48 calories, 3 g protein, .33 g carbohydrates, 4 g total fat, 138 mg cholesterol, 41 mg sodium

TABLE #3: BEVERAGES

Offer a variety of beverages, including sherries, wines, and sparkling water.

In Spain, sherry is the traditional accompaniment to tapas, and part of the tapas experience is trying different sherries. Spanish and American sherries differ greatly in flavor and style; the Spanish types are generally considered more complex.

Spanish sherries vary by maker, but these are general guidelines. *Fino* is dry, crisp, light, and best chilled; its color is usually deep amber. *Manzanilla* looks and tastes quite similar but tends to be drier with subtler nuances; serve chilled.

Amontillado has a medium-dry, nutlike flavor. It's darker than fino and has more taste and body. Offer it at room temperature. *Oloroso* may be dry or sweet, and medium- to full-bodied (your wine merchant can recommend drier brands best with tapas). Serve chilled.

American sherries good with tapas are *dry* and *cocktail* or *golden* (medium-dry).

For wine, try a dry Sauvignon Blanc or lightly oaked Chardonnay, and a mature, smooth Cabernet Sauvignon.

INDEX